DRAMA CLASSIC COLLECTIONS

These volumes collect together the most popular plays from a single author or a particular period. Both affordable and accessible, they offer students, actors and theatregoers a series of uncluttered texts in impeccable editions, accompanied by concise introductions. Where the originals are in English, there is an end-glossary of unfamiliar words and phrases. Where the originals are in a foreign language, the translations aim to be both actable and accurate – and are made by translators whose work is regularly staged in the professional theatre.

Other Drama Classic Collections

CHEKHOV – FOUR PLAYS

The Seagull
Uncle Vanya
Three Sisters
The Cherry Orchard

GREEK TRAGEDY

Antigone
Bacchae
Medea

RESTORATION COMEDY

The Country Wife
The Rover
The Way of the World

IBSEN
THREE PLAYS

A Doll's House
Ghosts
Hedda Gabler

Henrik Ibsen

translated and introduced by
KENNETH MCLEISH
and
STEPHEN MULRINE

NICK HERN BOOKS
London
www.nickhernbooks.co.uk

A Drama Classic Collection

This edition first published in Great Britain as a paperback original in 2005 by Nick Hern Books Limited, 14 Larden Road, London W3 7ST. Each play originally published in the Drama Classics series.

A Doll's House translation copyright © 1994 by Kenneth McLeish
Ghosts translation copyright © 2002 by Stephen Mulrine
Hedda Gabler translation copyright © 1995 by Kenneth McLeish

Introduction copyright © 2005 by Nick Hern Books

Kenneth McLeish and Stephen Mulrine have asserted their moral right to be identified as the translators of this work

Typeset by Country Setting, Kingsdown, Kent CT14 8ES
Printed by Bookmarque Ltd, Croydon, Surrey

ISBN-13   978 1 85459 846 2
ISBN-10   1 85459 846 5

Contents

Introduction

Henrik Johan Ibsen: a Brief Overview

When Ibsen was 23, he was appointed writer-in-residence at the newly-established Norwegian National Theatre in Bergen. Six years later he was made Director of the Norwegian Theatre in Kristiania (now Oslo), a post he held until 1862.

Ibsen found his years in the theatre intensely frustrating. The towns were small and the audiences parochial and frivolous-minded. His own plays at the time were chiefly historical dramas, some in verse, modelled on those of Shakespeare, Schiller and Hugo. In the end, the Norwegian Theatre lost its audience, ran out of money, and in 1864, after two years of poverty (aggravated by alcoholism and depression), Ibsen left Norway for Italy and Germany, countries in which he spent the next 27 years.

The first two plays Ibsen wrote in self-imposed exile, the verse dramas *Brand* (1866) and *Peer Gynt* (1867), established his reputation. With characteristic iron will, however, he immediately changed his style. He dropped verse for prose (which was more suitable, he said, for 'serious subjects') and, from 1877 onwards, wrote no more plays on historical or folk-inspired subjects. His subsequent plays (a dozen from *Pillars of the Community*, 1877, to *When We Dead Awaken*, 1899) all dealt with contemporary social or philosophical issues, and were set among the provincial bourgeoisie. They regularly caused scandal, and took time to find favour with critics and the middle-class audiences whose lives and concerns they dramatised. Other critics (notably Archer and Shaw in Britain) rallied to his cause, and by his sixties (the time of his greatest plays), he had become the grand old man not only of Scandinavian literature but of European theatre in general. The 'problem play' of which he was a pioneer has been a staple theatre genre ever since.

Ibsen returned to Norway in 1891. He wrote four more plays, but in 1900 suffered the first of a series of debilitating strokes, the last of which proved fatal.

Henrik Ibsen (1828-1906)

Henrik Ibsen was born on 20 March 1828 in Skien, a small
town to the south of Kristiania (modern Oslo), into a prosperous
middle-class family. His mother, Marichen, took a lively interest
in the arts, and Ibsen was introduced to the theatre at an early
age. When he was six, however, his father's business failed, and
Ibsen's childhood was spent in relative poverty, until he was
forced to leave school and find employment as an apprentice
pharmacist in Grimstad. In 1846, an affair with a housemaid
ten years his senior produced an illegitimate son, whose
upbringing Ibsen had to pay for until the boy was in his teens,
though he saw nothing of him. Ibsen's family relationships in
general were not happy; after the age of twenty-two, he never
saw either of his parents again and kept in touch with them
only through his sister Hedvig's letters.

While still working as a pharmacist, Ibsen was studying for
university, in pursuit of a vague ambition to become a doctor.
He failed the entrance examination, however, and at the age of
twenty launched his literary career with the publication in 1850
of a verse play, *Catiline*, which sold a mere fifty copies, having
already been rejected by the Danish Theatre in Kristiania.
Drama in Norwegian, as opposed to Swedish and Danish, was
virtually non-existent at this time, and the low status of the
language reflected Norway's own position, as a province of
Denmark, for most of the preceding five centuries. Kristiania,
the capital, was one of Europe's smallest, with fewer than
30,000 inhabitants, and communications were primitive.

However, change, as far as the theatre was concerned, was
already under way, and Ibsen and his younger contemporary
Bjørnson were among the prime movers. Another was the
internationally famous violinist, Ole Bull, who founded a
Norwegian-language theatre in his home town of Bergen, and
invited Ibsen to become its first resident dramatist in 1851, with
a commitment to write one play each year, to be premièred on
January 2nd, the anniversary of the theatre's founding.

During his time at Bergen, Ibsen wrote five plays, mainly
historical in content: *St. John's Night*, a comedy which he later
disowned, loosely based on *A Midsummer Night's Dream*; *The
Warrior's Barrow*, a reworking of a one-act verse play first staged
in Kristiania; *Lady Inger of Østråt*, a five-act drama set in 16th-
century Trondheim, on the theme of Norwegian independence;

The Feast at Solhaug, which went on to be commercially published; and a romantic drama, *Olaf Liljekrans*, to complete his contractual obligations in Bergen.

Ibsen had meanwhile met his future wife, Suzannah Thoresen, and the offer of the artistic directorship of the newly-created Norwegian Theatre in Kristiania must have been very welcome. Ibsen took up this post in September 1857, with a specific remit to compete for audiences with the long-established Danish Theatre in Kristiania. A successful first season was accordingly crucial, and his own new play, *The Vikings at Helgeland*, set in 10th-century Norway, and based on material drawn from the Norse sagas, was an important contribution. By 1861, however, the Danish Theatre was clearly winning the battle, in part by extending its own Norwegian repertoire, and Ibsen's theatre was forced to close, in the summer of 1862.

Now unemployed, Ibsen successfully applied for a government grant to collect folk-tales in the Norwegian hinterland. During this period he also wrote *Love's Comedy*, a verse play on the theme of modern marriage, and a five-act historical drama, *The Pretenders*, now regarded as his first major play, premièred at the Kristiania Theatre in January 1864, under Ibsen's own direction. A few months later, financed by another government grant, Ibsen left Norway for Copenhagen on 2 April 1864, beginning a journey that would take him on to Rome, and international recognition.

Brand, the first fruit of Ibsen's self-imposed exile, sees him abandoning historical themes, and drawing on his own experience more directly, basing his uncompromising hero on a fanatical priest who had led a religious revival in Ibsen's home town of Skien in the 1850s. Like all of Ibsen's plays, *Brand* was published before it was staged, in March 1866, and received its first full performance almost twenty years later, in 1885 at the Nya Theatre in Stockholm, though it seems clear that like his next play, *Peer Gynt*, *Brand* was intended to be read, rather than acted.

Ibsen wrote *Peer Gynt* in Rome, Ischia and Sorrento, through the summer of 1867, using material from Asbjørnsen's recently-published *Norwegian Folk-Tales*, as well as the darker corners of his own life, but the end result is regarded as containing some of his finest dramatic writing, with the irrepressible Peer at the other end of the moral spectrum from Brand, a typical example of Ibsen's fondness for opposites or antitheses in his dramatic work.

The following spring, Ibsen left Rome for Berchtesgaden in the Bavarian Alps, to work on a new play, *The League of Youth*, which was premièred at the Kristiania Theatre in October 1869, and attracted some hostility for its satirical portrayal of contemporary politicians. A few weeks later, Ibsen travelled to Egypt, to represent his country at the official opening of the Suez Canal.

On his return, Ibsen began work on what he regarded as his greatest achievement, the mammoth ten-act *Emperor and Galilean*, dramatising the conflict between Christianity and paganism, through the life of Julian the Apostate. Published in Copenhagen in October 1873, to critical acclaim, the play nonetheless had to wait over a century before it was staged in full, an eight-hour marathon in Oslo in 1987.

By this time, Ibsen's fame had brought him tempting offers to return to Norway, as well as recognition at the highest level in the form of a knighthood, of the Order of St Olaf. However, apart from a brief sojourn in Kristiania in the summer of 1874, he remained in Germany, moving from Dresden to Munich the following year, to commence writing *Pillars of the Community*, completed in 1877, the first in a series of 'problem' plays, although its large cast requirements make it nowadays something of a theatrical rarity. By contrast, his next play, *A Doll's House*, has seldom been absent from the stage since its Copenhagen première in December 1879, and the challenge it offers to male hypocrisy and so-called 'family values' has ensured its continuing popularity.

In Ibsen's characteristic manner, *Ghosts* in effect is the obverse of *A Doll's House*. Whereas in the latter play Nora flees the family home, in *Ghosts* Ibsen shows the tragic consequences of a wife's failure to break free from a disastrous marriage. Its exposure of taboo subjects like venereal disease, however, still retains the power to shock, and it was at first rejected by all Ibsen's preferred theatres. After publication in 1881, almost two years elapsed before *Ghosts* was staged in Scandinavia, the world première having already taken place in Chicago, in May 1882.

Ibsen was angered by his countrymen's reception of *Ghosts*, so that *An Enemy of the People*, with its ill-concealed attack on the Norwegian establishment, is, to an extent, a vehicle for that anger, as well as for Ibsen's sceptical views on democracy. The play thus offended liberals and conservatives alike, but not enough to impede its staging; it was premièred in Kristiania in January 1883, to mixed reviews.

The initial reaction to *The Wild Duck*, published in November of the following year, was largely one of bewilderment, although it was produced without delay in all the major Scandinavian venues. While the 'original sin' of the drama, the housemaid made pregnant by her master and married off to a convenient dupe, echoes that of *Ghosts*, Ibsen's use of symbolism appeared to sit uneasily with the naturalistic dialogue, and indeed still troubles modern audiences.

However, Ibsen was moving away from the concerns of the 'problem' play towards a more personal, oblique utterance, and the controversy which dogged his work scarcely lessened with the publication of *Rosmersholm*, in November 1886, following a brief return to Norway, after an eleven-year absence. Partly inspired by Ibsen's disillusionment with Norwegian politics, it is especially noteworthy for the creation of Rebecca West, one of his most compelling characters, though its witches' brew of ingredients caused something of a scandal.

Ibsen's reputation was by now unassailable, however, and in Germany particularly, the innovative productions of the Saxe-Meiningen company had won him an eager following. In England, the enthusiasm of Edmund Gosse, and later William Archer, ensured that several of his plays were at least available in print in translation, but the first significant staging of his work in London had to wait until June 1889, with the Novelty Theatre production of *A Doll's House*.

Meanwhile, *The Lady from the Sea* fared well enough at the box office, with simultaneous premières in Kristiania and Weimar, on 12 February 1889, though again its complex amalgam of dreamy symbolism, evolutionary theory, and the daily routine of the Wangel household in northern Norway, tended to confuse audiences and is still something of an obstacle to production.

Hedda Gabler, premièred in Munich at the Residenztheater in January 1891, is now Ibsen's most popular play, but attracted fierce criticism in its day, largely on account of the character of Hedda herself. Arguably Ibsen's finest creation, Hedda's contempt for the sacred roles of wife and mother seemed the more offensive in that Ibsen provided no explanation for it, no inherited moral taint, and she continues to unnerve us even today, like a glimpse into the abyss.

In that same year, 1891, there were no fewer than five London productions of Ibsen plays, including *Hedda Gabler*, and the publication of George Bernard Shaw's seminal critique, *The Quintessence of Ibsenism*, helped assure his place in the permanent English repertoire. Ibsen himself finally returned to Norway in July, a national hero, though he suffered the indignity of hearing his achievement disparaged by the rising young novelist Knut Hamsun, at a public lecture in October.

In his declining years, Ibsen increasingly sought the company of young female admirers, and his relationships with Emilie Bardach, Helene Raff, and finally Hildur Andersen, find their way into his later plays, notably *The Master Builder*, in which Ibsen also revisits the theme of self, which had inspired his early master-pieces, *Brand* and *Peer Gynt*. The burden of fame, the generational conflict between age and youth, Ibsen's personal concerns, are all explored in the relationship between the successful middle-aged architect Solness and the twenty-something 'free spirit' Hilde Wangel. Although the all-pervasive tower metaphor puzzled some critics, given that Freud had still to explain such things, the play was an instant success, going on from its première in Berlin in January 1893, to productions in Scandinavia, Paris, Chicago and London within the year.

Ibsen's next play, *Little Eyolf*, despite having the distinction of a public reading in English, at the Haymarket Theatre in December 1893, even before it was published in Copenhagen, has enjoyed little success on the stage, where its mixed modes of realism and symbolism can fail to blend, with unintentionally comic results. However, *John Gabriel Borkman*, published three years later, and premièred in Helsinki in January 1897, achieves in prose the poetic grandeur of *Brand*. The play is drawn in part from Ibsen's own experience of humiliating dependency, in the wake of his father's financial ruin, and explores Ibsen's cherished themes: marital disharmony on the one hand, and, on the other, the cor-rupting influence of materialism, personal freedom and self-doubt.

Ibsen was now permanently resident in Kristiania, venerated wherever he went, and his seventieth birthday, on 20 March 1898, was the occasion for widespread rejoicing. His collected works were in preparation in both Denmark and Germany, and his international fame rivalled that of Tolstoy. It is fitting, there-fore, that Ibsen's last play, *When We Dead Awaken*, should have been premièred on 15 January 1900, in effect launching the next century, at Kristiania's new National Theatre, the confident expression of that Norwegian identity which Ibsen and Bjørnson, whose statues graced its entrance, did so much to promote.

Finally, like almost all of Ibsen's plays, *When We Dead Awaken* is a response to the author's psychic needs, part confession, part exorcism. It can be argued that the ageing sculptor Rubek's return to his first inspiration, Irene, now confined in a sanatorium, represents Ibsen's feelings of guilt over his neglect of his wife Suzannah, and his belated acknowledgement that she had been the real sustaining force behind his work. The tone of *When We Dead Awaken* is accordingly elegiac, an appropriate coda to Ibsen's long career. Two months later, in March 1900, he suffered the first of a series of strokes which was to lead to his death, in Kristiania, on 23 May 1906.

The 'Problem' Play and the 'Well-Made' Play

The 'problem' play was a response, in mid-19th-century European theatre, to an upsurge in public discussion of 'big' social and philosophical issues. Favoured topics were the differing natures and social roles of women and men, family relationships, sexual behaviour, religion, politics and social ethics. The plays were set among ordinary, contemporary people, whose dilemmas onstage embodied the questions under discussion. The 'problem' plays of some writers – for example Bjørnson in Norway, Sardou in France, Grundy and Jones in Britain – were often creaking and contrived: sermons or newspaper leaders disguised as art. (Shaw coined the nickname 'Sardoodledum'; Wilde memorably said, 'There are three rules for the young playwright. The first rule is not to write like Jones. The second and third rules are the same.') But in other hands, notably Ibsen's, concentration on character and on personal tragedy elevated the form. Even such preachy plays as *Ghosts* or *An Enemy of the People* make their impact through the vitality of their characters and situations rather than the underlying issues they address.

Rules for the 'well-made' play were formulated in France in the early 19th century, and quickly spread throughout Europe. They were as strict as those Aristotle laid down for ancient tragedy (see below). In a 'well-made' play, action should be organised in three sections: exposition of the central problem, alarms and excursions, dénouement. The plot should hinge on a secret or a dilemma which affects the main character; the audience should be allowed only hints and glimpses of this as the play proceeds, and all should be fully revealed only as the action moves towards dénouement. There should be reversal of fortune – 'up' in a 'well-made' farce, 'down' in a 'well-made' melodrama.

And finally, settings, dialogue and behaviour should be contemporary and conventional. Tens of thousands of 'well-made' plays were written, and most are justly forgotten. (Victorian melodramas are typical examples.) But in the hands of fine writers – Dumas' *Lady of the Camellias* and Labiche's farces spring to mind, not to mention Maugham's or Rattigan's plays in a later age – the recipe has led to masterpieces. 'Well-made' conventions, in whole or in part, were particularly useful to writers of 'problem' plays, whose effect on their audience depended, in part, on putting a spin on familiar-seeming characters and situations and on received ideas.

A Doll's House: Moral Identity

Ibsen wrote *A Doll's House* in 1879, much of it in a holiday apartment in Amalfi; it was first published, and first performed, in December that year. From the start it attracted critical praise, and – rather more unexpectedly, perhaps, in view of the bourgeois nature of its audiences – full houses. Critics applauded its technical innovation, the way it gave tragedy a domestic setting, with no more than five main characters and an almost total absence of histrionics. It is impossible to say what drew audiences, though the fact that the 'message' of the play was much discussed, as if Ibsen had preached some kind of sermon about contemporary life, suggests that this may have been at least part of what attracted people to the theatre or made them buy the printed text (a bestseller). Possibly also the racking-up of emotional tension, which is such a feature of the action, made its impression, so that word-of-mouth soon guaranteed the playgoing public a cathartic, if uncomfortable, night out.

Right from the start, *A Doll's House* has been the prey of people who saw in it confirmation of their own prejudices about society. Calvinists in Ibsen's own country, and fundamentalist Christians of other kinds in the US, railed against its 'denunciation of marriage'; women's guilds were disgusted by its 'laxity of language', and by its depiction onstage of drunkenness, domestic wrangling and an extortioner with – horror of horrors – redeeming characteristics. The play's supporters could be equally dogmatic. In particular, from Shaw onwards (in *The Quintessence of Ibsenism*) it has regularly been claimed as a major document of women's emancipation, a trumpet-call to blow down the walls of Western, male oppression. It is still regularly overlaid with feminist interpretations, in both academic books and stage productions. Ibsen's theme *is* emancipation, but his play is, so to speak, as much 'peoplist' as feminist. He is concerned that everyone, of either gender, should break free of conventional shackles and discover his or her own moral identity; however painful or destructive this process proves to be, Ibsen's claim is that moral truth is always better than moral lie. Nora in the play may be the most spectacular adventurer along the path to self-knowledge, but she is by no means the only one. As the action develops, all the other main characters approach a similar point of discovery in different ways and from different directions, and make their own decisions about how that discovery will affect their future actions. (Only Helmer's future action is left undecided; as the curtain falls he is at the very moment of self-discovery.)

Assertion of moral identity involves not rejection of the way other people treat us, or we them, but an examination of where we stand in relation to ourselves and others; the results of that examination may be revolt against the status quo, or acceptance, but the important thing, for Ibsen and his characters, is not the action which follows the examination but the moral purgation which precedes it. In 1880 the actress Hedwig Niemann-Raabe, about to play Nora in the German première, refused to perform the original ending on the grounds that she herself, as a mother, would never desert her children as Nora deserted hers. Ibsen, unwillingly, wrote an alternative ending (in which Helmer persuades Nora to 'think again of the little ones', and leads her to the children's door, where she collapses as the curtain falls). This subverts the entire point of the play, restores the status quo and destroys Nora's moral character – something Ibsen acknowledged by describing it as a 'barbaric outrage' on the play, and which the actress admitted by dropping the ending as soon she could, in favour of the original.

Characterisation and Irony in *A Doll's House*

The role of Nora is one of the most challenging and rewarding in all Ibsen's work. In the first two acts she barely leaves the stage, and runs the gamut from simpering flirtation (ironically underscored by our knowledge that she is deliberately playing the part of a child-wife) to energetic hysteria. As the third act opens (after her strenuous dancing which ends Act Two) the actress has a respite offstage, before coming on to experience a seduction, a domestic quarrel and the total change of direction which has been implicit from the start but which now carries the action to its bleak conclusion. The volatility of the part is brilliantly offset by Helmer's rocklike steadiness: his and Nora's relationship is like a darkly tragic version of the vaudeville double act in which an anarchic, unpredictable comedian bounces off the 'straight man', whose assumption of control is constantly challenged but never abandoned. Ibsen trumps this by the ending: Helmer's collapse, in terms of what he is, is a moment of moral self-discovery as huge, and as open-ended, as anything which happens to Nora in the play.

In 19th-century Scandinavian theatre companies of the traditional kind, there were five main performers. They took the roles, respectively, of Hero, Heroine, Confidante, Villain and 'Fifth Business'. 'Fifth Business' brought about the dénouement of the action: either the hero's or heroine's recognition that he/she was careering to self-inflicted doom, or the revelation or incident which brought destruction or salvation from outside the characters. (If coincidence brought happiness at the end of a melodrama, that coincidence was manipulated by 'Fifth Business'.) In *A Doll's House* Ibsen uses all five of the standard categories, but all – and especially 'Fifth Business' – are fluid. Save in numbers of lines (not, of course, the least consideration in some acting-companies then, and now) Helmer is not exclusively the hero; Nora is not solely the heroine; the roles of villain, confidante and 'Fifth Business' circulate among the other characters. In particular, characters we initially think are 'good' are shown to have 'bad' qualities and motives, and vice versa. Mrs Linde's motives seem confused and opaque, until she reveals that everything she does is the result of a process of self-examination (long past) similar to the one which Nora is currently undergoing and which Mrs Linde both encourages and compels. Krogstad seems a heartless villain until – melodramatically – he is 'redeemed' in Act Three and shown to have been acting, however wickedly, out of morally understandable motives. (This revelation is one of the least 'prepared' moments in the play, hardly forseeable from what we learn of Krogstad's character and history in earlier scenes.) Rank is that favourite Ibsen secondary character, the apparently amoral, sardonic bystander – but in this play, he has a 'terrible secret' which explains, if it never excuses, his outlook on life, and which makes him a fascinating foil for Helmer's apparently flawless rectitude.

If the details of Ibsen's plot are occasionally melodramatic, his over-riding theme (moral self-examination) removes the play

entirely from mechanistic cliché. The blurring and ambiguity
of character (never features of melodrama) allow him a greater
degree of irony than in any of his other plays. Almost from the
beginning of Act One, we know that Nora is nursing a terrible
secret, and that her behaviour with Helmer is desperate play-
acting – a knowledge which is itself ironically undercut because
she herself half believes in, and certainly assents in, the 'reality'
of the part she plays. We know that Helmer's unquestioning self-
certainty is a house of cards, that Rank's apparent bonhomie
will have its darker side, that Mrs Linde has some hidden
purpose in coming back to town. Above all, and although we
know that Krogstad will not easily surrender his hold on Nora,
we still know less than he does about his motives and his
intentions, matters which are themselves to change in view of
factors of which he himself is unaware. The irony in *A Doll's
House* is on many interlocking levels, and it shifts as the action
develops, creating and enhancing the play's extraordinary
psychological tension. Consistently, we are less intrigued by the
characters' motives and nature than by what they know, and by
how soon and in what way they will find out more than they
know. In his third act, Ibsen exploits this state of affairs between
dramatist and audience to give his moral theme more power.
Nora's (apparent) volte-face is shocking because it is (apparently)
unexpected; the irony is that it is inevitable, and predictable,
almost from the opening line.

The Language of *A Doll's House*

Ibsen was concerned, in his prose plays, to write the kind of
language which ordinary people spoke in everyday life. (He
objected strongly to 'literary' translations, insisting that the plays
should be rendered as far as possible in the vernacular of the
place and period in which they were to be performed.) *A Doll's
House* is remarkable for the ordinariness of its language. There are
so few literary or histrionic flights that the simplest of metaphors
(the singing bird), the plainest of images (Krogstad's vision of the
'deep dark depths' into which Nora may throw herself) or the
briefest of fancies (Nora's and Rank's flirtatious – desperately
flirtatious – discussion of the foie gras and oysters which may
have comprised Rank's father's dissipation) all impact like bombs.
Because voices are seldom raised, Nora's hysteria at the end of
the second act, and Helmer's fury after he reads the letter, seem
almost unbearably violent. Helmer's attempted seduction, half a

dozen lines of suggestion and murmur, shrieks, in context, like a
scream in church. (This passage was one of those which provoked
outrage among Ibsen's more staid contemporaries.) The play's
impression of frankness comes not from the words spoken, but
from the feeling that we are walking on the characters' very
nerve-ends, on the raw flesh of their relationships. When the
characters in Osborne's *Look Back in Anger* use baby-talk, it repels
because we know they hate it; when Nora and Helmer use it,
our horror is intensified because we know that they both believe,
or wish, that it may be 'real'. Without ever being overt, the play
is consistently frank about matters which had never before been
so laid out for public inspection. Before the spectators' eyes,
intimacy is violated – not the intimacy of Man and Woman in
general, but the intimacy of one particular woman and one
particular man – and this is why, even today, when Ibsen's
'messages' have long been part of our emotional, psychological
and dramatic baggage, *A Doll's House* can still seem one of his
most uncomfortable, most shocking and most moving plays.

A Doll's House in Performance

Following its first performance, in Copenhagen in December
1879, the play was quickly taken up in Germany; it was
performed in New York in 1882 and in London in 1884 – the
first of Ibsen's plays to reach America and Britain, in each case
initially in an adapted and somewhat emasculated form; by the
mid-1890s it was part of the international repertoire, a main
cause of Ibsen's worldwide reputation. The first English Helmer
was Herbert Beerbohm Tree; distinguished British Noras have
included Janet Achurch, Gwen Ffrangçon-Davies, Sybil Thorndike,
Flora Robson and Claire Bloom (who filmed it in 1973 with
Anthony Hopkins as Helmer and Ralph Richardson as Rank);
distinguished American Noras have included Beatrice Cameron
(whose production caused nationwide controversy in the late
1880s), Ruth Gordon (in an adaptation by Thornton Wilder) and
Jane Fonda (in a 1973 film notable for its feminist emphasis).

Ghosts: Realism and Fate

While critical estimates vary, the consensus view of Ibsen's *Ghosts*
remains unchanged from that expressed by his Danish contemporary Georg Brandes: it may not be his greatest work, but it is
'certainly his noblest deed'. Ibsen's awareness of the revolution

he was about to make in European theatre is plain in his own comment about the necessity, as he saw it, of shifting the 'boundary posts' – not only those restricting what could be said in the theatre, but in what manner, and by whom. *Ghosts*, written in 1881 at Sorrento, where he had completed the equally daring *Peer Gynt* some fourteen years before, is thus the first modern tragedy, dealing with the lives of an ordinary middle-class family, and spoken in everyday prose.

Ibsen was also well aware that it would ruffle some feathers in his homeland, but he could scarcely have anticipated the violence of the reaction to *Ghosts*, from critics and public alike. Ibsen's plays in general spring from a sense of 'unfinished business', and *Ghosts* was written in part as a response to criticism directed at his previous work, *A Doll's House*, in which Nora Helmer, with the playwright's implicit approval, abandons her husband and children. *Ghosts* shows the disastrous consequences of a wife choosing to stay.

Unfortunately, while critical reservations about *A Doll's House* had very little impact on the play's popularity, *Ghosts* was another matter entirely, and Ibsen's publisher Hegel took a heavy loss on its publication. Ibsen was especially upset at being attacked by so-called 'progressives', who lacked the courage of their professed convictions, and who would become a target for his wrath in *Rosmersholm*, some years later. However, it is little wonder that *Ghosts* caused such an uproar, given the bleak picture Ibsen paints of the sacred institutions of marriage and the family, and its open discussion of the taboo subjects of 'free love', incest, and venereal disease, which Osvald, by implication, has inherited from his father.

In fact, despite what was perceived as its innovative and shocking naturalism, *Ghosts* rigorously observes the classical unities of time, place and action: the narrative, constructed for the most part as a series of debates, unfolds over a period of a day, in one location, the Alvings' drawing-room, while the drama is sharply focused almost to the point of obsession. So far from being a 'problem' play, in which Ibsen exposes the social and physical ills of his day, *Ghosts* has more in common with Greek tragedy, in the sense that it demonstrates the inexorable workings of Fate, which no human intervention can reverse. Retribution, the sins of the fathers visited upon the children, is Ibsen's recurring theme, with inherited character traits taking the place of divine wrath.

However, there are some difficulties with seeing Ibsen as a modern Sophocles, not least the relentless determinism of the characters' situation, the outcome of which is arguably more depressing than cathartic. And indeed, interpretations which focus too strongly on the tragic destiny of Osvald, as did most earlier readings, run the risk of becoming static, especially in the latter part of the play. In more recent times, the emphasis has shifted to the theme of enlightenment, as personified in Mrs Alving's spiritual journey from meek acceptance of that wifely duty which will ultimately destroy her child, through growing financial, intellectual, and moral independence, to a belated realisation of her own shortcomings, as the sun finally rises over the wreckage of her life. Mrs Alving must now confront that truth, towards which the play has been inching, in its full horror, but the choice she is left with – to kill or not to kill her son – is no choice at all, and it is no surprise that Ibsen himself declined to guess at what she might do, once decently screened by the final curtain.

Despite its reputation as the first great realist tragedy, Ibsen's *Ghosts* has more than its share of artifice, and critics have not been slow to point out a number of flaws, e.g., Ibsen's imperfect understanding of the nature of syphilis; Osvald's risibly idyllic portrait of the artistic community in Paris; Manders's too-easy acceptance of blame for the Orphanage fire; its fortuitous timing, just as Mrs Alving is on the point of revealing all, in the manner of a soap-opera cliff-hanger. More serious criticisms have been levelled at the characterisation: Pastor Manders at times seems more of a target for Ibsen's anti-clericalism than a fully-rounded human being; Osvald, with his taste for strong drink and serving-maids, is a little too plainly the Captain's son; and Regine also, with her easy virtue, Johanne's daughter. However, it is hard to see how else Ibsen could have proceeded, in a play whose dominant theme, announced in its very title, is the influence of heredity, the dead hand of the past choking the natural life out of the present.

And Ibsen's artifice extends to the creation of 'reflections', intensifying the effect of his theme: Manders's hypocrisy is the more exposed in being contrasted with Engstrand's, who could assuredly give the Pastor lessons in the art; Regine's eventual return to the Engstrand family 'home', as it were, invites comparison with Osvald's own homecoming, to a womb-like state of dependence. And despite the gulf that separates Engstrand and Mrs Alving, it may be asked whether, in some deep, dark recess of her being, Mrs Alving does not also achieve her desire, i.e., to possess her son utterly. We should not forget, moreover, that Mrs Alving's original plan for Regine was to pack her off to a life of drudgery in the Orphanage, ridding herself of a living reminder of the Captain's shame, while the bricks and mortar of his memorial performed the same function.

Ghosts, realism notwithstanding, is alive with symbols, actual and potential, ranging from Engstrand's Oedipal deformed foot to the very light, or lack of it, by which we watch the action unfold. Its obvious parallels, coincidences, contrivances, may trouble the logical mind, but they result in an extraordinary degree of concentration and dramatic force. Thus the 'convenient' interruption of the fire, at the close of Act II, is not simply a crude device to hold off Mrs Alving's climactic revelation; it actually *is* that revelation – the fact that Captain Alving's public fame is a total sham – delivered wordlessly, as a powerful metaphor.

Among Ibsen's most important contributions to European theatre is the multi-layered structure of his dialogue, in which the past, brought into the present by a series of carefully-timed revelations, exerts pressure not only on what is said, but perhaps more significantly, what is unsaid. Subtext is thus crucial to the understanding of Ibsen's characters, and in *Ghosts* this is nowhere more obvious than in the relationship between Manders and Mrs Alving, as they negotiate their tortuous passage to mutual understanding, if not enlightenment. Without that sense of engagement on two levels, conscious and subconscious, in which the remembered, or indeed forgotten, past constantly works to re-position the present, the play is at risk of seeming mechanistic, a grim moral fable on the sins of the fathers. That leaves out of account not only Ibsen's humour, but also the genuine complexity of the characters. Pastor Manders may have all the stereotypical traits of his calling – naivety, pomposity, self-righteousness – but a charge of hypocrisy is hardly justified against a man who lives by his religious convictions, however absurd. Manders neither lines his own pocket, nor seduces his young parishioners, and he is certainly no Tartuffe. Moreover, Mrs Alving was, and perhaps still is to some extent, in love with him. Even the chief villain, Engstrand, deserves a fair hearing, and while Ibsen tells us nothing about the carpenter's antecedents, we may guess that he would have needed a thick skin to survive the daily torment of married life with Johanne, bringing up another man's child. The case-hardened Engstrand, indeed, may bear witness to the influence of environment, rather than heredity, on shaping character. And Mrs Alving, so often the focus of the play in the modern theatre, as she advances line by line to her final, terrible realisation, is by turns shallow and perceptive, strong-willed and pusillanimous, uncaring and compassionate, as changing circumstances dictate. However, the very contradictions in *Ghosts* are potentially a source of strength, keeping the play open to interpretation, and its characters essentially mysterious.

While Ibsen's 'noblest deed' remains a puzzle in many respects, there is no denying its concentrated power, and the sense that the doomed Alving family, in their remote Nordic fastness, have something of permanent value to communicate to us about Ibsen's society and our own – no longer shockable, it may be, but still under threat from the 'ghosts' of the past, dead conventions, hollow reputations, empty gestures.

Ghosts in Performance

In common with all Ibsen's plays, *Ghosts* was published, in December 1881, before being staged, though the playwright's hopes of profiting from the Christmas rush encountered a severe setback, and indeed the scandal provoked by its publication had a damaging effect on sales of all Ibsen's work. The earlier performance history of the play is accordingly a catalogue of rejections, beginning with the prestige theatres in Scandinavia, the Royal Theatres in Copenhagen and Stockholm, and the Kristiania in the Norwegian capital. Ibsen was by this time very popular in Germany, but not until 1886 was *Ghosts* produced there, by the Saxe-Meiningen players at Augsburg. In fact, the very first performance of *Ghosts* took place in Chicago, on 20 May 1882, in Dano-Norwegian, with a Danish professional actress, Helga von Bluhme, and a scratch company of Scandinavian immigrants. Its Norwegian première took place some eighteen months later, on 17 October 1883, at the tiny Møllergaten Theatre in Kristiania, a venue which Ibsen himself regarded as quite unsuitable, while the Kristiania Theatre, from which *Ghosts* was banned until 1900, performed a no-account French farce.

Interestingly, Ibsen's great defender William Archer was in the audience for the Norwegian première of *Ghosts*, which gives his account of the press reaction to its first English staging an added piquancy. A year after Antoine's famous Théâtre Libre boldly

introduced French audiences to Ibsen with *Ghosts*, J.T. Grein's
one-off production at the Royalty Theatre in Soho on 13 March
1891, met with a positive torrent of critical abuse, which Archer
wittily surveys in an article for the *Pall Mall Gazette* a few weeks
later, titled 'Ghosts and Gibberings'. The *Daily Telegraph* leader is
perhaps the most damning, describing the play as: 'an open
drain; a loathsome sore unbandaged; a dirty act done publicly;
a lazar house with all its doors and windows open' while the
reviewer in *The Gentlewoman* thought it 'just a wicked nightmare',
and Ibsen himself: 'a gloomy sort of ghoul, bent on groping for
horrors by night, and blinking like a stupid old owl when the
warm sunlight of the best of life dances into his wrinkled eyes.'

The general tenor of the five hundred-odd articles prompted by
Ibsen's masterpiece was sufficiently hostile to ensure that the
play could not be performed in a public theatre in England
until 1914, though there were some dissenting voices, among
them the critic of *The Star*, who asked: 'Have they no eyes for
what stares them in the face: the plain simple fact that *Ghosts* is
a great spiritual drama?' But as Archer concludes: 'Who can
carry on a rational discussion with men whose first argument is
a howl for the police?'

Slowly but surely, however, Ibsen's great achievement in *Ghosts*
came to be recognised, not least with the Berlin Freie Bühne
production at the Lessing Theater in the autumn of 1890, which
Archer claims to have inspired a new generation of German
dramatists. In London, as the shock waves of the Royalty
production gradually subsided, *Ghosts* came to be among the
most performed of Ibsen's plays, with the first licensed staging at
the Haymarket in July 1914, initially promoted by a women's
suffrage group. Mrs Patrick Campbell and the young John
Gielgud came together in a Wyndham's Theatre production in
March 1928, and, in a 1930 production at the Everyman, Sybil
Thorndike played Mrs Alving, a role which Beatrix Lehmann
filled at the Duke of York's Theatre in 1943, and reprised at the
Embassy in 1951. Flora Robson played Mrs Alving to Michael
Hordern's Manders at the Lyric, Hammersmith, in 1959.
Catherine Lacey, at the Theatre Royal, Stratford East, in 1965,
and Irene Worth at the Greenwich Theatre in 1974, brought
their several talents to the same role, as did Jane Lapotaire with
the Royal Shakespeare Company at the Barbican in 1994. If
anything, productions of *Ghosts* have increased in frequency over
the years, and hardly a theatre season passes without a fresh
assault somewhere on Ibsen's 'noblest deed'. Radio, as early as

1934, found an audience for the play, followed in 1951 by the first of several television productions, notably that of 1968, directed by Michael Elliott, and starring Celia Johnson, Tom Courtenay, and Donald Wolfit. *Ghosts* was televised again in 1987, with Judi Dench, Kenneth Branagh, and Michael Gambon. More recently, there have been new productions of *Ghosts* in 2001, at the Comedy Theatre in April, with Francesca Annis and Anthony Andrews, and on BBC Radio 3, in December, with Penelope Wilton, Paul Rhys, and Patrick Malahide. The translation in this volume was premièred, by English Touring Theatre, with Diana Quick as Mrs Alving, in February 2002.

Hedda Gabler: Formal Structure

Hedda Gabler was first staged in 1890. It deals with a favourite Ibsen theme, the conflict between individual spiritual freedom and the claims of convention and society. It resembles the plays which preceded it (*Pillars of the Community, A Doll's House, Ghosts* and *An Enemy of the People*) in that it is entirely realistic, tragedy in a domestic setting. (In fact domesticity is one of the main causes of the tragedy.) At the same time, it anticipates some of the symbolism and 'otherness' of such later plays as *The Master Builder* or *Rosmersholm*. There are times when it is not just to herself, but to the other characters and to us as well, that Hedda seems to come from a different planet from everyone else. Ibsen may have had this quality in mind when he talked of the play's 'demonism'.

Ibsen's later plays are formally dazzling: tightly structured, without a loose end or a wasted word. But even among them, *Hedda Gabler* is exceptional. One of the most striking things about it is its harmonisation of the conventions of the 'well-made' play with a much grander set of 'rules': those deduced from classical Greek tragedy and noted by Aristotle. *Hedda Gabler* observes the unities: it happens in one place, in a single stretch of time, in a sequence of action which proceeds without inter-ruption or divergence from beginning to end. Characters and action are totally integrated: even Aunt Rina, lying unseen on her death-bed, plays a crucial role in the unfolding of events. The plot concerns a 'tragic flaw' in the leading character: a psychological failing, at first unperceived, which is gradually revealed and which engenders the character's doom. That doom is inevitable from the beginning of the play, and is worked out inexorably before our eyes. There is a moment of recognition: a climactic point when the leading character realises that she is trapped by her own nature and actions and that her destruction is inevitable. The cathartic event of violence takes place offstage.

Aristotelian ideas influence the play's structure as well as its themes. The characteristic organisation of structure in surviving Greek tragedy is an introduction and five sections, of which the last is a kind of extended musical 'coda'. These are interspersed with choral sections which link, frame and counterpoint the main action. The five-act division of Renaissance tragedy probably imitated this pattern, without the choruses. In *Hedda Gabler*, Ibsen follows a four-act pattern, dispensing with the coda. Each act, like each spoken section in Greek tragedy, is a contained thematic unit, advancing the action in a single direction, moving it a few more irretraceable steps towards ultimate catastrophe. The content of Acts 2-4 is not guessable at the end of Act One; that of Acts 3-4 is not guessable at the end of Act Two, and so on – and yet, in retrospect, we recognise that each later event has been prepared and prefigured in what has gone before. The sense of inevitable progression is also achieved by the narrowing focus of the action. Each act is shorter than the one before, and the broad sweep of the opening (exhibiting Berta's character, for example, before revealing something of Hedda's and Tesman's characters in the way they treat Aunt Julia) is never repeated, yielding instead to extremely close attention on single moments, individual relationships, single plot-developments. The way in which, in the play's last three or four pages, Hedda is left with nothing, and with nowhere to turn, is remarkable given that the rhythms of the writing are as easy and everyday as in the entire rest of the play. Its power comes from the inexorable elimination of the inessential, the irising-in, which has preceded it and has continued, uninterrupted, from the first moments of Act One.

Fate and Hubris in *Hedda Gabler*

Although Ibsen follows the 'rules' of Greek tragedy (so closely that it seems unlikely to be by chance), he studiously avoids one of its major themes. Greek tragedies were part of a religious occasion, and their action – usually drawn from myth – arose from the attempts of human beings to come to terms with the nature and demands of the supernatural. The gods in Greek tragedy are devious, all-powerful and implacable, and the fate they oversee for mortals is arbitrary (at least in mortal eyes) and inescapable. The tragic flaw which destroys the protagonist is often hubris: the arrogance which makes mortals think they can transcend their own mortality. None of this applies in Ibsen. Sternly atheist, unswervingly rationalist, he allows religion no part in the events of *Hedda Gabler*. When characters do invoke God (Tesman; Mrs Elvsted; Miss Tesman) it is a superficial, conventional way of talking, to add emphasis to otherwise bland remarks – and Ibsen the ironist takes it one step further when he makes Brack invoke, for the same purpose, not the deity but the devil. The only 'supernatural' force in *Hedda Gabler* is a bleak certainty that to think is to suffer and to take a moral stand is to die. Two of the most 'religious' characters, Tesman and Mrs Elvsted, are involved in the greatest compromises of principle. This is not Fate but a kind of personification of Ibsen's characteristic pessimism: inevitability of failure seen almost as an enabling force, at least until you fail.

The second main force on Ibsen's characters, as dominating as the power of religious observance in Greek tragedy, is social convention. Society and its rules may be human constructs (but so, Ibsen the atheist might have argued, are religious dogma and ritual); but their weight, in this play, is as great as if they had been ordained by God. Characters may take a dozen different approaches to them, from unthinking observance through ironical lip-service to manipulation and challenge, but the rules themselves seldom change. Given Hedda's 'station' in life, and given the situations of Tesman and his aunts, no meeting of minds is possible without self-destructive compromise on someone's part. For Tesman (essentially not a 'noble' character), marriage with Hedda was a gift of chance, a stroke of luck to be snatched, like some wish in a fairy tale, before it disappeared. For Hedda (a 'noble' character), marriage with Tesman was an act of hubris, whose unlikelihood of success she very well knew before she did it. They, and indeed all characters in the play, are imprisoned in themselves, each in what they are – another of Ibsen's commonest, iciest themes.

The Language of *Hedda Gabler*

Throughout *Hedda Gabler*, tightness of form and thematic concentration are balanced by the extraordinary freedom and colloquialism of the language. (The stylistic tension this sets up embodies, in an entirely unforced way, the pull between

Apollonian control and Dionysian abandon which underlies the plot.) Only Miss Tesman speaks with an old-fashioned, faintly artificial turn of phrase, as if she were using a language learned from books or samplers rather than from real life. All other characters speak brisk, unambiguous prose whose self-confident slanginess must have fallen like a cold shower on the ears of Ibsen's first audience. There is no hint of literary stodginess, of the kind sometimes imparted by translators over-respectful of Ibsen's status as a 'literary classic'. The language is intentionally ordinary, and its vernacular simplicity gives pace, verve, and opportunity for darkly comic points-scoring and irony. (All characters, even Berta, use irony.)

For all its insouciant appearance, Ibsen handles this continuum of everyday looseness and naturalness of speech with a virtuosity matching his use of form. The rhythms of the dialogue, both in individual characters' utterances and in whole scenes and acts, are precisely controlled. Early 20th-century critics somewhat fancifully compared *Hedda Gabler* to a symphony. Its four acts, they said, like symphonic movements, might differ in theme and content but were all recognisably part of the same overall conception, aspects of the same mental landscape. In fact the musical analogy aids our understanding of the play's language more than of its form. Ibsen controls pace, for example, or presents, repeats and varies crucial ideas or turns of phrase, as a symphonic composer develops musical themes. A simple example is the by-play between Hedda, Brack, Løvborg and (in a minor way) Mrs Elvsted on the notions of trust, comradeship and the need for, and nature of, a single 'beautiful', existentially self-defining action in each person's life. These exchanges play with a dozen repeated words, as children might pick up toys, look at them and pass them from hand to hand.

A more complex example, articulating Ibsen's presentation of the formality of the society in which the characters move, is the enormous variety of modes of address employed. In English we have perhaps a dozen ways of addressing strangers, acquaintances and intimates. Nineteenth-century Norwegian had many more, and the nuances were far more scrupulously noted. Ibsen makes constant use of this, freighting slight changes of address with emotional and psychological meaning. Thus, the ways in which Hedda addresses Tesman, Løvborg and Brack – and the way she varies modes of address almost from speech to speech – vitally reflect her changing state of mind and the attitudes she strikes. This happens not just in obvious places (such as her first scene alone with Løvborg, where it is almost possible to deduce, from the ways they address each other, the depth of passion in their relationship before Hedda's marriage), but also in the apparently bland ebb and flow of ordinary dialogue. For example, Hedda's changing feelings about Tesman, and her sense of what she wants from him, are reflected by what she calls him. A single instance makes the point: Ibsen's careful placing of the very few occasions when she calls her husband by his first name, 'Jørgen'.

Hedda Gabler in Performance

Hedda Gabler quickly became established, not least because it offers such a superb challenge to the leading actress. Within a few months of its premiere, it was staged in Norway, Britain and the USA, and it has been revived more frequently than any Ibsen play except *The Wild Duck*. Notable English-language Heddas, over the years, have included Janet Achurch, Mrs Patrick Campbell, Sonia Dresdel, Peggy Ashcroft and Fiona Shaw. More recently, Hedda has been played by leading actresses ranging from Glenda Jackson on stage and screen in the 1970s to Eve Best in a production by Richard Eyre in 2005. It has influenced playwrights from Shaw (*Candida* follows its structure particularly closely) to Albee (*Who's Afraid of Virginia Woolf* plays bleak variations on its themes of marital incompatibility and emotional dependence and predation), and its legacy is also apparent in hundreds of excellent film melodramas, from Joan Crawford's and Bette Davis' 1940s vehicles to more recent, more explicitly feminist 'problem films' featuring such actresses as Jane Fonda and Meryl Streep.

Further Reading

In addition to a valuable introduction to *Ghosts*, the fifth volume
of the Oxford *Ibsen*, ed. James McFarlane, Oxford University
Press, contains an appendix of Ibsen's early drafts of the play,
and a selection of important letters. Edited by the same author,
The Cambridge Companion to Ibsen, Cambridge University Press,
1994, is a varied collection of essays by a distinguished
international cast, while George B. Bryan's *An Ibsen Companion*,
Greenwood Press, Westport, Conn., 1984, is a very useful guide,
in dictionary format, to Ibsen's life and work. A similar function
is served by Michael Meyer's compact little *Ibsen on File*,
Methuen, 1985. Meyer's three-volume *Henrik Ibsen*, revised in
1992, and also available in a single, condensed volume, is justly
regarded as the authoritative work in English on Ibsen's life,
and the theatre and politics of his day. The pioneer endeavours
of William Archer in bringing Ibsen to the attention of the
English-speaking world, are commemorated in *William Archer
on Ibsen: The Major Essays 1889-1919*, ed. Thomas Postlewait,
Greenwood Press, Westport, Conn., 1984, and John S.
Chamberlain's *Ibsen: The Open Vision*, Athlone Press, 1982,
includes a particularly thought-provoking discussion of *Ghosts*.
The revised version of Halvdan Koht's *Life of Ibsen*, translated by
Haugen and Santaniello, and published by Benjamin Blom, Inc.,
New York, 1971, despite its venerable age (first published in
1928 to mark Ibsen's centennial) is also worth reading, while
Robert Ferguson's *Henrik Ibsen – A New Biography*, Richard Cohen
Books, 1996, is a fascinating warts-and-all portrayal of a deeply
troubled spirit. Finally, Michael Goldman's *Ibsen: The Dramaturgy
of Fear*, Columbia University Press, New York, 1999, is a
perceptive contribution to Ibsen scholarship.

A Note on Stage Directions

To modern eyes, Ibsen's plays can seem cluttered with unnecessarily explicit stage directions. In particular, his instructions to the actors about how to deliver the lines can seem both pedantic and fustian. Modern conventions, we might argue, are different; we play by our own rules. But it seems at least plausible that Ibsen, so scrupulous about every other kind of artistic effect, might have organised the emotional blocking of each scene with as much care as he did everything else. What we have, in short, may be analogous less to the stage-directions in an 'acting edition' than to the instructions for performing-nuance which composers write on music. For this reason, the present translations retain all original directions, whether they look over-explicit or not.

A DOLL'S HOUSE

translated by Kenneth McLeish

Characters

HELMER

NORA, *his wife*

DOCTOR RANK

MRS LINDE

KROGSTAD

Helmer's three young CHILDREN

ANNE-MARIE, *their nanny*

MAID

PORTER

The action takes place in Helmer's apartment.

ACT ONE

Room in HELMER's *apartment. The decoration is not extravagant, but comfortable and stylish. Back right, door to the hall; back left, door to* HELMER's *study. Between the doors, a piano. Centre left, a door, and beyond it a window; beside the window a round table, easy chairs and a small sofa. Upstage right, a door, and below it a stove, two easy chairs and a rocking chair. Between the door and the stove, a side-table. Engravings on the walls. A cabinet filled with china and other small objects; a small bookcase with expensively-bound books. Carpet on the floor; fire in the stove. Winter.*

A bell rings in the hall, off, and soon afterwards we hear the door being opened. Enter NORA. *She is happy, humming a tune. She is dressed in outdoor clothes, and carries a number of parcels, which she puts down on the table, right. She leaves the hall door open, and through it can be seen a* PORTER, *carrying a Christmas tree and a basket. He gives them to the* CHAMBERMAID, *who has opened the door.*

NORA. Make sure you hide it, Helene. The children mustn't see it till tonight, after it's trimmed. (*To the* PORTER, *taking out her purse.*) How much is that?

PORTER. Fifty øre.

NORA. Keep the change.

The PORTER *thanks her and goes.* NORA *closes the door. She takes off her coat, laughing to herself. She takes a bag of macaroons from her pocket and eats two of them. Then she goes cautiously and listens at* HELMER's *door.*

He is home.

Still humming, she goes to the table right, and starts opening the parcels.

HELMER (*off*). Is that my little songbird piping away out there?

NORA. Yes it is.

HELMER (*off*). Is that my little squirrel rustling?

NORA. Yes.

HELMER (*off*). When did squirrelkin come home?

NORA. Just now.

She puts the macaroons in her pocket and wipes her mouth.

Come out here, Torvald, and see what I bought.

HELMER (*off*). Just a moment.

After a short pause, he opens the door and looks in, pen in hand.

Did you say bought? All those? Has my little songbird been spending all my money again?

NORA. Oh Torvald, this year we can let ourselves go a little. It's the first Christmas we don't have to scrimp and save.

HELMER. That doesn't mean we've money to burn.

NORA. Can't we burn just a little? A tiny little? Now you're getting such a big pay-packet, pennies and pennies and pennies.

HELMER. After January the first. And even then we won't see the money till the end of the first quarter.

NORA. Oh fiddle, we can borrow till then.

HELMER. Nora!

He takes her playfully by the ear.

What a little featherbrain it is! I borrow a thousand kroner today, you spend it all by Christmas, and on New Year's Eve a tile falls on my head and kills me –

NORA (*hand to mouth*). Don't say that.

HELMER. But suppose it did?

NORA. If it did, why would I care if I still owed people money?

HELMER. But what about them? The people I borrowed it from?

NORA. Who cares about them? I don't even know their names.

HELMER. Just like a woman! But seriously, you know what
I think. No borrowing. No debt. When a household relies
on debt, it's slavery, it's vile. We've struggled this far
without, the two of us – and we'll struggle on for a few
more weeks, till we don't have to struggle any more.

NORA (*crossing to the stove*). Yes, Torvald.

HELMER (*following*). There, there. Poor little songbird,
drooping her wings? Little squirrel, making sulky faces?

He takes out his wallet.

Nora, what have I here?

NORA (*turning quickly*). Pennies!

HELMER. Look. (*Giving her money.*) Heavens, d'you think I
don't know what it costs at Christmastime?

NORA (*counting*). Ten, twenty, thirty, forty. Oh thank you,
Torvald, thank you. Now I'll manage.

HELMER. You must.

NORA. I will. Now come here, and see what I've bought.
Bargains! A new outfit for Ivar, and a little sword. A
horse and a trumpet for Bob. A dolly and a dolly's bed
for Emmy. Nothing expensive: they'll soon be broken,
anyway. Dress-lengths and hankies for the maids. Old
Anne-Marie should really have something better.

HELMER. What's in this one?

NORA (*with a shriek*). No, Torvald. Not till tonight!

HELMER. And what about my own little spendthrift? What
would she like, herself?

NORA. Oh fiddle. Me? I don't want anything.

HELMER. Of course you do. Tell me some little thing you'd
like more than all the world.

NORA. I really don't . . . Unless . . . Torvald . . .

HELMER. Yes?

NORA (*playing with his buttons, not looking at him*). If you really
want to give me something, you could . . . you could . . .

HELMER. Out with it.

NORA (*blurting it*). Give me some pennies of my own. Just what you can spare. I could keep them till I really wanted something . . .

HELMER. Oh, Nora –

NORA. Please, Torvald, please. I'll wrap them in pretty paper and hang them on the tree. They'll be so pretty.

HELMER. What do they call little birds that are always wasting money?

NORA. Featherbrains. I know. But why don't we try it, Torvald, try it? Give me time to think what I'd really like? It would be a good idea.

HELMER (*smiling*). Of course it would – if you really did manage to save it, to spend on yourself. But it'll just go into the housekeeping, you'll spend it on this or that, and I'll end up forking out again.

NORA. No, Torvald.

HELMER. Darling Nora, yes.

He puts his arm round her waist.

What a sweet little featherbrain it is. But it swallows up so many pennies. It costs a lot of pennies, to keep a little featherbrain.

NORA. Don't be horrid. I do save, all I can.

HELMER (*with a laugh*). All you can. That's right. The whole trouble is, you can't.

NORA (*smiling gently and playfully*). Oh Torvald, songbirds, squirrels, you know how we spend and spend.

HELMER. What a funny little thing it is. Daddy's daughter. A thousand little ways of wheedling pennies – and as soon as you've got them, they melt in your hands. You never know where they've gone. It's in the blood, little Nora, it's inherited.

NORA. I wish I'd inherited some of Daddy's other qualities.

HELMER. I wouldn't have you any different. Dear little bird, little darling. But what is it? There's something, isn't there? There is.

NORA. What?

HELMER. Look at me.

NORA (*looking at him*). There.

HELMER (*wagging his finger*). Was little Miss Sweet-tooth naughty in town today?

NORA. What d'you mean?

HELMER. Did she visit the sweetie-shop?

NORA. No, Torvald. I promise.

HELMER. She's not been nibbling?

NORA. No. No.

HELMER. Not one tiny macaroon?

NORA. Torvald, I swear –

HELMER. It's all right. I was only joking.

NORA (*crossing to the table right*). You told me not to. You don't really think I'd – ?

HELMER. Of course not. You promised.

He goes to her.

Darling Nora, keep all your Christmas secrets to yourself. They'll all come out this evening, when we light the tree.

NORA. Did you remember to invite Dr Rank?

HELMER. There's no need: he'll eat with us, goes without saying. I'll ask him when he comes this morning. I've ordered good wine. Nora, you can't imagine how much I'm looking forward to this evening.

NORA. So am I. Oh Torvald, what fun the children will have!

HELMER. A secure job, a good income – isn't it wonderful?

NORA. Wonderful.

HELMER. Remember last Christmas? How you shut yourself in here evening after evening for three whole weeks, making tree-decorations and all the other surprises? The dullest three weeks I've ever spent.

NORA. I wasn't bored.

HELMER (*smiling*). It's not as if anything much came of it, Nora.

NORA. Don't be horrid. How could I guess that the cat would get in and tear everything to bits?

HELMER. There, there, of course you couldn't. You wanted to please us all, that was the main thing. But thank goodness, even so, that those hard times are past us now.

NORA. It's really wonderful.

HELMER. No more Torvald sitting all alone and bored. No more Nora wearing out her lovely eyes, her pretty little fingers −

NORA (*clapping her hands*). No, Torvald, never again! (*Taking his arm.*) Now, shall I tell you what we ought to do? As soon as Christmas is over −

Ring at the bell, off.

A visitor.

She begins tidying the room.

What a nuisance.

HELMER. I'm not at home.

MAID (*at the door*). There's a lady, madam . . . a stranger.

NORA. Show her in.

MAID (*to* HELMER). The doctor's here too.

HELMER. In the study?

MAID. Yes, sir.

HELMER *goes into the study. The* MAID *shows in* MRS LINDE, *who is wearing travelling clothes, and shuts the door after her.*

MRS LINDE (*timidly, rather ill-at-ease*). Good morning, Nora.

NORA (*hesitantly*). Good morning.

MRS LINDE. You don't recognise me.

NORA. No, I . . . just a minute . . . (*Suddenly.*) Kristine!

MRS LINDE. That's right.

NORA. Kristine! To think I didn't recognise you. (*More subdued.*) You've changed, Kristine.

MRS LINDE. Nine, ten years –

NORA. Is it really so long? I suppose it is. I've been so happy these last eight years. And now you've come back to town. Such a long journey, in winter too. Aren't you brave?

MRS LINDE. I came on the steamer this morning.

NORA. Just in time for Christmas. What a lovely surprise! What a time we'll have. Take your coat off. You can't be cold. (*Helping her.*) There. Let's be cosy, by the stove. This armchair. I'll sit in the rocking chair. (*Taking her hands.*) That's better. Now you're like you always were. It was just that first moment. You're paler, Kristine, thinner.

MRS LINDE. Older.

NORA. A tiny bit.

Suddenly she breaks off, and speaks seriously.

How thoughtless of me, sitting here chattering. Kristine, darling, I'm sorry.

MRS LINDE. What d'you mean?

NORA (*with sympathy*). Dear Kristine, you lost your husband.

MRS LINDE. Three years ago.

NORA. I read it in the paper. I did mean to write. I thought about it, often. But I kept putting it off . . . there was always something . . .

MRS LINDE. Don't worry.

NORA. It was horrid of me. Poor Kristine. Did he leave you enough to live on?

MRS LINDE. No.

NORA. You've children?

MRS LINDE. No.

NORA. You've nothing?

MRS LINDE. Not even sad memories.

NORA (*looking at her in amazement*). But surely – ?

MRS LINDE (*smiling sadly, stroking her hair*). It happens, Nora.

NORA. Completely alone. That must be awful. I've got three beautiful children. They aren't here now, they're out with Nanny. But tell me everything.

MRS LINDE. No, no, you first.

NORA. No, you. Today I won't be selfish. I'll put you first. But there is just one thing – d'you know what a stroke of luck we've had?

MRS LINDE. What is it?

NORA. They've made my husband manager. At the Bank!

MRS LINDE. That's wonderful.

NORA. Unbelievable. He was a lawyer. But that's not secure, especially if you won't take on cases for people you don't approve of. Torvald never would, and of course I agree with him. But now! Imagine! He starts in the New Year. A big salary and lots of bonuses. Our lives'll be so different. We'll be able to do anything we want. Oh Kristine, I'm so relieved, so happy. To have no more worries, all one needs. Isn't it wonderful?

MRS LINDE. Wonderful, yes, to have all one needs.

NORA. Not just all one needs, but lots of money, lots.

MRS LINDE (*lightly*). Nora, Nora, have you still not grown up? You were an extravagant little thing at school.

NORA (*with a light laugh*). That's just what Torvald calls me. (*Wagging a finger.*) 'Nora, Nora' – she's not all featherbrain. Not all you both think. We've never had the money for me to waste. We've had to work, both of us.

MRS LINDE. You, as well?

NORA. Odds and ends. Sewing, embroidery, things like that. (*In a low voice.*) And other things too. You know Torvald set up on his own when we got married? He'd no prospects at the office, and he had to earn more money. In the first year, he overworked terribly. It was because of the money. He worked every hour there was. It was too much for him. He had a breakdown, and the doctors said he had to get away, go South.

MRS LINDE. You went to Italy, didn't you? A year in Italy.

NORA. It was hard to get away. It was just after Ivar was born. But we simply had to. It was wonderful, Kristine, and it saved Torvald's life. The only thing was, it cost a fortune.

MRS LINDE. I can imagine.

NORA. Four thousand, eight hundred kroner. A fortune.

MRS LINDE. You were lucky to have it, just when you needed it.

NORA. Ah well, it came from Daddy.

MRS LINDE. I remember, your father died about that time.

NORA. Can you imagine, I couldn't go and look after him? I was expecting Ivar, any day. Torvald was really ill. Poor, darling Daddy. I never saw him again, Kristine. It was the worst time of my whole married life.

MRS LINDE. I know how fond you were of him. But then you all went to Italy.

NORA. We had the money then, and the doctors insisted. So we went, a month later.

MRS LINDE. And your husband recovered?

NORA. Oh yes, yes.

MRS LINDE. But . . . the doctor?

NORA. Pardon?

MRS LINDE. I thought the maid said that was the doctor, that man who arrived at the same time I did.

NORA. Oh, Dr Rank. It's not because anyone's ill. An old friend – he comes every day. No, since Italy, Torvald hasn't had a moment's illness. The children are fine, and so am I.

She jumps up and claps her hands.

Kristine, it's all so wonderful. We're so happy, so lucky. Oh . . . how awful of me. Talking of nothing but myself.

She sits on a stool beside her, and rests her arms on her knee.

Don't be cross. Is it really true, you didn't love him, your husband? Why ever did you marry him?

MRS LINDE. My mother was still alive: bedridden, helpless. I'd two younger brothers to look after. When he proposed, how could I not accept?

NORA. He'd money too, hadn't he?

MRS LINDE. Then, he did. I think. But his business was shaky. After he died, it collapsed entirely. There was nothing left.

NORA. So how did you – ?

MRS LINDE. Whatever I could find. A shop . . . a little school . . . It's been endless hard work, these last three years. I haven't had a moment. But now it's finished. My mother's passed on, needs nothing more. The boys have jobs, they don't need me either –

NORA. You must feel so relieved!

MRS LINDE. No, empty. No one left to live for.

She gets up, in distress.

I couldn't bear it any longer, life in that backwater. Better to find something here, to occupy me, to fill my mind. If I could get a job, some kind of office job –

NORA. But that'll be exhausting, Kristine. Draining. You look worn out. Why don't you go away somewhere, have a holiday?

MRS LINDE (*crossing to the window*). Dear Nora, I've no Daddy to pay the bills.

NORA (*getting up*). Don't be cross with me.

MRS LINDE (*going to her*). Nora, don't you be cross. The worst thing about a situation like mine is that it makes you hard. No one else to work for; always out for yourself; survival, it makes you selfish. You won't believe this: when you told me how well things were going for you, I was delighted – not for you, for me.

NORA. Pardon? Oh. If Torvald did something for you . . .

MRS LINDE. Yes.

NORA. Of course he will, Kristine. Leave it to me. I'll see to it. I'll find a way. Put him in a good mood. I'd love to help you.

MRS LINDE. You're so kind. To be so eager to help me. Especially you, when you've so little idea how difficult life can be.

NORA. Me – ?

MRS LINDE (*with a smile*). Sewing, embroidering . . . Nora, you're a babe in arms.

NORA (*moving away, with a toss of the head*). Don't be so snooty.

MRS LINDE. What d'you mean?

NORA. You're all the same. None of you think I can manage anything . . . serious.

MRS LINDE. No, no.

NORA. You think I don't know how hard life is.

MRS LINDE. But you've just told me yourself. Your problems.

NORA. Fiddle. They were nothing. (*Quietly.*) I haven't told you the real one.

MRS LINDE. What real one?

NORA. You don't take me seriously. You should. Aren't you proud of all you did, all that hard work for your mother?

MRS LINDE. I take everyone seriously. Of course I'm proud, I made my mother's last months a little easier.

NORA. And your brothers – you're proud of what you did for them.

MRS LINDE. I've a right to be.

NORA. Of course you have. And so do I. I've a right to be proud too.

MRS LINDE. Why? What d'you mean?

NORA. Sh! Torvald must never hear. He mustn't ever – no one in the world must ever know, except you, Kristine.

MRS LINDE. Know what?

NORA. Come over here.

She pulls her to the sofa and sits beside her.

I *have* got something to be proud of. The person who saved Torvald's life – it was me.

MRS LINDE. Saved his life? How?

NORA. The trip to Italy. I told you. If he hadn't gone –

MRS LINDE. But your father –

NORA (*smiling*). That's what everyone thought. Torvald . . . everyone.

MRS LINDE. But –

NORA. We didn't have a penny from Daddy. I paid. I got the money.

MRS LINDE. All of it?

NORA. Four thousand, eight hundred kroner.

MRS LINDE. Nora, how? Did you win the Lottery?

NORA (*scornfully*). The Lottery! Pff! *That* wouldn't have been clever.

MRS LINDE. How did you get it, then?

NORA (*smiling mysteriously, humming*). Hm, hm, hm.

MRS LINDE. You didn't – *borrow* it?

NORA. Why not?

MRS LINDE. A wife can't borrow without her husband's permission.

NORA (*tossing her head*). Unless she knows about business . . . knows her way around.

MRS LINDE. I don't understand.

NORA. Never mind. I didn't say I *did* borrow it. There are plenty of other ways.

She stretches out on the sofa.

Perhaps it was one of my admirers. I'm such a pretty little thing . . .

MRS LINDE. You are silly.

NORA. And you're nosy.

MRS LINDE. Nora. Are you sure you haven't done something . . . rash?

NORA (*sitting up straight*). Saving my husband's life?

MRS LINDE. I mean rash, if he didn't know − ?

NORA. That's the whole point. He wasn't to know. Don't you understand? He was never to know how ill he was. The doctors came to me, to me, and told me his life depended on it. Time in the South, in the sun. D'you think I didn't try to wheedle him? I told him it was for me, how lovely it would be to go abroad, like other young wives. I begged, I cried. I told him to think of my condition, he had to be kind to me, humour me. I hinted that he took out a loan. Kristine, he almost lost his temper. He said I was featherbrained, and his duty as a husband was not to indulge my . . . my little whims, he called them. Right, right, I thought. If you won't save yourself . . . So I . . . found a way myself.

MRS LINDE. Torvald never knew the money wasn't from your father?

NORA. Of course not. Daddy died about that time. I'd wanted to tell him, to ask him to help. But first he was too ill, then it was too late.

MRS LINDE. And you've never told your husband?

NORA. For heaven's sake! When he thinks the way he does.
In any case, Torvald, a man, proud to be a man – how
d'you imagine he'd feel if he knew he owed anything to
me? It would break us apart. Our lovely home, our
happiness – all gone.

MRS LINDE. You won't ever tell him?

NORA (*thoughtfully, with a light smile*). One day. Perhaps.
When I'm not quite such a pretty little thing. Don't laugh.
I mean when Torvald isn't as smitten as he is now, when
he's tired of me dancing, reciting, dressing up. Then I
may need something in reserve. (*Abruptly.*) Da, da, da. It'll
never happen. Well, Kristine? What d'you think of my
great big secret? D'you still think I'm silly? No cares in all
the world? Don't think it's been easy, meeting the
payments on time, each time. Quarterly accounts,
instalments – I can tell you all about that sort of thing.
Keeping up with them's not easy. I've saved a little bit
here, a little bit there. Not much from the housekeeping,
because of Torvald's position. The children couldn't go
without nice clothes. Every penny he gave me for my little
darlings, I spent on them.

MRS LINDE. Oh, Nora! It came out of your own
allowance?

NORA. What else? That was mine to do as I liked with.
Every time Torvald gave me money for clothes, I put half
of it away. I bought the simplest, cheapest things. Thank
heavens everything looks good on me: Torvald never
noticed. But it was hard, Kristine, often. It's nice to wear
nice clothes. Don't you think?

KRISTINE. Oh . . . yes, yes.

NORA. Fortunately there were other things I could do. Last
winter I was lucky: I got a lot of copying. I locked myself
in every evening and sat and wrote, into the small hours.
It was exhausting. But it was thrilling too, to be sitting
there working, earning money. Almost like a man.

MRS LINDE. How much have you paid back?

NORA. I really don't know. Business: it's hard to keep track of. All I know is, I paid every penny I could scrape together. The number of times I didn't know *how* I'd manage! (*Smiling.*) When that happened, I used to sit and daydream. A rich old man was head over heels in love with me –

MRS LINDE. What? Who?

NORA. Sh! He died, and when they read his will, there it was in capital letters: ALL MY CASH TO BE PAID OVER INSTANTER TO THAT DELIGHTFUL NORA HELMER.

MRS LINDE. Nora! Who on Earth was it?

NORA. Heavens, can't you guess? He didn't exist, he just came into my head every time I sat here thinking how to get some money. It doesn't matter now, anyway. The silly old nuisance can stay away; I don't need him and I don't need his will. I'm free of it! (*Jumping up.*) Free, Kristine, free of it! I can play with the children . . . make the house pretty, make everything the way Torvald likes it. It'll soon be spring, the wide blue sky. We could have a holiday . . . the seaside. Free of it! I'm so happy, so happy.

A bell rings, off.

MRS LINDE (*getting up*). I'd better go.

NORA. No, stay. It'll be for Torvald.

MAID (*in the doorway from the hall*). Excuse me, madam. There's a gentleman here to see the master.

NORA. To see the Bank Manager.

MAID. Yes, madam. But I didn't know if . . . Dr Rank's still there.

NORA. Who is the gentleman?

KROGSTAD (*at the door*). Me, Mrs Helmer.

MRS LINDE *starts, then goes over to the window.* NORA *goes closer to* KROGSTAD, *and speaks in a low, strained voice.*

NORA. You. What is it? What d'you want with my husband?

KROGSTAD. Bank business. I work for the Bank, very
    junior. Your husband's the new manager, and so –

NORA. So it's –

KROGSTAD. Business, Mrs Helmer. Nothing else.

NORA. Please go in, then. Into the study.

*She inclines her head casually, closes the hall door, then goes and
starts making up the stove.*

MRS LINDE. Nora, who was that?

NORA. Krogstad. Used to be a lawyer.

MRS LINDE. Oh yes.

NORA. You knew him?

MRS LINDE. A long time ago. He was a solicitor's clerk.

NORA. That's right.

MRS LINDE. How he's changed.

NORA. Unhappy marriage.

MRS LINDE. Didn't his wife die? Isn't he a widower?

NORA. With a houseful of children. There, that's better.

She shuts the stove and moves the rocking chair to one side.

MRS LINDE. What does he do now?

NORA. I don't know. Don't let's talk about business: it's
    boring.

DR RANK *comes out from* HELMER's *study.*

RANK (*at the door*). No, no, my dear chap. I'll get out of
    your way. I'll talk to Nora.

He shuts the door, then notices MRS LINDE.

Oh, excuse me. Company here as well.

NORA. It's all right. (*Introducing them.*) Dr Rank, Mrs Linde.

RANK. Dear lady. We often hear your name in this house.
    Didn't I pass you on the stairs just now?

MRS LINDE. I go slowly; I find stairs hard.

RANK. You're not well?

MRS LINDE. Overworked.

RANK. Ah. So you came to town for our . . . distractions?

MRS LINDE. To find work.

RANK. Is that the best cure for overwork?

MRS LINDE. One has to live.

RANK. Yes. So they say.

NORA. Oh Doctor . . . you know *you* want to live.

RANK. Most certainly. However dreadful I feel, I want to
prolong the agony as long as possible. My patients all feel
the same way. Not to mention those who are morally sick
– one of whom, very far gone, is with Helmer even as we
speak.

MRS LINDE (*distressed*). Oh.

NORA. Whoever do you mean?

RANK. Krogstad, his name is. An ex-lawyer. No one you
know. Totally depraved. But even he was prattling on
about how he had to *live*.

NORA. Why did he want to talk to Torvald?

RANK. Something about the Bank.

NORA. I didn't know Krog – Mr Krogstad – was connected
with the Bank.

RANK. He's got some sort of position there. (*To* MRS
LINDE.) I don't know if it's the same where you are.
Some people go round sniffing out weakness . . . and as
soon as they find it, they back the person concerned into
a corner, a . . . profitable corner. No escape. If you're
strong, they leave you alone.

MRS LINDE. You don't need curing unless you're sick.

RANK (*shrugging*). – and that makes all society a nursing home.

NORA *has been absorbed in her own thoughts; now she smothers a
laugh and claps her hands.*

How else would you describe society?

NORA. What do I care about silly old society? I'm laughing at something else. Dr Rank, it's true, isn't it? Everyone who works at the Bank has to answer to Torvald now?

RANK. You find that funny?

NORA (*smiling, humming*). No, no. (*Pacing.*) It's just odd to think that we – that Torvald has power over so many people. (*Taking the sweet packet from her pocket.*) Dr Rank, a macaroon?

RANK. I thought they were forbidden.

NORA. Kristine gave me these.

MRS LINDE. What?

NORA. It's all right. You didn't know Torvald had forbidden them. He thinks they'll ruin my teeth. Fiddle! Just once in a while. Dr Rank, don't you agree? Have one.

She puts a macaroon in his mouth.

You too, Kristine. I'll have one too. Just a little one. Perhaps two. (*Pacing again.*) I'm really so happy. There's only one thing left –

RANK. What's that?

NORA. I'd like to say something straight out. Something to Torvald.

RANK. Why don't you, then?

NORA. I daren't. It's too terrible.

MRS LINDE. Terrible?

RANK. If it's terrible, you'd better not. Say it to us, if you like. What is it you'd say to Helmer, if he was here?

NORA. I'd say – Good God!

RANK. Tut, tut.

MRS LINDE. Don't be silly, Nora.

RANK. He *is* here. Say it.

NORA (*hiding the macaroon-packet*). Sh!

HELMER *comes out of his study, with his coat over his arm and his hat in his hand.* NORA *runs to him.*

Torvald, darling, did you get rid of him?

HELMER. Yes, he's gone.

NORA. Let me introduce you. This is Kristine. She's come to town.

HELMER. I'm sorry . . . Kristine . . . ?

NORA. Mrs Linde, darling. Kristine Linde.

HELMER. Oh yes. One of Nora's schoolfriends?

MRS LINDE. We knew each other once.

NORA. Just imagine, she's come all this way just to talk to you.

HELMER. Pardon?

MRS LINDE. No, no, I —

NORA. Kristine's a genius at book-keeping. All she needs is the right man to work for, someone who'll show her even more than she knows already.

HELMER. Very commendable, Mrs Linde.

NORA. So of course, as soon as she heard that you were the new Bank Manager — they sent a telegram — she came here as fast as she could . . . Torvald, won't you find her something? For my sake?

HELMER. It's not a bad idea. Madam, are you a widow?

MRS LINDE. Yes.

HELMER. You've book-keeping experience?

MRS LINDE. A bit.

HELMER. I may well have something —

NORA *(clapping her hands)*. See? See?

HELMER. In fact, Mrs Linde, you could hardly have come at a better time.

MRS LINDE. How can I ever thank you?

HELMER. Oh, that's all right. (*Putting on his coat.*) But for the moment, if you'll excuse me . . .

RANK. Wait. I'll go with you.

He takes his fur coat and warms it at the stove.

NORA. Don't be too long, darling.

HELMER. An hour, no more.

NORA. Are you going too, Kristine?

MRS LINDE (*putting on her coat*). I need to find a room.

HELMER. We'll walk along together.

NORA (*helping her*). It's a shame we're so cramped here. We just can't −

MRS LINDE. No, no. Bye-bye, Nora − and thanks.

NORA. Till tomorrow. Yes, come tomorrow. You too, Dr Rank. What − if you're well enough? Of course you will be. Wrap up well.

They go towards the hall, all talking. Children's voices on the stairs outside.

They're here! They're here!

She runs to open the door. ANNE-MARIE, *the nanny, comes in with the* CHILDREN.

Come in. Come in.

She bends to kiss them.

Darlings. Dear little darlings. Kristine, aren't they darlings?

RANK. Let's get out of the draught.

HELMER. This way, Mrs Linde. This'll soon be no place to be, except for mothers.

He, RANK *and* MRS LINDE *go downstairs.* ANNE-MARIE *and the* CHILDREN *come into the room, followed by* NORA, *who closes the hall door. The* CHILDREN *chatter to her during what follows.*

NORA. Haven't you had fun? Such rosy cheeks. Like little red apples. Have you had a lovely time? What, both of

them? Emmy *and* Bob? Both on the sledge at once. And
you pulled them, Ivar? What a clever boy. Let me hold
her a moment, Anne-Marie. My own little dolly-baby.

She takes the smallest CHILD *and dances with her in her arms.*

Yes, Bob. I'll dance with you too. Did you? Snowballs? I
wish I'd been there. It's all right, Anne-Marie, I'll take
their coats off. No, no, I enjoy it. You go in. You look
frozen. There's coffee on the stove.

ANNE-MARIE *goes into the room left.* NORA *helps the*
CHILDREN *out of their coats and scatters them about, as the*
CHILDREN *all talk to her at once.*

A big dog? Ran after you? Of course it didn't bite. Dogs
don't bite dear little dolly-babies. Don't touch those, Ivar.
Wait and see. A surprise. Let's play a game. Let's play . . .
hide and seek. Bob hide first. What? Mummy hide first?
All right. You try to find me.

She and the CHILDREN *play, laughing and shouting, running in*
and out of the room on the right. Eventually NORA *hides under*
the table. The CHILDREN *run in, but can't find her, till they*
hear her smothered laughter, lift up the ends of the tablecloth and see
her. Shrieks of delight. She crawls out, pretending to frighten them.
Louder shrieks. Meanwhile someone has knocked at the hall door,
unheard. The door is half opened, and KROGSTAD *appears. He*
waits in the doorway. The game continues.

KROGSTAD. Excuse me. Mrs Helmer.

NORA *gives a stifled cry, and gets to her knees.*

NORA. Ah! What is it?

KROGSTAD. I'm sorry. The door was on the latch . . .

NORA (*getting up*). Mr Krogstad, my husband's out.

KROGSTAD. I know.

NORA. Then . . . what is it?

KROGSTAD. It's you I want to talk to.

NORA. Me? (*Gently, to the* CHILDREN.) Go in there, to
Anne-Marie. What? No, the man won't hurt Mummy.
When he's gone, we'll have another game.

She takes the children into the room left, and shuts the door behind them. She is uneasy, and speaks tightly.

You want to talk to me?

KROGSTAD. Yes.

NORA. It's not the first of the month.

KROGSTAD. It's Christmas Eve. And what sort of Christmas Day you have, depends on you.

NORA. I can't do anything today.

KROGSTAD. It's not that. Later. It's something else. You have got a moment – ?

NORA. Yes. Of course. I . . . Yes.

KROGSTAD. I was in Olsen's Restaurant and saw your husband in the street.

NORA. Yes?

KROGSTAD. With a woman.

NORA. What of it?

KROGSTAD. Pardon me for asking, but was that Mrs Linde?

NORA. Yes.

KROGSTAD. Just arrived?

NORA. Today.

KROGSTAD. A friend of yours?

NORA. I don't –

KROGSTAD. Mine too. Once.

NORA. I know.

KROGSTAD. Ah. Well, I'll ask straight out: has Mrs Linde been given a job in the Bank?

NORA. Mr Krogstad, you shouldn't ask me that. An employee. But since you have . . . Yes, Mrs Linde has been given a job. On my recommendation. Satisfied?

KROGSTAD. I thought she had.

NORA (*pacing*). One isn't without influence. Just because one's a woman. And employees, Mr Krogstad, people in positions of dependence, should be careful not to annoy people who, people who . . .

KROGSTAD. Have influence?

NORA. Exactly.

KROGSTAD (*changed tone*). Mrs Helmer, you'll oblige me by putting your influence to work for me.

NORA. What d'you mean?

KROGSTAD. You'll oblige me by making sure that I keep my . . . position of dependence in the Bank.

NORA. Is someone taking it away?

KROGSTAD. Don't pretend you don't know. It's obvious that your friend doesn't want to bump into me again – and it's also obvious who I've got to thank for getting me the sack.

NORA. But –

KROGSTAD. Never mind. I'm telling you: use your influence to see it doesn't happen.

NORA. Mr Krogstad, I don't have any influence.

KROGSTAD. That's not what you said just now.

NORA. I didn't mean . . . you shouldn't have . . . What makes you think I can influence my husband?

KROGSTAD. I've known your husband for years. He can be influenced, Mr Manager, just like anyone else.

NORA. If you're impertinent about my husband, you can leave my house.

KROGSTAD. Oh, very brave.

NORA. I'm not afraid of you. Not any more. As soon as it's New Year, I'll be finished with the whole business.

KROGSTAD (*with control*). Mrs Helmer, understand one thing: if it comes to it, I'll fight for my job as if I was fighting for my life.

NORA. That's obvious.

KROGSTAD. The money's not important. It's something else. It's . . . ah . . . You must be aware that some time ago, a long time ago, I . . . slipped up a little.

NORA. I heard.

KROGSTAD. It never came to court. But it . . . blocked me, barred doors against me. That's why I began my business. You know what I mean. I had to make a living – and I wasn't one of the worst. But now I want done with it. My sons are growing up; for their sakes I want to be respectable again, as much as possible. That job at the Bank was the first step – and now your husband is kicking me down to the mud again.

NORA. Mr Krogstad, for heaven's sake, I can't help you.

KROGSTAD. Can't? Won't. But I think you must.

NORA. You'd tell my husband I owe you money?

KROGSTAD. Why not?

NORA. How can you? (*Fighting back tears.*) My secret, my pride, my treasure – and he hears it from *you*. It's horrid. It'll be so *awkward*.

KROGSTAD. *Awkward?*

NORA (*angrily*). Do it, do it, and see where it gets you. My husband'll see what sort of man you are. You'll never get your job back.

KROGSTAD. What I meant was, is it just awkwardness you're afraid of?

NORA. As soon as my husband hears, he'll pay you every penny. Naturally. At once. And then we'll be rid of you for good.

KROGSTAD (*closer*). Mrs Helmer. Pay attention. Either you've a very bad memory, or you know nothing of business. I'd better remind you.

NORA. What?

KROGSTAD. Your husband was ill. You came to me for a loan. Four thousand, eight hundred kroner.

NORA. Where else was I to turn?

KROGSTAD. I said I'd find the money –

NORA. You did find it.

KROGSTAD. – on certain conditions. You were so upset about your husband, so eager for the money to cure him, I don't think you noticed the conditions. So I'd better remind you. I said I'd find the money; I wrote a contract.

NORA. And I signed it.

KROGSTAD. That's right. But underneath your signature was a clause saying that your father would guarantee the repayments. Your father should have signed that clause.

NORA. He did.

KROGSTAD. I left the date blank. Your father was to fill it in: the date he signed the document. You remember that, Mrs Helmer?

NORA. I think so.

KROGSTAD. I gave you the contract, to post to your father. You remember that?

NORA. Yes.

KROGSTAD. You must have done it immediately, because you brought it back in less than a week, with your father's signature. Then I gave you the money.

NORA. And I've been paying it back, haven't I? As arranged?

KROGSTAD. Let's keep to the point, Mrs Helmer. That must have been a very difficult time for you.

NORA. Yes.

KROGSTAD. Your father was desperately ill.

NORA. Yes.

KROGSTAD. In fact he died soon after?

NORA. Yes.

KROGSTAD. Mrs Helmer, can you remember the exact date? The date he died?

NORA. 29th September.

KROGSTAD. Yes indeed. I checked. That's what makes it so extraordinary . . .

He takes out a paper.

So hard to explain . . .

NORA. What's hard to explain?

KROGSTAD. The fact that your father signed this document three days after he died.

NORA. What d'you mean?

KROGSTAD. Your father died on the 29th September. But he dated his signature – here, look – on the 2nd October. As I say, Mrs Helmer: extraordinary.

NORA says nothing.

Can *you* explain it?

No answer.

Even more extraordinary: the words 2nd October, and the year, aren't in your father's writing, but in someone else's. I think I know whose. It's easily explained. Your father forgot to date his signature, so someone else dated it, someone who didn't know the date he died. But none of that's important. What's important is that the signature's genuine. There's no doubt about that, is there, Mrs Helmer? This is your father's signature?

Short pause. Then NORA lifts her head and looks defiantly at him.

NORA. No, it isn't. I signed father's name.

KROGSTAD. Mrs Helmer, you shouldn't have admitted that.

NORA. You'll get your money.

KROGSTAD. Tell me: why didn't you send your father the contract?

NORA. He was too ill. I couldn't. I'd have had to tell him what the money was for. He was so ill, I couldn't tell him my husband was at death's door too. I couldn't.

KROGSTAD. You should have cancelled the trip abroad.

NORA. My husband's life! How could I?

KROGSTAD. It never worried you, that you were cheating me?

NORA. I couldn't let it. I couldn't consider you. I hated you . . . all that coldness, those conditions, when you knew how ill my husband was.

KROGSTAD. Mrs Helmer, you've obviously no idea just what you've done. But I'll tell you, it was nothing more or less than my own . . . mistake. All those years ago.

NORA. You took a risk, that kind of risk, to save your wife?

KROGSTAD. The law's not interested in reasons.

NORA. Then it's a fool.

KROGSTAD. Fool or not, it's what you'll be judged by, if I take this document to court.

NORA. Nonsense. A daughter can't save her dying father from care and worry? A wife can't help her sick husband? I know nothing about the law, but there must be laws about that. You were supposed to be a lawyer – didn't you know about them? You can't have been much of a lawyer.

KROGSTAD. Maybe not. But contracts, the kind of contract you made with me, I know all about those. You understand? Good. Do as you please, but remember one thing: if I lose everything a second time, you keep me company.

He bows and goes out through the hall. NORA *is lost in thought for a moment, then tosses her head.*

NORA. Ridiculous. He was trying to scare me. I'm not so silly.

She starts gathering the CHILDREN*'s clothes. Stops suddenly.*

But suppose – ? No. I did it for love.

CHILDREN (*at the door, left*). Mummy, he's gone, the man.

NORA. That's right, he's gone. Don't tell anyone he came. Not even Daddy.

CHILDREN. Mummy, let's play another game.

NORA. No. No. Not now.

CHILDREN. You promised.

NORA. I can't just now. I'm too busy. Go in. Darlings, go in.

She manages to get them out of the room and shuts the door. She sits on the sofa, takes up some sewing and does a stitch or two, then stops.

No!

She puts the sewing down, goes to the hall door and calls.

Helene! Bring in the Christmas tree.

She goes to table, left, opens a drawer then stops again.

I can't. I can't.

The MAID *brings in the tree.*

MAID. Where shall I put it, madam?

NORA. There, in the middle.

MAID. Can I get anything else?

NORA. No thank you. I've all I need.

The MAID *puts the tree down, and goes.* NORA *starts trimming it.*

A candle here . . . flowers here . . . That dreadful man. No, no, it's all right. The tree, the tree must be beautiful. Torvald, I'll do whatever you want. I'll sing for you, dance for you −

HELMER *comes in, with papers.*

Ah! Back so soon?

HELMER. That's right. Has anyone called?

NORA. No.

HELMER. I saw Krogstad at the gate.

NORA. Krogstad? Ah. He was here, just for a moment.

HELMER. Nora, I know what it is. He was asking you to put in a word for him.

NORA. Yes.

HELMER. You were to pretend it was your idea? You were to pretend he hadn't been here? Did he ask that too?

NORA. Oh, Torvald –

HELMER. Nora, how could you? Talk to a man like that, make promises, lie to me?

NORA. Lie?

HELMER. No one called, you said. (*Wagging his finger.*) Little bird must never do that again. Little bird must only sing pretty songs. No nasties. (*Putting his arm round her waist.*) Isn't that right? Of course it is. (*Letting her go.*) Let's have no more about it. (*Sitting by the stove.*) It's lovely and warm in here.

He turns over his papers. NORA *busies herself with the tree for a moment, then:*

NORA. Torvald . . .

HELMER. What?

NORA. I can't wait for Boxing Day. The Stenborgs. The fancy-dress party.

HELMER. And I can't wait to see your surprise.

NORA. I'm such a goose.

HELMER. What d'you mean?

NORA. The surprise. I can't think what to wear. Every idea I have seems silly, silly.

HELMER. Dear little Nora realises that at last?

NORA (*behind him, arms on the back of his chair*). Torvald, are you busy?

HELMER. Mm?

NORA. Those papers.

HELMER. Bank business.

NORA. Already?

HELMER. The retiring manager has authorised me to review staffing and duties. I have to do it this week, have it ready by New Year.

NORA. That's why poor Mr Krogstad –

HELMER. Hm.

NORA (*leaning over the chair, playing with his hair at the neck*).
Torvald, if you hadn't been so busy, I was going to ask
you a big favour.

HELMER. What favour?

NORA. No one has taste like yours. I want to look nice for
the fancy-dress party. Torvald, won't you settle it? Tell me
what to wear, what I ought to go as?

HELMER. Aha! My independent little creature needs a
helping hand?

NORA. I can't manage without you.

HELMER. I'll think about it. We'll sort it out.

NORA. You are nice.

She goes to the tree. Pause.

Aren't these red flowers pretty? Did Krogstad do
something really terrible?

HELMER. Forged someone's name. Can you imagine?

NORA. If he'd no alternative – ?

HELMER. If he'd made a mistake . . . I'm not heartless;
I wouldn't condemn a man for one mistake.

NORA. Torvald . . .

HELMER. Plenty of people make mistakes, admit them, take
the punishment –

NORA. Punishment?

HELMER. But not Krogstad. He wriggled out of it. That's
what I can't forgive.

NORA. You can't?

HELMER. Imagine someone like that. Lies, hypocrisy,
tricking everyone in sight, his family, his wife, his children.
That's the worst thing of all, the children.

NORA. What d'you mean?

HELMER. An atmosphere like that, a stench of lies and deceit, poisons the whole household. Each breath children take in a house like that is a lungful of deadly germs.

NORA (*going closer*). D'you really believe that?

HELMER. Darling, when I worked in the law I saw hardly anything else. Almost always, when people go bad young in life, the cause is a deceitful mother.

NORA. Just – a mother?

HELMER. It's usually the mother. Though a father can be just as bad. Every lawyer knows. This Krogstad has been poisoning his children for years. Lies, cheating . . . you see what I mean, depraved.

He holds out his hands to her.

That's why darling little Nora must promise: never ask me to help him. Mm? Mm? Take hold. What's the matter? Take hold. There. I just couldn't work with him. People like that literally make me ill.

NORA *lets go his hands and crosses to the other side of the tree.*

NORA. It's so hot in here. And I've such a lot to do.

HELMER (*getting up, bundling up his papers*). I must try to get through some of this before dinner. And there's your fancy dress to think about. And I may – I *may* – have a little something in gold paper, to hang on the tree. (*Putting his hand on her head.*) My darling, my little songbird.

He goes into the study and shuts the door. Pause. Then NORA whispers:

NORA. It can't be. No. It *can't*.

ANNE-MARIE *appears at the door, left.*

ANNE-MARIE. The children are crying for you. Shall I bring them in?

NORA. No! No! I don't want to see them. Stay with them.

ANNE-MARIE. As madam wishes.

She closes the door.

NORA (*white with terror*). Poison them? My children, my family?

Pause. Then she lifts her head.

Never. Impossible.

Curtain.

ACT TWO

The same. In the corner beside the piano, the Christmas tree stands stripped of its decorations and with its candles burned to stumps. On the sofa, NORA's evening cape. NORA, alone in the room, is pacing restlessly. She picks up her cape, then puts it down again.

NORA. Someone's coming.

She goes to the door and listens.

No one. Of course not, it's Christmas Day. Not tomorrow, either. Unless –

She opens the door and looks out.

No. No letters. The box is empty. (*Pacing.*) Stupid. Of course he didn't mean it. Things like that don't happen. They don't. I've got three small children.

ANNE-MARIE *comes from the room left, with a large cardboard box.*

ANNE-MARIE. I've found it. The box with the fancy dress.

NORA. Thanks. Put it on the table.

ANNE-MARIE (*as she does so*). It needs mending.

NORA. I wish I'd torn it to pieces.

ANNE-MARIE. You can fix it. Just a little patience.

NORA. I'll ask Mrs Linde to help.

ANNE-MARIE. Out again? In this weather? You'll catch a chill, make yourself poorly.

NORA. Never mind that . . . Are the children all right?

ANNE-MARIE. Playing with their Christmas presents. If only –

NORA. Are they still asking for me?

ANNE-MARIE. They're used to having their Mummy there.

NORA. No, Anne-Marie. I've no time any more.

ANNE-MARIE. Well, little ones get used to anything.

NORA. D'you think so? D'you think if their Mummy went far away, they'd forget her?

ANNE-MARIE. Far away!

NORA. Anne-Marie, I want to ask you something. I've often wondered. How could you do it? How could you bear it? To give your own child to be fostered.

ANNE-MARIE. I'd no choice. How else could I have been nurse to baby Nora?

NORA. But did you *want* to?

ANNE-MARIE. To get such a good position? A poor girl in trouble. *He* wasn't about to help.

NORA. I suppose your daughter's long forgotten you.

ANNE-MARIE. No, no. She wrote to me, when she was confirmed, and when she got married.

NORA (*hugging her*). Dear old Anne-Marie. You were such a good mother to me when I was little.

ANNE-MARIE. Poor baby, you'd no one else.

NORA. I know if my little ones had no one else, you'd . . . Tsk, tsk. (*Opening the box.*) Go back to them. I must . . . Tomorrow you'll see how pretty I'll look.

ANNE-MARIE. You'll be the prettiest one there.

She goes into the room left. NORA *starts taking things out of the box, then pushes it aside.*

NORA. If I dared go out. If I knew no one would come, nothing would happen. Stupid. No one's coming. Don't think about it. Brush my muff. What pretty gloves. Think about something else. One, two, three, four, five six . . . (*Screams.*) Ah! Someone's there!

She tries to go to the door, but can't move. MRS LINDE *comes in from the hall, where she has taken off her coat.*

It's you, Kristine. There's no one else out there? Oh, thanks for coming.

MRS LINDE. They said you'd called and asked for me.

NORA. I was passing. Something you can perhaps help me with. Let's sit on the sofa. Look. There's a fancy-dress party tomorrow. The Stenborgs. The apartment upstairs. Torvald wants me to go as a Neapolitan fishergirl, and dance the tarantella I learned in Capri.

MRS LINDE. Quite a show.

NORA. Torvald insists. This is the dress. Torvald had it made for me. But it's all torn . . . I don't . . .

MRS LINDE. It's easy. The frill's come undone, here and here. That's all. Have you a needle and thread? Ah yes.

NORA. It's kind of you.

MRS LINDE (*sewing*). So tomorrow you'll be all dressed up? I'll pop in, see how you look. I never said thank you for that lovely evening, yesterday.

NORA (*getting up, pacing*). It could have been even better. If you'd come to town sooner. Well. Torvald certainly knows how to make a place welcoming.

MRS LINDE. And so do you. Not your father's daughter for nothing. Is Dr Rank always as gloomy as yesterday?

NORA. He was bad. He's seriously ill. Lesions in the spine. Poor man. His father was horrible. Woman after woman. That's why the son . . . tainted blood . . .

MRS LINDE (*putting down the sewing*). Nora, how do you *know* about things like that?

NORA (*pacing*). Oh, fiddle, if you've got three children, people are always calling. Married women. Medical things . . . they mention this and that . . . they know.

MRS LINDE (*resuming her sewing, after a short pause*). Does he come every day, Dr Rank?

NORA. He's been Torvald's best friend for years. Since they were children. My friend too. One of the family.

MRS LINDE. You're sure he's . . . all he seems? Not just . . . making himself agreeable?

NORA. Of course not. Why d'you think so?

MRS LINDE. When you introduced us yesterday, he said he'd often heard my name here. But your husband had no idea who I was. So how could Dr Rank − ?

NORA. That's no mystery. Torvald's so fond of me, wants me all to himself, he says. He was always so jealous, if I mentioned people I'd known before. So I didn't. But I often gossip with Dr Rank. He enjoys all that.

MRS LINDE. Nora, you are a child, sometimes. Listen to me. I'm older, more experienced. Finish all this with Dr Rank.

NORA. Finish all what?

MRS LINDE. Yesterday you talked about a rich admirer, someone who'd leave you all his money −

NORA. That's right. Imaginary, alas. What of it?

MRS LINDE. Is Dr Rank . . . well off?

NORA. Oh yes.

MRS LINDE. No dependants?

NORA. What about it?

MRS LINDE. Calls here every day?

NORA. I told you.

MRS LINDE. How could a good friend be so . . . presumptuous?

NORA. I don't know what you mean.

MRS LINDE. Nora. Don't pretend. D'you think I can't guess who lent you all that money?

NORA. You're crazy. A friend, who calls in every day − d'you think I could bear it?

MRS LINDE. It isn't him?

NORA. Of course it isn't him. I'd never have dreamed . . . In any case, in those days he hadn't a penny to lend. He came into money later.

MRS LINDE. That could be lucky for you.

NORA. Dr Rank? You don't think I'd ever ask him . . . ?
Though I'm sure if I did . . .

MRS LINDE. Which you won't.

NORA. Of course I won't. But if I *did* . . .

MRS LINDE. Behind your husband's back?

NORA. I'll finish with the other one. That's also behind his
back. I've got to finish it.

MRS LINDE. I said so yesterday. But –

NORA (*pacing*). It's easy for a man to end that kind of thing.
But a wife . . .

MRS LINDE. Her husband could do it.

NORA. Oh no. (*Stands still.*) When you pay off a debt, you
do get your contract back?

MRS LINDE. I imagine so.

NORA. And you can tear it to bits, burn the nasty, filthy
thing.

MRS LINDE *looks at her, then puts down the sewing and goes to
her.*

MRS LINDE. What is it, Nora?

NORA. What?

MRS LINDE. Something's happened since yesterday.

NORA (*going close*). Kristine . . . (*Listens.*) Sh! Torvald. Look,
go in there, with the children, d'you mind? Torvald hates
seeing dress-making. Anne-Marie'll help you.

MRS LINDE *gathers some of her things.*

MRS LINDE. All right, but I won't leave the house till
we've talked about this properly.

She goes into the room, left, as HELMER *comes in from the hall.*

NORA (*going to greet him*). Darling. I've been waiting . . .

HELMER. Was that the dressmaker?

NORA. No, Kristine. She's helping me. I'll look splendid.

HELMER. Wasn't it a good idea?

NORA. And aren't I good to do it?

HELMER (*chucking her under the chin*). Good, to agree with your husband? Tut, tut, tut. Well, I'll keep out of the way. You'll be wanting to try it on.

NORA. You've work to do?

HELMER. Yes. (*Showing her a sheaf of papers.*) I've just been into the Bank . . .

He is about to go into the study, when she stops him.

NORA. Torvald.

HELMER. Yes?

NORA. If your little squirrel asked for something, very, very nicely . . .

HELMER. Yes . . . ?

NORA. Would you do it?

HELMER. Depends what it was.

NORA. If you'd be good and kind and say yes, little squirrel would dance and do lots of tricks.

HELMER. Come on.

NORA. Little songbird would chirp and sing in every room.

HELMER. Songbird does that anyway.

NORA. I'd play fairies, dance in the moonlight. Torvald.

HELMER. Nora: this isn't what you were asking this morning?

NORA (*going to him*). Eth, Torvald. I'th athking vewwy nithely.

HELMER. How can you bring that up again?

NORA. Please. For me. Give Krogstad his job back. Please.

HELMER. Nora, darling, I've given Mrs Linde Krogstad's job.

NORA. And that was very kind of you. But surely you can sack some other clerk instead of Krogstad.

HELMER. I don't believe this. Obstinacy! Because *you* made him a stupid promise, *I'm* supposed to –

NORA. Torvald, that isn't why. It's for your sake. He writes articles in dreadful newspapers. You told me so. He can do you a lot of harm. I'm scared of him, scared –

HELMER. Because of the past.

NORA. What d'you mean?

HELMER. Well, obviously: your father.

NORA. Oh. Yes. When those spiteful men wrote about him in the papers. Lies and slander. He'd have lost his job if you hadn't been sent to enquire, if you hadn't been so kind to him, so helpful . . .

HELMER. Nora, there's a vital difference between your father and me. Your father wasn't a respected public official. I am. And I hope I'll always be so, as long as I stay in office.

NORA. Who knows what terrible things they'll do, those men? We could be so happy here, Torvald, you, me, the children, in our carefree, peaceful home. All I ask, please –

HELMER. It's because you plead for him that I can't help him. Everyone at the Bank knows I've sacked him. If it comes out that the new manager changes his mind when his wife demands it –

NORA. What's wrong with that?

HELMER. You mean if my little terrier got her way? I'd be a laughing stock. Before the whole staff. They'd think anyone could work on me. I couldn't have that. In any case, I can't take Krogstad back, under any circumstances.

NORA. Why not?

HELMER. I could overlook his character if I had to –

NORA. Of course you could.

HELMER. And they say he's a good worker. But I knew
him when we were both children. We were friends – one
of those stupid friendships you regret later in life. I mean,
we used first names. And that tactless oaf won't let it lie,
even now, even when we're in company. Thinks it's quite
in order to stroll up any time he feels like it – 'Hey,
Torvald, Torvald . . . ' Highly embarrassing. It would
make my position in the Bank impossible.

NORA. Torvald, you're joking.

HELMER. You think so?

NORA. I can't believe you're so small-minded.

HELMER. You think I'm small-minded?

NORA. Of course I don't. So –

HELMER. Right. You think I'm small-minded. Small-
minded. I'll settle this right away.

He goes to the hall door and calls:

Helene!

NORA. What are you doing?

HELMER (*fishing among his papers*). Settling it.

The MAID *comes in.*

Here. Take this letter. Run downstairs, find a porter and
tell him to deliver it. Right now. The address is on it.
Here's some money.

MAID. Yes, sir.

She goes. HELMER *gathers his papers.*

Now then, little Miss Stubborn . . .

NORA (*hardly able to breathe*). Torvald, what was it, that letter?

HELMER. Krogstad's dismissal.

NORA. Call her back, Torvald. There's still time. Oh
Torvald, call her back – for me, for you, for the children.
Please, Torvald, please. You don't know what it'll do to us.

HELMER. Too late.

NORA. Yes, too late.

HELMER. Darling, I don't blame you for being upset, even though it's so insulting to me. That's right, insulting. To think that I'd be afraid of that . . . that worn-out pen-pusher. I don't blame you, because it shows how much you love me. (*Taking her in his arms.*) My own dear darling, this is how it'll be. Whatever happens, I'll be strong enough, brave enough. I'm a man, I'll carry the burden alone.

NORA (*terrified*). You mean − ?

HELMER. All of it.

NORA (*recovering her composure*). You'll never have to do that.

HELMER. Darling, we'll share it, then: husband and wife. That's how it'll be. (*Stroking her.*) Happy? It's all right, all right. Poor little trembling dove. Silly, silly. Why don't you play that tarantella? Practise your tambourine. I'll go into the office and shut the door. I won't hear; make all the noise you want.

He goes to the door, then turns.

When Rank comes, tell him where to find me.

He nods to her, goes into the study with his papers and shuts the door.

NORA *stands rooted, terrified and unsure.*

NORA (*whisper*). He was ready to do it. He can. He will. Nothing can stop him. No. He mustn't. But how? What?

Doorbell, off.

Rank! Anything . . .

She passes her hands over her face, pulls herself together and goes to open the door to the hall. RANK is in the hall, hanging up his coat. During the scene which follows, it begins to get dark.

Hello, Doctor. I recognised your ring. Don't disturb Torvald: he's busy just now.

RANK. What about you?

He comes into the room, and she shuts the door.

NORA. You know I've always got time for you.

RANK. Thank you. I'll make the most of it, as long as I can.

NORA. As long as you can?

RANK. What's the matter?

NORA. It sounded odd, that's all. As if you were expecting something to happen.

RANK. I've been expecting it for a long time. Not quite so soon, that's all.

NORA (taking his arm). What is it? Doctor, tell me.

RANK (sitting by the stove). I'm done for. Incurable.

NORA (sighing with relief). Oh, it's you.

RANK. No point lying to oneself. Mrs Helmer, I'm in the worst state of all my patients. I've spent the last few days reviewing my own case. Terminal. In a month I'll be rotting in the churchyard.

NORA. Don't be horrid.

RANK. It is horrid. And it won't get any less horrid. One more examination; as soon as that's done, I'll know the exact moment when the decline begins. Mrs Helmer, one thing. Torvald's a fastidious man. Ugliness disgusts him. I won't have him in my sickroom.

NORA. Doctor –

RANK. Absolutely not. Door barred. As soon as I know the worst, I'll send you one of my cards, marked with a cross. You'll know that the dissolution, the vileness, has begun.

NORA. You're being ridiculous. I wanted you to be in such a good mood . . .

RANK. With Death at my elbow? For someone else's guilt? How fair is that? I think it's the same in every family in the world: retribution, one kind or another, unavoidable –

NORA (covering her ears). La, la, la! Be nice, be nice.

RANK. It's a joke. The whole thing's a joke. My father indulged himself; my poor blameless spine has to pay the bill.

NORA (*at the table, left*). Foie gras? Asparagus?

RANK. And truffles.

NORA. Oysters.

RANK. Naturally.

NORA. Port, champagne – what a shame such delicious things take it out on our poor old bones.

RANK. Especially poor old bones that never had the pleasure of them.

NORA. That's the worst of all.

RANK (*looking hard at her*). Hmm.

NORA (*after a short pause*). Why did you smile?

RANK. You were laughing.

NORA. Doctor, you smiled.

RANK (*getting up*). You're even wilder than I thought.

NORA. I'm in a wild mood today.

RANK. So it seems.

NORA (*both hands on his shoulders*). Doctor, darling, please don't die. For Torvald, for me, don't die.

RANK. You'll get over me. Out of sight, out of mind.

NORA (*distressed*). Don't say that.

RANK. You'll find someone else. People do.

NORA. Who does? Who will?

RANK. You. Torvald. You've started already. Mrs Linde – why else was she here yesterday?

NORA. Hoho. You're jealous.

RANK. Of course I am. She'll take my place. When I'm dead and done for, she'll be the one –

NORA. Sh! She's in there.

RANK. You see?

NORA. She's doing some sewing. What a bear you are! (*Sitting on the sofa.*) Be good now, Doctor, and tomorrow

you'll see how nicely I dance. You can pretend it's all for
you – well, for Torvald too.

She starts taking things out of the box.

Doctor Rank, sit down here. I want to show you
something.

RANK (*sitting*). What?

NORA. These.

RANK. Silk stockings.

NORA. Aren't they pretty? It's dark now, but tomorrow . . .
No no, look at the feet. Oh well, the legs as well.

RANK. Hm –

NORA. What's the matter? Don't you think they'll fit?

RANK. I've no possible way of telling.

NORA (*glancing at him*). Tut tut!

She flicks his ear with the stockings.

Bad boy!

RANK. What other delights am I to see?

NORA. None at all, you're far too naughty.

Humming, she turns the things over. Short pause.

RANK. When I sit here with you, so friendly, I can't . . .
it's hard to . . . what would my life have been like if I'd
never known this house?

NORA (*smiling*). You really feel at home here.

RANK (*low, looking straight ahead*). To have to leave it for
ever –

NORA. Fiddlededee. You don't.

RANK (*as before*). To have to leave without a single token of
what it's meant to me . . . hardly a backward glance . . .
just an empty place for the next person, anyone, to fill . . .

NORA. What if I asked you . . . No!

RANK. Asked what?

NORA. For a token. Of friendship . . .

RANK. Go on.

NORA. I mean, a really big favour.

RANK. I'd be delighted −

NORA. You don't know what it is, yet.

RANK. Tell me.

NORA. I can't. It's too much. Advice, help, a favour −

RANK. The bigger the better. I can't imagine what you mean. Tell me. Don't you trust me?

NORA. You're my truest, dearest friend. You know you are. Doctor, it's something you can help me prevent. You know how Torvald loves me . . . deeply, beyond words . . . he'd give his life . . .

RANK (*leaning forward to her*). Nora. D'you think he's the only one?

NORA (*starting*). What?

RANK. The only one who'd give his life for you?

NORA (*heavily*). Ah.

RANK. I swore I'd tell you before I . . . went. Now. Nora, now you know. And you know that you can rely on me, as on no one else.

NORA (*getting up, calmly and evenly*). Excuse me.

RANK (*sitting still, but making room for her to pass*). Nora −

NORA (*at the hall door*). Helene, bring the lamps.

She crosses to the stove.

Doctor, dear Doctor, that was uncalled for.

RANK (*getting up*). To love you as much as . . . another man? Uncalled for?

NORA. To tell me. There was no need.

RANK. You knew?

The MAID *brings in the lamps, puts them on the table and goes out again.*

Nora . . . Mrs Helmer . . . are you saying you knew?

NORA. I don't know what I knew. How could you be so . . .
clumsy?

RANK. All that matters is, you know I'm at your service,
body and soul. Tell me what it is.

NORA (*staring at him*). What?

RANK. Please.

NORA. Not now.

RANK. Don't punish me. Let me help you . . . whatever a
man can do.

NORA. There's nothing you can do. I don't really need
help. It was just . . . a game, a silly game.

She sits on the rocking chair, and smiles at him.

Doctor, what a man you are! Aren't you embarrassed,
now, in proper light?

RANK. Not in the least. But perhaps I'd better go . . .
forever.

NORA. Of course not. Come. Don't change. You know
what it means to Torvald.

RANK. And to you?

NORA. I'm always delighted to see you.

RANK. That's why I . . . I don't understand you. I've often
thought that you enjoy my company almost as much as
Torvald's.

NORA. Company. We enjoy some people's company.
Others, we love.

RANK. Yes.

NORA. When I was a child, I loved Daddy more than
anyone. But I kept thinking how nice it would be to slip
down to the servants' room. They never told me what to
do. They were such fun to talk to.

RANK. And it's *their* place I've taken.

NORA *jumps up and goes to him.*

NORA. I didn't mean that. I didn't mean that. It's just that . . . Torvald and Daddy . . . Don't you see?

The MAID *comes in.*

MAID. Madam . . .

She whispers to her and gives her a visiting card.

NORA (*glancing at it*). Ah!

She puts it in her pocket.

RANK. Nothing wrong?

NORA. No, no. Just . . . my new dress.

RANK. It's in there, your dress.

NORA. One of them is. This is another one. I ordered it . . . I don't want Torvald to know.

RANK. Hoho. *That* was the great big secret.

NORA. Yes. Go in to him now. He's in the study. Keep him there.

RANK. Don't worry. He won't get away.

He goes into the study.

NORA (*to the* MAID). He's in the kitchen? Waiting?

MAID. He came to the back door.

NORA. You told him no one was in?

MAID. It didn't do any good.

NORA. He wouldn't go?

MAID. He said he had to talk to you.

NORA. Well, bring him in. But quietly. Helene, keep it a secret. It's a surprise for my husband.

MAID. Yes, madam. I understand.

She goes.

NORA. It's happening. I can't stop it. I can't. I can't.

She locks the study door. The MAID *ushers* KROGSTAD *in from the hall, and shuts the door behind him. He is wearing boots and a fur coat and cap.* NORA *hurries to him.*

NORA. Keep your voice down. My husband's here.

KROGSTAD. Doesn't matter.

NORA. What d'you want?

KROGSTAD. I want you to explain something.

NORA. Be quick.

KROGSTAD. You know I've been sacked?

NORA. There was nothing I could do. I tried, but it was no good.

KROGSTAD. Your husband cares so little for you? He knows the harm I can do you, and still he –

NORA. What makes you think he knows?

KROGSTAD. Ah. I thought he didn't. I could hardly imagine Torvald Helmer being so brave –

NORA. I'll thank you to show a little more respect.

KROGSTAD. As much as he deserves. But since milady's kept the whole thing so carefully to herself, I imagine it's sunk in since yesterday, exactly what you've done.

NORA. No thanks to you.

KROGSTAD. I'm a very bad lawyer, remember?

NORA. What is it you want?

KROGSTAD. Mrs Helmer, I was anxious about you. I've had you in my thoughts all day. A cashier, a pen-pusher, a nonentity like me, can still feel sympathy.

NORA. Feel some, then. For my children.

KROGSTAD. As much as you and your husband felt for me? Never mind. I just want to tell you, there's no need to take this business to heart. There'll be no accusations made from this side.

NORA. I didn't think there would be.

KROGSTAD. It can be settled easily. Amicably. No one has to know but the three of us.

NORA. My husband must never find out.

KROGSTAD. How will you prevent that? Are you saying you can pay the balance?

NORA. Not at the moment.

KROGSTAD. You've some quick way to find it?

NORA. None I intend to use.

KROGSTAD. In any case, it wouldn't help now. However much you pay, I'm not giving up that paper.

NORA. What are you going to do with it?

KROGSTAD. Keep it, that's all. Safe. No third party need ever hear of it. So if you'd any crazy ideas –

NORA. I had.

KROGSTAD. – of running away, for example –

NORA. Who told you?

KROGSTAD. – don't bother.

NORA. How did you know I – ?

KROGSTAD. We all think of that at first. I did, too. But I wasn't brave enough.

NORA (*tonelessly*). Neither am I.

KROGSTAD (*lightly*). Exactly. You aren't brave enough, either.

NORA. No.

KROGSTAD. It would be stupid, anyway. Once the first storm at home blows over . . . I've a letter here for your husband.

NORA. Telling him everything?

KROGSTAD. As objectively as possible.

NORA (*blurted*). He mustn't see it. Tear it up. I'll find the money.

KROGSTAD. I'm sorry, Mrs Helmer, but I thought I just told you –

NORA. I don't mean the loan. Tell me how much you're demanding from my husband, and I'll find the money.

KROGSTAD. I'm not asking him for money.

NORA. What, then?

KROGSTAD. I told you. Mrs Helmer, I want to make
myself respectable. I want to get on. I want your husband
to help me. I've had clean hands for eighteen months,
and things have been very difficult. I didn't mind: I was
working my way up, step by step. But now I've been
sacked, I won't be satisfied with simply getting my job
back. I want something better. Reinstatement − in a
higher position. Your husband will find one −

NORA. He won't.

KROGSTAD. I know him. He won't dare argue. Once I'm
back, just wait and see! In one year − less − I'll be the
Manager's right hand. Not Torvald Helmer, but Nils
Krogstad, will run that bank.

NORA. No. Never.

KROGSTAD. You mean you'll − ?

NORA. I'm brave enough now.

KROGSTAD. You don't scare me. A fine lady, airs and
graces −

NORA. Wait and see.

KROGSTAD. Under the ice, perhaps? In the deep, dark
depths? Floating up in the spring, bloated, unrecognisable,
your hair fallen out −

NORA. You don't scare me.

KROGSTAD. And you don't scare me. Mrs Helmer, no one
does things like that. In any case, what good would it do?
I'd still have him just where I wanted him.

NORA. You mean even after I . . . even if I was − ?

KROGSTAD. Have you forgotten? I own your reputation.

NORA *stares at him speechlessly.*

So, you stand warned. Don't do anything stupid. Helmer
will get my letter. I'll wait for a reply. And remember this:

it was him, your husband, who forced me to do this. I'll never forgive him for that. Good afternoon.

He goes out through the hall. NORA, *at the door, holds it open and listens.*

NORA. He's going. He's not leaving the letter. Of course he is. (*Opening the door further.*) What is it? He's standing there. Not going downstairs. He's changing his mind. He's –

A letter falls into the box, and we hear KROGSTAD'*s steps dying away as he goes down the stairs. With a stifled shriek,* NORA *crosses to the table by the sofa. Short pause.*

In the letter-box.

She creeps across to the hall door.

Torvald, oh Torvald, he's finished us.

MRS LINDE *comes in from the room left. She carries the fancy dress.*

MRS LINDE. That didn't take long. Shall we try it on – ?

NORA (*hoarse whisper*). Kristine, come here.

MRS LINDE (*throwing the costume down on the sofa*). What's the matter? You look terrified.

NORA. Come here. D'you see that letter?

MRS LINDE. Yes.

NORA. It's from Krogstad.

MRS LINDE. The man who lent you the money?

NORA. Now Torvald'll know everything.

MRS LINDE. It's really best, for both of you.

NORA. You don't understand. I forged a signature.

MRS LINDE. For heaven's sake!

NORA. Kristine, you must speak for me.

MRS LINDE. What d'you mean?

NORA. If I . . . go crazy.

MRS LINDE. Nora.

NORA. Or if anything happened . . . if I had to go away . . .

MRS LINDE. What are you saying, Nora?

NORA. If someone else wants to take all the blame – d'you understand? –

MRS LINDE. Yes.

NORA. *Then* you must speak for me. I'm not crazy. I know what I'm doing. And I'm telling you: no one else knew anything about it. I did it, not another soul. Remember.

MRS LINDE. I still don't understand.

NORA. Why should you understand? What's going to happen . . . is a miracle!

MRS LINDE. A miracle?

NORA. It's a miracle. And it mustn't happen, Kristine, mustn't happen for all the world.

MRS LINDE. I'm going to see Krogstad.

NORA. No. He'll hurt you.

MRS LINDE. Once, he'd have done anything for my sake.

NORA. Krogstad?

MRS LINDE. Where does he live?

NORA. I don't . . . (*Fishing in her pocket.*) Yes, here's his card. But the letter, the letter . . .

HELMER (*in his room, knocking*). Nora!

NORA (*scream*). Ah! What is it?

HELMER. Don't be alarmed. We won't come in. You've locked the door. Are you trying the dress?

NORA. Yes. Yes. I'll be so pretty, Torvald.

MRS LINDE (*who has read the card*). It's just round the corner.

NORA. It's too late. We're finished. The letter's in the box. There, in the hall.

MRS LINDE. And your husband has the key?

NORA. The only one.

MRS LINDE. Krogstad must ask for his letter back, unopened. He must find some excuse . . .

NORA. But it's now that Torvald always –

MRS LINDE. Delay him. Go in there. I'll be as quick as I can.

She hurries out through the hall. NORA *goes to* HELMER's *door, opens it and peeps in.*

HELMER (*out of sight*). Ah! We can use our own front room again. Come on, Rank, now we'll see – (*In the doorway.*) What's the matter?

NORA. What d'you mean, darling?

HELMER. Rank said I was to expect a transformation.

RANK (*in the doorway*). I must have been mistaken.

NORA. No one's to admire my dress till tomorrow morning.

HELMER. Nora, you look worn out. Have you been practising too hard?

NORA. I haven't been practising.

HELMER. You ought to.

NORA. I will, Torvald. But you've got to help. I can't remember it all.

HELMER. We'll soon bring it back.

NORA. Yes, Torvald, help me. Promise. I'm terrified . . . all those people. Help me, this evening. No business. No pen, no papers. Please, Torvald.

HELMER. I promise. This evening I'm yours, and yours alone. Little Miss Helpless. Just a moment, though –

He makes for the hall door.

NORA. Where are you going?

HELMER. Just to see if the post has come.

NORA. Torvald, don't.

HELMER. What's the matter?

NORA. Torvald, I beg you. There isn't any.

HELMER. I'll just have a look.

He is about to go, when NORA *runs to the piano and plays the first few bars of the tarantella. He stops.*

Aha!

NORA. I can't dance tomorrow, unless I rehearse with you.

HELMER *(going to her)*. You're really nervous?

NORA. Let me practise. There's time, before dinner. Please, Torvald, sit down and play for me. Play, and watch, and put me right.

HELMER. Of course. Whatever you like.

He sits at the piano. NORA *takes a tambourine and a long shawl out of the box. She drapes herself in the shawl, jumps centre front and cries:*

NORA. I'm ready! Play!

HELMER *plays and she dances.* RANK *looks on, standing by the piano.*

HELMER. Slower, slower.

NORA. This way.

HELMER. Not so violently.

NORA. Yes. Yes.

HELMER *stops playing.*

HELMER. It isn't right.

NORA *(laughing, swinging the tambourine)*. I *told* you.

RANK. Let me play.

HELMER *(getting up)*. Good idea. I'll be able to see better.

RANK *sits and plays.* NORA *dances, ever more wildly.* HELMER *has taken his place by the stove, and directs her as she dances. She seems not to hear him. Her hair falls over her shoulders, and she pays no attention. She is engrossed in the dance.* MRS LINDE *comes in, and stands at the door, amazed.*

MRS LINDE. Ah!

NORA *(as she dances)*. Look, Kristine, look!

HELMER. Nora, darling, anyone'd think your life depended on this dance.

NORA. It does.

HELMER. Rank, stop. This is ridiculous. Stop.

RANK *stops playing, and* NORA *stands suddenly still.* HELMER *goes to her.*

It's incredible. You've forgotten the whole thing.

NORA (*throwing down the tambourine*). I *told* you.

HELMER. You need a lot of practice.

NORA. Yes, Torvald. I must practise, and you must watch. Like you did before. Please, Torvald, please.

HELMER. I said I would.

NORA. Today, tomorrow, concentrate on me. Nothing else. No letters. Don't even open the postbox.

HELMER. You're still afraid of him.

NORA. Yes.

HELMER. He's written a letter. It's here.

NORA. I don't know. I think so. But don't read it. Not now. Nothing nasty must come between us, not now, not now.

RANK (*aside to* HELMER). Better humour her.

HELMER (*taking her in his arms*). Whatever my darling wants. But tomorrow night, when you've done your dancing –

NORA. Then you're free.

MAID (*at the door, right*). Madam, dinner's served.

NORA. We'll have champagne, Helene.

MAID. Yes, madam.

She goes.

HELMER. What do I hear? A celebration?

NORA. A banquet, all night long. Champagne! (*Calling.*) And macaroons, Helene. Platefuls of macaroons!

HELMER *takes her hands.*

HELMER. Calm down. Sh, sh. Little singing bird, there there.

NORA. Go in. You too, Doctor. Kristine, help me put up my hair.

RANK (*to* HELMER *as they go in*). She's not . . . ah . . . ?

HELMER. No, no, no. My dear fellow! Over-excited, that's all.

They go out, right.

NORA. Well?

MRS LINDE. Gone. Out of town.

NORA. I knew. As soon as I saw you.

MRS LINDE. He'll be back tomorrow afternoon. I wrote him a note.

NORA. I wish you hadn't. You can't stop it. A miracle's going to happen, and we're celebrating.

MRS LINDE. What miracle?

NORA. You can't guess. Go in. I won't be long.

MRS LINDE *goes into the dining room.* NORA *stands quite still, as if gathering herself. Then she looks at her watch.*

Five o'clock. Seven hours till midnight. Then twenty-four hours till tomorrow midnight. Twenty-four and seven. Thirty-one. Thirty-one hours left, to live.

HELMER *comes to the door, right.*

HELMER. What's keeping my little singing bird?

NORA. Here she is! Here!

She runs to him with open arms.

Curtain.

ACT THREE

The same. The table and chairs have been moved centre. There is a lighted lamp on the table. The hall door is open, and dance-music can be heard from the upstairs apartment. MRS LINDE is sitting at the table, turning the pages of a book. She is trying to read, but finds it hard to concentrate. She looks at her watch.

MRS LINDE. Still not. It's almost time. Perhaps he won't –

She listens again.

Here he is.

She goes into the hall and carefully opens the main door. Light steps can be heard on the stairs outside. She whispers:

Come in. There's no one here.

KROGSTAD (*in the doorway*). You left me a note. What is it?

MRS LINDE. I must talk to you.

KROGSTAD. Here?

MRS LINDE. Not at my lodgings: I don't have my own entrance. Come in. There's no one here. The servants are asleep, and the Helmers are upstairs at a party.

KROGSTAD (*coming in*). A party? Tonight of all nights?

MRS LINDE. Why shouldn't they?

KROGSTAD. No reason.

MRS LINDE. Nils, we've got to talk.

KROGSTAD. Do we?

MRS LINDE. It's important.

KROGSTAD. Really?

MRS LINDE. You've never understood.

KROGSTAD. What's to understand? It was obvious to anyone. A heartless woman, jilting a man as soon as a better chance turned up.

MRS LINDE. Heartless? D'you really think so? You think it was easy?

KROGSTAD. Wasn't it?

MRS LINDE. You really thought so?

KROGSTAD. If it wasn't, why did you write . . . what you wrote?

MRS LINDE. What else could I do? I had to break with you. It was essential to kill everything you felt for me.

KROGSTAD (*wringing his hands*). Yes. I see. And all that . . . for money.

MRS LINDE. I'd a bedridden mother and two small brothers. We couldn't wait for you, Nils. You'd no prospects then.

KROGSTAD. You'd no right to throw me away for someone else.

MRS LINDE. Who can judge?

KROGSTAD (*slowly*). When I lost you, it was like being shipwrecked. Look: I'm drowning.

MRS LINDE. Help may be near.

KROGSTAD. It was near, until you came and interfered.

MRS LINDE. Until today, I'd no idea it was your job they were giving me.

KROGSTAD. If you say so. But now you know. What will you do now – turn it down?

MRS LINDE. That wouldn't help you.

KROGSTAD. What's help to do with it?

MRS LINDE. Life, hard need . . . I've learned.

KROGSTAD. And I've learned to distrust fancy speeches.

MRS LINDE. Fine words, yes. But deeds?

KROGSTAD. What d'you mean?

MRS LINDE. You said you were drowning.

KROGSTAD. It's true.

MRS LINDE. Well, so am I. No one to weep for, to care for.

KROGSTAD. You chose it.

MRS LINDE. I had to — then.

KROGSTAD. What d'you mean?

MRS LINDE. Nils, two drowning people — can't we help each other?

KROGSTAD. You —

MRS LINDE. Two together, support each other.

KROGSTAD. Kristine.

MRS LINDE. Why else d'you think I came?

KROGSTAD. You thought of me?

MRS LINDE. All my life, as long as I can remember, I've worked. It's been my greatest pleasure, my only pleasure. Now I'm alone . . . empty, thrown away. Where's the satisfaction in working for oneself? Nils, give me someone, something to work for.

KROGSTAD. Hysteria. Female hysteria. Extravagant self-sacrifice, that's what this is.

MRS LINDE. From *me*?

KROGSTAD. You know . . . all about me? My past?

MRS LINDE. Yes.

KROGSTAD. And what I count for here?

MRS LINDE. You said just now, hinted, that if I'd been with you, things would have been different.

KROGSTAD. Quite different.

MRS LINDE. And now?

KROGSTAD. Kristine, you mean this. I can see it. You really would —

MRS LINDE. I need someone to mother; your children need a mother; you and I need each other. I trust you, Nils, the man you really are.

KROGSTAD (*taking her hands*). Thank you. Kristine, thank you. Now I can . . . climb again. No. I forgot . . .

MRS LINDE. Sh! The tarantella. Go, now.

KROGSTAD. What?

MRS LINDE. As soon as it's done, they'll be coming.

KROGSTAD. I'll go. But there's nothing we can do. You don't know what . . . steps I've taken with the Helmers.

MRS LINDE. Nils, I do.

KROGSTAD. And still you – ?

MRS LINDE. Despair – I know what it makes people do.

KROGSTAD. If I could only cancel it.

MRS LINDE. You can. Your letter's still there, in the box at the door.

KROGSTAD (*giving her a long look*). It's her you want to save. Your friend. That's what this is.

MRS LINDE. Nils, someone who's sold herself once for someone else, doesn't do it twice.

KROGSTAD. I'll ask for my letter back.

MRS LINDE. No.

KROGSTAD. Yes. I'll wait for Helmer. I'll tell him I want my letter . . . it's just about my dismissal . . . he's not to read it . . .

MRS LINDE. No, Nils. You mustn't. Don't ask for it back.

KROGSTAD. That's why you wrote, why you asked me here.

MRS LINDE. It was, yesterday. I was in a panic. But since then, you won't believe the sights I've seen in this house. Helmer must know the truth. The secret must come out. No more lies, tricks, they must understand each other.

KROGSTAD. Whatever you say. But there's one thing I can

do, and I'll do it now.

MRS LINDE (*listening*). Hurry. Go. They've finished. We're not safe a moment longer.

KROGSTAD. I'll wait downstairs.

MRS LINDE. Yes: they may see me to the door.

KROGSTAD. This is the luckiest day of my life!

He goes out through the hall, leaving the hall door open. MRS LINDE tidies the room, and puts her coat ready to put on.

MRS LINDE. At last. Someone to work for, live for. A home. There. It's all I want. If only they'd *come*.

She listens.

They're here. Coat on.

HELMER and NORA can be heard off. Key in the door, then HELMER all but pulls NORA into the hall. She is wearing the Italian dress and a large black shawl; he is in evening dress, with a black, swirling cloak. NORA stands in the doorway, resisting.

NORA. No. No. I want to go back up. It's too soon, too soon.

HELMER. Nora, darling –

NORA. Please, Torvald. Please. Another hour. For little Nora. Please.

HELMER. No, darling. Not another minute. We agreed. Go in. You'll catch cold out here.

She still resists, but he brings her into the room.

MRS LINDE. Good evening.

NORA. Kristine!

HELMER. Mrs Linde, good evening. Isn't it rather late – ?

MRS LINDE. I'm sorry. I was dying to see Nora in her dress.

NORA. You've been sitting, waiting?

MRS LINDE. I just missed you, you'd gone upstairs. I couldn't go home again without seeing you.

HELMER (*taking off* NORA's *shawl*). Well, here she is. Isn't she pretty? Isn't she delightful?

MRS LINDE. She's –

HELMER. They all thought so, upstairs. But what an obstinate little thing it is. What are we to do with her? D'you know, I almost had to steal her away by force.

NORA. Torvald, it would have been all right. Just half an hour.

HELMER. You see, Mrs Linde? She danced her tarantella. A triumph. As well it should have been. A little . . . energetic, a little more . . . enthusiastic than artistic . . . but still a triumph. Was I going to let her stay after that? Spoil the effect? Of course I wasn't. I took my little Capri fishergirl – my delicious, capricious little fishergirl – on my arm . . . swift tour round the room, curtsey here, curtsey there – and the vision of loveliness was gone, as they say in fairy tales. Always make a good exit, Mrs Linde – that's what I keep telling her. Fff, it's hot in here.

He throws his cloak over a chair, and opens the study door.

Dark? It's dark. Excuse me.

He goes into the study and lights a couple of candles. Meanwhile, NORA *whispers to* MRS LINDE, *quickly and breathlessly:*

NORA. Well?

MRS LINDE (*in a low voice*). I've talked to him.

NORA. And – ?

MRS LINDE. Nora, you must tell Torvald. Everything.

NORA (*tonelessly*). I knew it.

MRS LINDE. You've nothing to fear from Krogstad. But you must tell Torvald.

NORA. I won't do it.

MRS LINDE. Then the letter will.

NORA. Thanks, Kristine. Now the miracle – Sh!

HELMER (*coming back in*). Well, Mrs Linde? Have you gazed your fill?

MRS LINDE. I'll say goodnight.

HELMER. Is this yours, this knitting?

MRS LINDE (*taking it*). I'd forgotten all about it.

HELMER. You knit as well?

MRS LINDE. Yes.

HELMER. Have you ever tried embroidery?

MRS LINDE. Why?

HELMER. Far more becoming. Look, when you embroider, you hold the frame like this, in the left hand, the needle like this, in the right hand . . . a graceful, easy movement . . .

MRS LINDE. Yes.

HELMER. Whereas knitting . . . no gracefulness . . . elbows in, needles pumping up and down . . . chopsticks . . . That was wonderful champagne.

MRS LINDE. Good night, Nora. And no more obstinate.

HELMER. Well said!

MRS LINDE. Good night, sir.

HELMER (*going to the door with her*). Good night, good night. You'll find your way home? I could easily . . . no, it's just round the corner. Good night, good night.

She goes, and he shuts the door and comes back into the room.

What a boring woman!

NORA. Torvald, you must be tired.

HELMER. Not at all.

NORA. Sleepy?

HELMER. Wide awake, full of beans. What about you? You look exhausted.

NORA. I must go to bed.

HELMER. You see! I was right, to make you come away.

NORA. You're always right.

HELMER (*kissing her forehead*). That's it. Little singing bird, making lots of sense. Did you notice Rank this evening? How happy he was?

NORA. I hardly spoke to him.

HELMER. Neither did I. But I've seldom seen him so jolly.

He looks at her for a moment, then goes closer.

Hmm. It's so nice to be back home again, just the two of us. Just you, and me.

NORA. Torvald.

HELMER. My darling. No one else's. My sweetheart, my treasure.

NORA *goes to the other side of the table.*

NORA. Don't look at me like that.

HELMER (*following her*). Aha! Little Miss Tarantella still? More delicious than ever. Listen! The guests are leaving. (*In a low voice.*) Nora, soon it'll be so still, so still . . .

NORA. I hope so.

HELMER. Darling, you know when I'm out with you, at a party, when I hardly talk to you, just glance at you now and then – d'you know why I do that? I'm pretending we're secret lovers, that we're promised to one another, and it's our secret, no one knows but us.

NORA. I know you were thinking of me.

HELMER. When it's time to come away, and I'm arranging the shawl on your pretty shoulders, your lovely neck, I imagine you're my new young bride, we've just come from the wedding, I'm bringing you home for the very first time . . . we're alone for the very first time . . . alone, my shy little, sweet little darling. All evening I've longed for nothing else but you. When I saw you twirling, swirling in the tarantella, my blood pounded, I couldn't bear it, I hurried you, hurried you down here –

NORA. Torvald! Let me go! I won't!

HELMER. Darling, you're joking, it's a game. Won't? Won't? I'm your husband.

Knock at the outer door.

NORA (*startled*). Listen!

HELMER (*at the hall door*). Who is it?

RANK (*off*). Me. Can I come in a moment?

HELMER (*low, crossly*). What does he want? (*Aloud.*) Just a minute.

He goes and opens the door.

Nice of you to drop by.

RANK. I thought I heard you. Just wanted to make sure.

He glances all round.

Yes, yes. These dear, familiar rooms. Such a happy, cosy little home.

HELMER. I see you enjoyed the party too.

RANK. Of course. Why shouldn't I? Why shouldn't we enjoy every blessed thing? As much as we can, as long as we can. Good wine –

HELMER. Especially champagne.

RANK. I was amazed how much I managed to put away.

NORA. Torvald drank plenty too.

RANK. Really?

NORA. It goes straight to his head, always.

RANK. No harm in a . . . jolly evening after a well-spent day.

HELMER. Well-spent? I can't quite claim that.

RANK (*slapping his back*). But I can, I can.

NORA. Scientific work, Doctor Rank? Investigation?

RANK. Exactly.

HELMER. Such big words for such a little girl! Scientific . . . investigation . . .

NORA. May I congratulate you on the result?

RANK. Indeed you may.

NORA. A good one?

RANK. For the doctor, and the patient, the very best.

NORA (*eagerly, anxiously*). Final?

RANK. Final. So didn't I deserve a jolly evening, after that?

NORA. Oh doctor, of course you did.

HELMER. Hear, hear. So long as you don't regret it in the morning.

RANK. No one must ever regret anything, ever.

NORA. You really enjoy fancy-dress parties?

RANK. If there are plenty of pretty costumes.

NORA. So what will we go as next time, you and I?

HELMER. Little featherbrain, thinking of next time already.

RANK. You and I? I know: you can be a good-luck pixie.

HELMER. What on Earth will she wear for that?

RANK. Just her ordinary clothes.

HELMER. Bravo! How gallant! And what will you go as?

RANK. I know, exactly.

HELMER. What?

RANK. At the next fancy-dress party, I shall be – invisible.

HELMER. Brilliant!

RANK. There's a big black hat – haven't you heard of it? You put it on . . . invisible.

HELMER (*checking a smile*). Absolutely right.

RANK. But I'm forgetting what I came for. Helmer, give me a cigar, one of the dark Havanas.

HELMER. Delighted.

He offers him the case. RANK *takes a cigar and cuts the end.*

NORA (*striking a match*). Let me light it for you.

RANK. Thank you.

He holds out the cigar, and she lights it.

And now, goodbye.

HELMER. Goodbye, dear old friend, goodbye.

NORA. Sleep well, Doctor.

RANK. Thank you.

NORA. Say the same to me.

RANK. If you like. Sleep well. And thanks for the light.

He nods to them both, and goes out.

HELMER (*glumly*). Too much to drink.

NORA (*absently*). Perhaps.

HELMER takes keys out of his pocket and goes into the hall.

Torvald! What are you doing?

HELMER. The letter box is full. If I don't clear it, they'll never get the papers in tomorrow.

NORA. You're not going to work tonight.

HELMER. You know I'm not. Hello. Someone's been at the lock.

NORA. The lock?

HELMER. Yes. But who? Not the servants . . . A broken hairpin. Yours, Nora.

NORA (*quickly*). One of the children must have –

HELMER. Make sure they never do it again. Hm, hm . . . there. Done it.

He takes the letters out and shouts to the kitchen.

Helene! Helene! Put out the front door lamp.

He comes in and shuts the hall door. He has the letters in his hand.

Just look at them all.

He turns them over.

What's this?

NORA (*at the window*). No, Torvald!

HELMER. Two visiting cards – from Rank.

NORA. Rank?

HELMER (*looking at the cards*). Lars Johan Rank, Bachelor of Medicine. They were on top. He must have posted them when he went out just now.

NORA. Is there anything on them?

HELMER. A cross of some kind, over the name. Look. What an odd idea. You'd think he was announcing his own death.

NORA. He was.

HELMER. You know about this? He told you?

NORA. He said, when the card came, it was to say goodbye. He'll lock himself in, to die.

HELMER. My friend. My poor friend. I knew we wouldn't have him long. But so soon, and shutting himself away like a wounded animal.

NORA. If it has to happen, it's better without a word. Don't you think so?

HELMER (*pacing*). He was like family. I can't imagine him . . . gone. Unhappy, lonely – he was like the sky, and our happiness was the sun. Well, perhaps it's best. For him, anyway. (*Standing still.*) And perhaps for us too, Nora. We've no one else now, just each other.

He puts his arms round her.

Darling wife, I can never hold you tight enough. D'you know, I've often wished you were in some deadly danger, so that I could give my heart's blood, my life, for you.

NORA (*firmly, disengaging herself*). You must open those letters, Torvald.

HELMER. Not tonight. I want to be with you, darling. With my wife.

NORA. But Rank, think of Rank –

HELMER. Yes. It's come between us − ugliness, death, a reminder of death. We must try to shake it off. Till then − separate rooms.

NORA *throws her arms round him.*

NORA. Darling, sleep well, sleep well.

HELMER (*kissing her forehead*). Sleep well, little songbird. Sleep well, Nora. I'll read those letters now.

He takes the letters into the study and shuts the door. NORA, wild-eyed, fumbles round, takes his cloak and throws it round herself. She speaks in a hoarse, broken whisper.

NORA. Never again. Never see him again. Never.

She puts her shawl over her head.

The children . . . never again. Never. Water . . . deep . . . black . . . Soon, soon, if only . . . He's opened it. He's reading it. Nothing, now. Torvald, little ones, goodbye

She is about to hurry out through the hall, when HELMER opens the study door and stands there. He holds an open letter.

HELMER. Nora.

NORA (*scream*). Ah!

HELMER. You know what this letter says?

NORA. I know. Let me go. Let me out.

HELMER. Where are you going?

He holds her back. She struggles.

NORA. You won't save me, Torvald.

HELMER (*stumbling*). It's true? What he writes, it's true? Unbearable. It's not, it can't be −

NORA. It's true. You were more than all the world to me.

HELMER. Never . . . mind . . . that.

NORA (*going to him*). Torvald!

HELMER. How could you?

NORA. Let me go. Don't help me. Don't take it over. Please.

HELMER. Stop playing games.

He locks the hall door.

You're staying. You have to come to terms. D'you understand what you've done? Do you understand?

NORA (*looking straight at him; frost forming in her voice*). Now, I understand.

HELMER (*pacing*). To wake up to this! Eight years . . . my joy, my life, my wife . . . Lies, deceit . . . a criminal. No way out. No end.

He stops and looks at her. She returns his gaze, without a word.

I should have expected it. I should have known. Like father – sh! – like daughter. No religion, no ethics, no sense of duty. I shut my eyes to what he was like – for your sake, for you – and this is what I get. This is how you repay me.

NORA. This is how I repay you.

HELMER. You've killed my happiness. You've destroyed my future. I'm trapped, in his claws. No mercy. He'll do whatever he likes to me, demand, insist, I can't refuse. No way out. A silly, empty-headed woman – and now I'm dead.

NORA. When I'm out of your way, you'll be free of it.

HELMER. Don't . . . talk. Your father was just the same. Talk! Even if you're out of the way, as you put it, what good is that to me? He'll tell his tale. They'll think I knew what you were doing, that I was part of it. Behind it, even – that the whole thing was my idea. And this from you, the wife I supported and cherished throughout our marriage. Now d'you understand what you've done to me?

NORA (*icy*). Entirely.

HELMER. It's beyond belief. I can't believe it. But it's happened; we have to cope with it. Take off that shawl. Take it off! I must try and calm him. It *must* be hushed up. Whatever it costs. As for you and me, we must go on

as if nothing had changed between us. In public. You'll
stay on here, obviously. But I won't have you near the
children. I can never trust you again. Fancy having to say
that to you – the woman I loved, I still . . . no. It's gone.
Happiness is gone. Rags, crumbs, pretence . . .

Doorbell, off. He jumps.

At this hour? It can't be, not *him*. Nora, hide yourself. Say
you're ill.

She stands motionless. He unlocks the hall door. The MAID *is in
the hall, in her nightclothes.*

MAID. A letter. For madam.

HELMER. Give it me.

He takes the letter and shuts the door.

Yes. It's from him. Leave it. I'll read it.

NORA. You read it.

HELMER (*by the lamp*). I . . . can't. It could be the end of
us, both of us. No, I must.

He tears open the letter, reads a few lines, then shouts with joy:

Nora!

NORA *looks at him enquiringly.*

Nora . . . no, just let me check. Yes, yes. I'm saved. Nora,
I'm saved.

NORA. And me?

HELMER. You as well. Naturally. Both of us are saved. He's
sent your contract back. Writes that he's sorry . . . his life
has changed . . . what does it matter what he writes?
We're saved. No one can touch you. Nora, Nora – wait.
First these must be got rid of. H'm . . .

He glances at the contract.

No, I won't look at it. Forget it, a nightmare.

*He tears the document and the letters in pieces, stuffs them in the
stove and watches while they burn.*

There you are: finished. He said that ever since Christmas Eve you've – Nora, these last three days have been dreadful for you.

NORA. I've fought hard these last three days.

HELMER. Racking yourself, no way out – no, don't let's think about it. It was dreadful; it's over; let's shout for joy. Nora, don't you understand? It's over. What's the matter? Such an icy face. Oh darling, Nora, I know what it is. You can't believe I've forgiven you. I have, I promise. Forgiven you everything. I know that everything you did, you did because you loved me.

NORA. Yes.

HELMER. You loved me as all wives should love their husbands. You were new to it, that's all: you didn't understand what you were doing. But don't think I love you any less, just because you don't know how to manage things. I'll guide you, darling, I'll protect you. Lean on me. I'd hardly be a man, if feminine weakness, your weakness, didn't make me love you even more. Those hard words, when I thought everything was lost – forget them. I've forgiven you, Nora, I swear I've forgiven you.

NORA. You're very kind.

She goes out, right.

HELMER. Wait. (*Looking in.*) What are you doing?

NORA (*off*). Changing. No more fancy dress.

HELMER (*at the open door*). Yes. Good. Be calm, be calm, my frightened little bird. Nothing will hurt you; I'll spread my wings, I'll shelter you. (*Pacing by the door.*) It's warm and cosy, our nest, our home. Nothing will hurt you. Poor frightened dove, I'll save you from the hawk, I'll keep you safe. Still, little fluttering heart, be still. It'll be all right. Darling, you'll see. Tomorrow . . . it'll all be like it was before. You'll soon understand, I won't need to remind you I've forgiven you. I'll never abandon you, never blame you – how can you think so? A husband's love, darling – a true husband's heart, how can you understand it? How sweet, how satisfying, to feel that he's forgiven his

wife, from the depths of his being, forgiven her? Made
her twice his own: given her life, identity, his wife, his
child. That's what you are to me now, poor, helpless little
darling. Don't ever be frightened, Nora. Tell me the truth,
and your will, your conscience – leave both to me. But
what – ? Not going to bed? You've changed.

NORA (*in her ordinary clothes*). I've changed.

HELMER. But why now? It's late.

NORA. I won't sleep tonight.

HELMER. Nora, darling –

NORA (*looking at her watch*). It's not very late. Sit here,
Torvald. We have to come to terms.

She sits at one side of the table.

HELMER. Nora? So cold –

NORA. Sit down. There's a lot to say.

HELMER *sits facing her across the table.*

HELMER. Nora? I don't understand.

NORA. Exactly. You don't understand me. And I've never
understood you – until just now. Don't say anything.
Listen. It's time to come to terms.

HELMER. What d'you mean?

NORA (*after a short pause*). It's strange. Isn't it?

HELMER. What is?

NORA. We've been married eight years. And this is the first
time we've sat down together, you and me, husband and
wife, to talk seriously.

HELMER. Seriously.

NORA. In eight years – no, since the first day we met –
we've never talked seriously about a single thing.

HELMER. You didn't expect me to tell you my worries all
the time – things you couldn't help me with?

NORA. I don't mean, business. I mean, we've never sat
down and settled anything.

HELMER. Darling, that wasn't your way.

NORA. That's it exactly. You've never understood me. You've done me great wrong, Torvald – you, and Daddy before you.

HELMER. The two men who loved you most in all the world?

NORA (*shaking her head*). You never loved me. Either of you. It pleased you, that's all – the idea of loving me.

HELMER. What are you telling me?

NORA. The truth, Torvald. When I lived with Daddy, he told me his views on everything, so I shared his views. If I disagreed I didn't say so: he'd have hated it. He called me his little dolly-baby, and played with me as I played with my dollies. Then I came here, to you –

HELMER. Is that how you describe our marriage?

NORA (*calmly*). I was transferred from Daddy's care to yours. You organised everything to suit yourself: your taste. So I shared your taste, or pretended to, I'm not sure which. Perhaps both: sometimes one, sometimes the other. I realise it now: I lived here hand to mouth, like a beggar. I've existed to perform for you, Torvald. That's what you wanted. You've done me great harm, you and Daddy: you've blocked my life.

HELMER. You're unreasonable, Nora, ungrateful. Haven't you been happy here?

NORA. No, never. I thought I was, but I wasn't.

HELMER. Not . . . happy . . . ?

NORA. Cheerful. You've always been kind to me. But it's as if we live in a Wendy house. I'm your dolly-wife, just as I used to be Daddy's dolly-baby. And my dolls were the children. When you played with me, I had a lovely time – and so did they when I played with them. That's our marriage, Torvald. That's what it's been like.

HELMER. Maybe you're right. Hysterical, overwrought, but a little bit right. And now things are going to change. Playtime ends; lessons begin.

NORA. Mine? Or the children's?

HELMER. Darling, yours *and* theirs.

NORA. Torvald, how could *you* ever teach me to be a proper wife? Your wife?

HELMER. You're joking.

NORA. And how could I ever teach the children?

HELMER. Nora!

NORA. You said so yourself just now. You'd never trust me again.

HELMER. I'd lost my temper. Surely, you didn't think I meant it?

NORA. It was the truth. I can't bring them up. I've someone else to bring up first – myself. You can't help. I must do it myself. That's why I'm leaving you.

HELMER (*jumping up*). What?

NORA. If I'm to come to terms with myself, understand myself, I have to be alone. I can't stay here.

HELMER. Nora, Nora.

NORA. I'll go right away. I'll sleep at Kristine's tonight.

HELMER. You're mad. I forbid this.

NORA. No more forbidding. I'll take what belongs to me. I need nothing of yours, either now or later.

HELMER. You're out of your mind.

NORA. Tomorrow I'll go home – I mean, where I was born. I'll find something there.

HELMER. You're blind. You don't know how –

NORA. I'll find out how.

HELMER. Deserting your home, your husband, your children. What will people say?

NORA. I must. Let them say what they like.

HELMER. It's unbelievable. You abandon your most sacred obligations –

NORA. You know what they are, then, my sacred obligations?

HELMER. You need me to tell you? To your husband, your children.

NORA. I've other obligations, just as sacred.

HELMER. Of course you haven't. What obligations?

NORA. To myself.

HELMER. You're a wife, a mother. They come first.

NORA. I don't think so, now. Not any more. I think that first I'm a human being, the same as you. Or at least that I'll try to be one. I know that most people would agree with you, Torvald, that that's what they teach in books. But I've had enough of what most people say, what they write in books. It's not enough. I must think things out for myself, I must decide.

HELMER. You should think about your place, here in your own home. Have you nothing to guide you? No . . . belief?

NORA. I don't know what that is.

HELMER. What?

NORA. All I know is what Pastor Hansen taught at confirmation class. Belief is this, and this, he said. I'll think about it, when I've time, when I've gone away. Work out if Pastor Hansen's belief was right – for me.

HELMER. You're a girl, a child! If belief doesn't affect you, what about conscience? Morality? Or have you none of that?

NORA. I can't answer. I don't know. I'm baffled. All I know is, you and I have different ideas about it all. And the law – I've discovered that's not what I always thought it was, and I can't believe it's right. A woman mustn't spare her dying father, or save her husband's life. I can't believe it.

HELMER. You're talking like a child. You don't understand the society you live in.

NORA. You're right: I don't. But I'm going to find out – which of us is right, society or me.

HELMER. Nora, you're ill. You're delirious. I think you're raving.

NORA. I've never felt better. My mind's never been clearer.

HELMER. Clearer? Leaving your husband, your children – ?

NORA. That's what I'm doing.

HELMER. There's only one explanation.

NORA. What?

HELMER. You've stopped loving me.

NORA. That's it exactly.

HELMER. How can you say that?

NORA. It hurts, Torvald. You've always been wonderful to me. But I can't help it. I've just stopped loving you.

HELMER (*controlling himself*). Something else you're clear about?

NORA. Completely clear. It's why I'm going.

HELMER. And what did I do? To lose your love? Can you tell me that?

NORA. It was tonight. The miracle didn't happen. I saw you weren't the man I'd imagined.

HELMER. You're not making sense.

NORA. For eight years I've waited patiently. Miracles don't happen every day, God knows. Then I was engulfed in catastrophe, and I was certain: it'll happen now, the miracle. When Krogstad sent his letter, I was certain you'd never give in to him. You'd tell him to publish and be damned. And then –

HELMER. When I'd exposed my own wife to disgrace and shame – ?

NORA. Then, I was certain, you'd take the whole thing on your own shoulders, and say, 'I did it. I was the guilty one.'

HELMER. Nora – !

NORA. You think I'd have denied it? Of course I would.
But what would my word have been worth, compared
with yours? That was the miracle I hoped for – and it
was to prevent it that I was going to kill myself.

HELMER. Darling, I'd work night and day for you. I'd
endure starvation, agony. But no man sacrifices his *honour*
for the one he loves.

NORA. Hundreds of thousands of women do just that.

HELMER. You're talking – thinking – like a child.

NORA. Perhaps. But you're not talking or thinking like the
husband I long for. As soon as you stopped panicking –
not panicking for me, but for what might happen to you
– when it was over, you behaved as if nothing at all had
happened. So far as you were concerned, I went back to
what I'd always been: your pet bird, your doll, which
you'd now have to treat with extra care because I was
fragile, breakable. (*Getting up.*) That's when I realised,
Torvald. For eight years I've lived with a stranger. Borne
him three children. I can't bear it. I'd like to tear myself
to pieces.

HELMER (*heavily*). It's clear. It's clear. There's a gulf opened
up between us. But surely we can bridge it, fill it?

NORA. The woman I am now is no wife for you.

HELMER. I'll change. I can change –

NORA. If your doll's taken away, perhaps.

HELMER. Nora. Don't leave me. I don't understand.

NORA. That's why I must.

*She goes into the room right, and comes back with her cloak and hat
and a small suitcase, which she puts on the chair by the table.*

HELMER. Not tonight. Tomorrow.

NORA (*putting on her cloak*). I can't spend the night in a
strange man's house.

HELMER. Brother and sister? Can't we live like that?

NORA (*putting on her hat*). It wouldn't last. You know that.

She puts on the shawl.

Goodbye, Torvald. I don't want to see the children.
They're in better hands than mine. The woman I am
now can do nothing for them.

HELMER. One day, Nora, one day − ?

NORA. How can I answer? I don't know what I'll be.

HELMER. Whatever you'll be, whatever you are, you're still
my wife.

NORA. Torvald, listen to me. When a wife deserts her
husband, as I'm deserting you, the law frees him of all
obligations towards her. And in any case, I set you free.
You're not bound in any way. You're free. We're both
free. On both sides: freedom. Take back your ring. Give
me mine.

HELMER. That too?

NORA. That too.

HELMER. There.

NORA. Thank you. It's over. I'll put the keys here. The
servants know where everything is − better than I do.
Tomorrow, as soon as I've left the town, Kristine will
come and pack my things − my own things, the things I
brought from home. I'll have them sent on.

HELMER. Over. Over. Nora, won't you ever think of me?

NORA. Often. You, the children, this house −

HELMER. Can I write to you?

NORA. No. It's forbidden.

HELMER. I could send you −

NORA. Nothing.

HELMER. If you needed help −

NORA. I'll take nothing from a stranger.

HELMER. Will I never be more to you?

NORA (*taking the case*). If the miracle happened −

HELMER. Tell me the miracle.

NORA. If we changed, both of us, if we – No, Torvald. I've stopped believing in miracles.

HELMER. I believe. Tell me. If we changed, if we –

NORA. If we discovered some true relationship. Goodbye.

She goes out through the hall. HELMER *slumps into a chair by the door and covers his face.*

HELMER. Nora! Nora!

He gets up, looks round.

Empty. She's gone.

A hope flashes across his face.

A miracle – ?

A door slams, off.

Curtain.

GHOSTS

translated by Stephen Mulrine

Characters

MRS HELENE ALVING, *the widow of Captain Alving, a former Court Chamberlain*

OSVALD ALVING, *her son, an artist*

PASTOR MANDERS

JAKOB ENGSTRAND, *a carpenter*

REGINE, *Engstrand's daughter, Mrs Alving's maid*

The action takes place on Mrs Alving's estate, near a large fjord in Western Norway.

Pronunciation of Proper Names

Engstrand – ENG-stran

Helene – Hay-LEH-na

Jakob – YA-kob

Johanne – Yo-HA-na

Osvald – OSS-vald

Regine – Ray-GHEE-na

ACT ONE

A spacious room looking onto a garden, with one door in the left-hand wall, and two in the right. In the centre of the room is a round table, with chairs, and on the table lie some books, magazines and newspapers. Downstage left is a window, near which stands a small sofa with a work-table in front of it. Upstage, the room is extended by a conservatory, which is slightly smaller, and the walls of which are largely glazed. In the right-hand wall of the conservatory is a door leading out into the garden. A gloomy fjord landscape may be discerned through the glass walls, dimly visible through the teeming rain.

The carpenter ENGSTRAND *is standing by the garden door. His left leg is slightly deformed, and he wears a boot with a built-up wooden sole.* REGINE, *holding an empty garden syringe, is trying to prevent him coming in.*

REGINE (*in a low voice*). What do you want? Stay where you are, you're soaking wet.

ENGSTRAND. It's God's good rain, that, my girl.

REGINE. It's the devil's rain, more like!

ENGSTRAND. Lord, you don't half talk, Regine. (*Limps a few paces into the room.*) Anyway, what I wanted to say was . . .

REGINE. Don't clump around like that, you idiot! The young master's asleep upstairs.

ENGSTRAND. Asleep at this hour? In the middle of the day?

REGINE. That's none of your business.

ENGSTRAND. Well, I was out on the town last night . . .

REGINE. I don't doubt it.

ENGSTRAND. And for all we're such feeble creatures, my girl . . .

REGINE. We are indeed.

ENGSTRAND. And there's no shortage of temptations in this world, you know – even so, I was still up and doing by half-past five this morning.

REGINE. Yes, yes – anyway, you'd better clear off. I can't stand here conducting a *rendez-vous* with you.

ENGSTRAND. You can't what?

REGINE. I don't want anybody to find you here. So clear off, go away.

ENGSTRAND (*moves a few steps closer*). No, dammit – not before I've had a few words with you. I'll have finished that job down at the school-house by this afternoon, and I'll be catching the ferry back to town tonight.

REGINE (*muttering*). Have a good trip!

ENGSTRAND. Eh? Oh, thanks. Anyway, they're dedicating the new orphanage tomorrow, and that'll be a rare old do, for sure, with plenty of free drink. So don't let them tell you Jakob Engstrand can't turn his back on temptation, right?

REGINE. Hah!

ENGSTRAND. Yes, well, everybody who's anybody'll be here tomorrow. Pastor Manders is supposed to be coming up from town.

REGINE. He's actually arriving today.

ENGSTRAND. There you are, you see? So I've got to watch my step – I'm damned if I want to get into his bad books.

REGINE. Oh, I see – so that's it?

ENGSTRAND. What do you mean by that?

REGINE (*gives him a knowing look*). What are you trying to talk him into this time?

ENGSTRAND. Oh, shush! Are you mad? Me try to put one over on the Pastor? No no, Pastor Manders has been too good a friend to me for that. Anyway, what I wanted to talk to you about was this business of me going back home tonight.

REGINE. Fine – the sooner the better.

ENGSTRAND. Yes, but I want you to come with me, Regine.

REGINE (*open-mouthed*). You want me to what? What are you talking about?

ENGSTRAND. I want you to come home with me, that's what.

REGINE (*scornfully*). Not on your life – I'm not coming home with you.

ENGSTRAND. We'll see about that.

REGINE. Damn right we will. What, me? After I've been brought up here by Mrs Alving? Who's treated me like one of her own family? And I'm to go home with you? To a house like that? Not a chance!

ENGSTRAND. What the hell's this? Are you talking back to your father, you little bitch?

REGINE (*mutters, without looking at him*). You've said often enough I was nothing to do with you.

ENGSTRAND. Oh, that – you don't want to pay any heed to that.

REGINE. And the number of times you've sworn at me, and called me a . . . *Fi donc!*

ENGSTRAND. As God is my judge, I never used that filthy word!

REGINE. Oh, I know only too well what word you used.

ENGSTRAND. Well, yes, but that was after I'd had a few, you know? There's no shortage of temptations in this world, Regine, as I said.

REGINE. Huh!

ENGSTRAND. And when your mother started narking at me, all right. I had to find some way of getting back at her, hadn't I? She was always so bloody high and mighty.

(*Mimicking.*) 'Oh, leave me alone, Engstrand! Don't annoy me! I've been in service for three years at Chamberlain Alving's house at Rosenvold, so there!' (*Laughs.*) Dear God! She couldn't ever forget that the Captain was made a Court Chamberlain while she was here.

REGINE. Poor mother! You drove her into an early grave.

ENGSTRAND (*squirming*). That's right. I get the blame for everything.

REGINE (*under her breath, as she turns away*). Oh God – and that leg!

ENGSTRAND. What's that you're saying, girl?

REGINE. *Pied de mouton.*

ENGSTRAND. What's that? English?

REGINE. Yes.

ENGSTRAND. Hm, yes – you've picked up a bit of learning out here. That might come in handy now, Regine.

REGINE (*after a brief silence*). So, what was it you wanted with me in town?

ENGSTRAND. How can you ask what a father wants with his only child? I'm a widower, aren't I, all on my lonesome?

REGINE. Oh, don't come that nonsense with me. What do you want me there for?

ENGSTRAND. Well, I'll tell you – the thing is, I've been thinking of taking up a new line.

REGINE (*snorts derisively*). I've heard *that* often enough. One mess after another.

ENGSTRAND. Ah, but just you watch me this time, Regine! I'll be damned if I . . .

REGINE (*stamps her foot*). Stop swearing!

ENGSTRAND. Sshhh! Right, right, my girl, you're absolutely right! All I wanted to say was that I've put a

fair bit of money aside, from the work I did on this new
Orphanage.

REGINE. Have you indeed? Good for you.

ENGSTRAND. Well, there's not much to spend your money
on, is there, stuck out here in the back of beyond?

REGINE. So?

ENGSTRAND. Anyway, I thought I'd put the money into
something profitable − a little sort of café-bar for sailors.

REGINE. Oh, God!

ENGSTRAND. Something with a bit of class, I mean − not
some pigs' trough for matelots. No, dammit, this'll be
captains and first mates and suchlike − people with class.

REGINE. And I suppose I'd have to . . .

ENGSTRAND. To give a hand, that's all. Put on a show,
you know what I mean. Dammit, girl, it's not as if it'll be
hard work. You can do pretty well what you like.

REGINE. Oh, can I, now?

ENGSTRAND. We've got to have some women about the
place, that's clear as day. We want a bit of fun in the
evenings, you know, singing, dancing, that sort of thing.
These are sailors, bear in mind, roaming the high seas.
(*Moves closer.*) Now, don't be stupid, Regine, don't stand in
your own light. What can you do with yourself stuck out
here, eh? All that expensive education she's given you, it
won't be much use, will it. You'll be looking after the kids
in the new Orphanage, from what I hear. What sort of a
job is that? Desperate to wear yourself out, is that it?
Ruin your health running after those dirty little brats?

REGINE. Not if I have my way, I won't − not if things work
out. Well, they just might!

ENGSTRAND. Just might what?

REGINE. Never you mind. So, you've managed to put some
money away?

ENGSTRAND. One way and another − yes. About seven or
eight hundred kroner, I reckon.

REGINE. That's not bad.

ENGSTRAND. Well, my girl, it's enough to get started.

REGINE. It never crossed your mind to give me some?

ENGSTRAND. No, dammit, it did not.

REGINE. You wouldn't have thought of sending me a measly dress-length, even?

ENGSTRAND. Come back with me to town, and you'll have all the dresses you want.

REGINE. Huh, I can manage that by myself, if I've a mind to.

ENGSTRAND. No, Regine, you'll do better with a father's hand to guide you. There's a nice house going in Little Harbour Street. They're not asking much as a down-payment, and it could be a sort of seamen's hostel, you know?

REGINE. Well, I certainly don't want to live with you. I don't want anything to do with you. Now clear off!

ENGSTRAND. I'm damn sure you wouldn't stay long with me, girl. There's not much chance of that. Not if you play your cards right. You've turned into a real good-looker this past year or two . . .

REGINE. So?

ENGSTRAND. Well, it wouldn't be too long before some nice officer'd come along – maybe even a captain . . .

REGINE. I wouldn't want to marry one of them. Sailors have no *savoir vivre*.

ENGSTRAND. They've no what?

REGINE. I know what sailors are like, believe me. They're not worth marrying.

ENGSTRAND. All right, you don't have to marry them. You can still do yourself a bit of good. (*Lowers his voice.*) That Englishman now, the one with the yacht – he paid three hundred dollars, and she wasn't a patch on you.

REGINE (*moving towards him*). Get out!

ENGSTRAND (*retreating*). Now, now – you wouldn't hit your own father, surely?

REGINE. Wouldn't I just! You say one word about my mother, and I'll hit you all right. Get out, I'm telling you! (*Shoves him towards the garden door.*) And don't go slamming any doors. Young Mr Alving . . .

ENGSTRAND. Yes, he's asleep, I know. You're making a great fuss over this young Mr Alving . . . (*Lowers his voice.*) You've not got your eye on *him*, have you?

REGINE. Get out, and hurry it up! You're off your head, you. No, not that way! Pastor Manders is coming – go down the kitchen stairs.

ENGSTRAND (*goes right*). All right, all right, I'm going. But you just have a talk with *him*, now that he's coming. He's the man to tell you what a child owes its father. I mean, I *am* your father, you know. I can prove it, it's in the Parish Register.

He goes out through the second door, which REGINE *opens for him, and closes after him.* REGINE *has a quick look in the mirror, flaps at herself with her handkerchief and adjusts her collar, then attends to the flowers.* PASTOR MANDERS, *wearing a topcoat and carrying an umbrella, with a small travel-bag slung over his shoulder, enters the conservatory through the garden door.*

MANDERS. Good morning, Miss Engstrand.

REGINE (*turns round, with a look of pleased surprise*). Why, good morning, Pastor Manders! Is the steamer here already?

MANDERS. Just this minute arrived. (*Enters the room.*) Goodness, what wretched weather we've been having these days.

REGINE (*following him in*). Well, it's a blessing for the farmers, I suppose.

MANDERS. Yes, you're absolutely right. We townsfolk never think of these things. (*Starts taking off his topcoat.*)

REGINE. Oh, let me give you a hand with that, Pastor. There you are! Heavens, it's soaking wet – I'll just hang

it up in the hall. And your umbrella, I'll leave it open
somewhere, let it dry out.

She carries the wet things out through the second door to the right.
MANDERS *takes off his travel-bag and places it along with his
hat on a chair. Meanwhile,* REGINE *re-enters.*

MANDERS. Oh, it's good to be in out of the rain. So –
how are things with you? Going well, I trust?

REGINE. Yes, thanks.

MANDERS. But pretty busy, I would imagine, getting ready
for tomorrow?

REGINE. Yes, there's a lot to be done.

MANDERS. And Mrs Alving is at home, I hope?

REGINE. Yes, indeed – she's just gone upstairs to make
some chocolate for the young master.

MANDERS. Ah, yes . . . I heard down at the pier that
Osvald was back home.

REGINE. Yes, the day before yesterday. We hadn't been
expecting him till today.

MANDERS. And he's fit and well, I trust.

REGINE. Yes, thanks, he's quite well. He's feeling dreadfully
tired after his journey, though. All the way from Paris
non-stop. I mean, he did the whole trip without a break.
He's having a nap just now, I think, so we'd maybe better
talk a little quieter.

MANDERS. Sshhh! We'll be quiet as mice.

REGINE (*moves an armchair up to the table*). Do sit down,
Pastor, please – make yourself at home. (*He sits down, she
places a footstool under his feet.*) There! Now, how's that – nice
and comfy?

MANDERS. Thank you, that's excellent. (*Looks closely at her.*)
You know, Miss Engstrand, I honestly think you've grown
since I last saw you.

REGINE. D'you think so, Pastor? The mistress says I've
filled out too.

MANDERS. Filled out? Hm, yes, perhaps a little. Not too much. (*A brief pause.*)

REGINE. Should I tell Mrs Alving you're here?

MANDERS. Thank you, my dear child, but there's no hurry. So, Regine, tell me – how is your father getting along out here?

REGINE. He's doing quite well, Pastor, thank you.

MANDERS. You know he dropped in to see me, last time he was in town?

REGINE. Really? Well, he's always pleased to have a talk with you, Pastor.

MANDERS. And I suppose you go down to see him pretty regularly?

REGINE. Me? Yes, I do – whenever I get the time.

MANDERS. Your father isn't a particularly strong character, Miss Engstrand. He's in sore need of a guiding hand.

REGINE. Yes, I've no doubt.

MANDERS. He needs someone at his side, someone he's fond of, and whose judgment he can respect. He admitted that himself, quite freely, the last time he came to see me.

REGINE. Yes, he said something like that to me too. But I'm not sure Mrs Alving would want to let me go – not now we've got the new Orphanage to look after. Besides which, I'd really hate to leave Mrs Alving, she's been so kind to me.

MANDERS. But it's a daughter's duty, my dear girl. Of course, we'd have to get your mistress's consent first.

REGINE. Anyway, I don't know that it's right, at my age – me keeping house for an unmarried man.

MANDERS. What? My dear Miss Engstrand, this is your own father we're talking about.

REGINE. That's as may be, but even so . . . Now, if it was a thoroughly respectable house, with a proper gentleman . . .

MANDERS. My dear Regine . . .

REGINE. Someone I could look up to, and feel affection for – be like a daughter to . . .

MANDERS. Yes, but my dear good child . . .

REGINE. I'd quite happily go back to town. It gets terribly lonely out here, and you know yourself, Pastor, what it's like to be alone in the world. And I think I can say I'm willing and quick to learn. You don't happen to know of a place like that for me, Pastor, do you?

MANDERS. Me? No, I certainly don't.

REGINE. But you will think of me, won't you, dear Pastor Manders, if you should ever . . .

MANDERS (*stands up*). Yes, I shall indeed, Miss Engstrand.

REGINE. Because if I . . .

MANDERS. Perhaps you'd be so kind as to fetch Mrs Alving?

REGINE. Yes, of course, Pastor – right away.

REGINE *goes out left.* MANDERS *paces up and down the room a few times, then stands upstage a moment, his hands clasped behind his back, gazing out at the garden. He then goes back towards the table, picks up a book and glances at the title-page. He starts in surprise, and looks at some of the others.*

MANDERS. Hm! Well, really!

MRS ALVING *enters through the door left. She is followed by* REGINE, *who immediately goes out again, downstage right.*

MRS ALVING (*holds out her hand*). Welcome, Pastor.

MANDERS. Good morning, Mrs Alving. As you see, I've kept my promise.

MRS ALVING. And punctual as ever.

MANDERS. Well, believe me, it's not easy getting away – all these blessed committees and boards I have to sit on.

MRS ALVING. Which makes it all the kinder of you to come so promptly. Now, perhaps we can settle our business before lunch? But where's your suitcase?

MANDERS (*hurriedly*). I've left my things down at the store.
I'll be staying there tonight.

MRS ALVING (*trying not to smile*). And we honestly can't
persuade you to spend the night here? Not even this time?

MANDERS. No no, Mrs Alving – thanks all the same. I'll
stay down there as usual. It's handy for getting the
steamer back.

MRS ALVING. Oh, well, please yourself. But I really
should've thought two old fogeys like us could . . .

MANDERS. Goodness me! You will have your little joke,
won't you. Anyway, of course you're feeling particularly
happy today. There's tomorrow's celebrations for a start,
and then you have Osvald at home too.

MRS ALVING. Yes, fancy that – isn't it wonderful? It's
more than two years since he was home last. And he's
promised to stay the whole winter.

MANDERS. Has he indeed? That's good of him, he's a
dutiful son. I daresay it must be very different, living in
Rome or Paris, with all those attractions.

MRS ALVING. Ah yes, but he has his mother here, you see.
Bless the dear boy, there's still a corner in his heart for his
mother.

MANDERS. Yes, it would be a sad thing if leaving home,
and taking up art and suchlike, were to deaden his
natural feelings.

MRS ALVING. It certainly would. But there's no fear of
that with him, indeed no. Anyway, I'll be interested to see
whether you recognise him again. He'll be coming down
later – he's just having a little rest upstairs on the sofa.
Now, do sit down, my dear Pastor.

MANDERS. Thank you. You're sure it's not inconvenient . . . ?

MRS ALVING. No, of course not. (*She sits down at the table.*)

MANDERS. Fine. Now, let's see . . .

He crosses to the chair on which his travel-bag is lying, takes out a
sheaf of papers, sits down at the other side of the table, and looks
for a space to put his papers.

Well, first of all, we have the . . . (*Breaks off.*) Mrs Alving,
tell me – what are these books doing here?

MRS ALVING. These books? They're mine – I'm reading
them.

MANDERS. Do you read this sort of thing?

MRS ALVING. Yes, of course I do.

MANDERS. And do you feel any better or happier, for
reading books like this?

MRS ALVING. I think I'm more confident, somehow.

MANDERS. That's remarkable. In what way?

MRS ALVING. Well, they seem to explain and confirm a lot
of things I've been puzzling over myself. What I find
strange, Pastor Manders, is that there's really nothing new
in these books – there's nothing in them but what most
people already believe. It's just that most people either
don't give any thought to these things, or else won't
admit it.

MANDERS. Good heavens! Do you seriously believe that
most people . . . ?

MRS ALVING. Yes, I do, absolutely.

MANDERS. Not in this country, surely? Not here.

MRS ALVING. Yes, of course here.

MANDERS. Well, really, I must say . . . !

MRS ALVING. Anyway, what exactly do you object to in
these books?

MANDERS. Object to? You don't think I spend my time
studying productions of this sort, do you?

MRS ALVING. So in fact you have no idea what it is
you're condemning?

MANDERS. I've read sufficient *about* these writings to
disapprove of them.

MRS ALVING. Yes, but your *own* opinion . . . ?

MANDERS. My dear lady, there are many occasions in life when one must rely on other people's judgment. That's the way of the world, and a good thing, too. How else would society survive?

MRS ALVING. Hm, yes. You may be right.

MANDERS. Of course, I don't deny that these sort of writings have a certain appeal. And I don't hold it against you that you want to keep up with the intellectual trends, which I'm told are current in the wider world – where you've allowed your son to roam free these past years. But . . .

MRS ALVING. But?

MANDERS (*lowers his voice*). Well, one doesn't talk about such things, Mrs Alving. One isn't bound to account to all and sundry for what one reads and thinks in the privacy of one's own room.

MRS ALVING. No, of course not. I quite agree.

MANDERS. I mean, think of your responsibilities towards the new Orphanage – which you decided to found at a time when your opinions on intellectual matters were rather different from what they are now – at least, as far as I can tell.

MRS ALVING. Well, yes, I grant you that. Anyway, speaking of the Orphanage . . .

MANDERS. It's the Orphanage we should be discussing, yes. However, discretion, dear lady! Now, let's get down to business. (*Opens a folder and takes out some papers.*) You see these?

MRS ALVING. The deeds?

MANDERS. All of them. The complete set. It wasn't easy assembling them all in time, as you can imagine. I had to put a lot of pressure on people. The authorities are pain-fully conscientious when it comes to making decisions. Anyway, we've got them. (*Leafs through the papers.*) This is the deed of conveyance for that part of the Rosenvold estate, known as the Solvik farmstead, together with the

buildings newly erected thereon, school, school-house and
chapel. And this is the legal sanction for the bequest,
and the statutes of the foundation. If you'd care to have a
look . . . (*Reads.*) 'Statutes of the Captain Alving Memorial
Children's Home'.

MRS ALVING (*stares long at the paper*). So there it is.

MANDERS. I chose 'Captain' rather than 'Chamberlain'.
'Captain' looks less pretentious.

MRS ALVING. Yes, yes, whatever you think.

MANDERS. And this is the bank-book showing the capital
sum deposited, the interest from which will be earmarked
for the running costs of the Orphanage.

MRS ALVING. Thank you. Actually, if you'd be so kind as
to hold on to them, for convenience . . .

MANDERS. With pleasure. I think we'll leave the money
with the bank for the time being. The interest isn't all
that attractive – four per cent at six months' notice. However, we might find a decent mortgage investment at some
point – of course it would have to be a first mortgage,
and absolutely sound – in which case we might
reconsider.

MRS ALVING. Yes, of course, dear Pastor Manders, you
know best.

MANDERS. Anyway, I'll keep my eyes open. There's just
one other thing I've been meaning to ask you.

MRS ALVING. And what's that?

MANDERS. Well, are the Orphanage buildings to be
insured?

MRS ALVING. Yes, of course, they must be insured.

MANDERS. Ah, now just a minute, Mrs Alving. Let's take a
closer look at this.

MRS ALVING. I keep everything insured – buildings,
contents, crops, livestock . . .

MANDERS. Well, obviously, yes. On your own property. I
do the same, of course. But this is quite a different matter,

you see. The Orphanage is to be consecrated, as it were, to a higher purpose.

MRS ALVING. Yes, but even so . . .

MANDERS. I mean, as far as I'm concerned personally, I don't see anything in the least offensive about securing ourselves against all eventualities.

MRS ALVING. No, absolutely not.

MANDERS. But . . . how will that go down with the local people, what will their reaction be? You'll know better than I.

MRS ALVING. Hm, their reaction . . .

MANDERS. Is there any considerable body of opinion here – opinion of some weight, that is – that might take exception to it?

MRS ALVING. What exactly do you mean by 'opinion of some weight'?

MANDERS. Well, I'm thinking mainly of people of independent means, people in positions of influence – such as make it difficult not to attach a certain weight to their opinions.

MRS ALVING. Oh, there are quite a few, I daresay, who might take exception if . . .

MANDERS. Well, there you are, you see? We have a great many people like that in town. People in the other churches, for example, the other denominations. They might interpret that as meaning that neither you nor I had sufficient trust in Divine Providence.

MRS ALVING. But as far as you yourself are concerned, my dear Pastor, you know perfectly well . . .

MANDERS. I know, I know – my conscience is clear, that's true. Even so, we might not be able to stop people from misrepresenting our action. And that might very easily have a damaging effect on the work of the Orphanage itself.

MRS ALVING. Well, if that's going to be the case . . .

MANDERS. And I can't entirely overlook the difficult –
indeed, I may say painful – position I might be placed in.
This Orphanage has been a frequent topic of conversation
among influential circles in the town. Of course, in one
respect it's intended to be an asset to the town, and
people are hoping it will make a substantial reduction in
the poor rate. But since I've been acting as your adviser,
looking after the business side of things, I do fear the
more fanatical types would make me their first target.

MRS ALVING. Well, you certainly don't want to risk that.

MANDERS. Not to mention the attacks that would
undoubtedly be launched against me in certain
newspapers and periodicals, which . . .

MRS ALVING. Say no more, dear Pastor Manders – that
settles it.

MANDERS. Then you won't be insuring it?

MRS ALVING. No, we'll leave it as it is.

MANDERS (*leans back in his chair*). But supposing there were
an accident? I mean, you never know . . . Would you be
able to cover the damage?

MRS ALVING. No, I can tell you now – I absolutely would
not.

MANDERS. Well, you must realise, Mrs Alving, this is a
very grave responsibility we're assuming.

MRS ALVING. But there's nothing else we *can* do, is there?

MANDERS. No, that's just it. There isn't. We mustn't leave
ourselves open to misrepresentation, and we mustn't under
any circumstances offend public opinion.

MRS ALVING. Not you, at any rate, a clergyman.

MANDERS. And you know, really, I think we have to
assume that an enterprise of this sort will have luck on its
side – indeed, that it will enjoy special protection.

MRS ALVING. Let's hope so, Pastor Manders.

MANDERS. So, shall we leave it at that?

MRS ALVING. Yes, definitely.

MANDERS. Good. Just as you wish. (*Makes a note.*) So . . . no insurance.

MRS ALVING. Actually, it's odd you should happen to mention this today . . .

MANDERS. Well, I kept meaning to ask you about it . . .

MRS ALVING. You know we almost had a fire down there yesterday?

MANDERS. What?

MRS ALVING. Well, it was nothing much, really. Some shavings caught fire in the carpenter's shop.

MANDERS. Where Engstrand works?

MRS ALVING. Yes. He's a bit careless with matches, so they say.

MANDERS. Well, he's got a lot on his mind, that fellow. All manner of distractions. From what I hear, though, he's making a genuine effort to keep to the strait and narrow, thank God.

MRS ALVING. Really? Who told you that?

MANDERS. He did, he assured me personally. And he's a good worker.

MRS ALVING. Yes, when he's sober.

MANDERS. Ah yes, his regrettable weakness. Actually, he's often forced to give in to it because of his bad leg, so he tells me. The last time he was in town, I was really quite touched. He came to see me, and thanked me most sincerely for getting him a job here, so he could be near Regine.

MRS ALVING. Well, he doesn't see that much of her.

MANDERS. Oh yes, he talks with her every day. He told me so himself.

MRS ALVING. Hm. Possibly.

MANDERS. He feels he needs someone by his side, someone who can keep him in check when temptation strikes. That's what's so endearing about Jakob Engstrand – the way he comes to one like a helpless child, so ready to accuse himself and admit his frailties. The last time he called in to see me . . . Look, Mrs Alving, supposing he did desperately need Regine back home with him . . . ?

MRS ALVING (*quickly stands up*). Regine!

MANDERS. You mustn't stand in their way.

MRS ALVING. Indeed I will, most certainly. Anyway, Regine has a position here at the Orphanage.

MANDERS. Don't forget, he *is* her father.

MRS ALVING. Yes, and I know best what sort of father. No no, she's not going back to him, not if I can help it.

MANDERS (*stands up*). My dear Mrs Alving, you mustn't get so excited. It really is a pity the way you misjudge poor Engstrand. It's almost as if you were frightened . . .

MRS ALVING (*calmer*). Never mind that. The point is, I've taken Regine into my house, and that's where she'll remain. (*Listens.*) Sshh . . . Enough, dear Pastor Manders, don't say any more. (*Her face lights up with pleasure.*) Listen . . . Osvald's coming downstairs. Let's just think about *him* now.

OSVALD ALVING *enters left, wearing a light overcoat, and carrying his hat. He is smoking a large meerschaum pipe.*

OSVALD (*standing in the doorway*). Oh, excuse me – I thought you were in the study. (*Approaches.*) Good morning, Pastor.

MANDERS (*staring at him*). Well! That's truly remarkable!

MRS ALVING. Now, Pastor Manders, what do you think of him, eh?

MANDERS. I think . . . I think . . . Can that really be . . . ?

OSVALD. Indeed it is, Pastor, the Prodigal Son.

MANDERS. Oh, my dear young friend . . .

OSVALD. Well, the returning son, at any rate.

MRS ALVING. Osvald's thinking of the time you were so dead set against him becoming an artist.

MANDERS. Yes, well, many a step seems hazardous at the time, to mortal eyes, but turns out . . . (*Shakes his hand.*) Anyway, welcome, welcome home, my dear Osvald! I may call you Osvald, mayn't I?

OSVALD. What else would you call me?

MANDERS. Splendid. Actually, what I wanted to say, my dear Osvald, is that you mustn't think I condemn the artistic profession as such. I daresay there are a great many, even in those circumstances, who can manage to keep the inner man free from corruption.

OSVALD. Let's hope so.

MRS ALVING (*beaming with pleasure*). Well, I know one who's kept both his inner and outer man uncorrupted. Take a good look at him, Pastor Manders.

OSVALD (*walks across the room*). Mother dear, please . . .

MANDERS. Oh, no doubt of it – nobody can deny that. And you've begun to make a name for yourself, I see. You're often mentioned in the newspapers, and in the most complimentary terms. I will say, though – things seem to have gone a little quiet recently.

OSVALD (*up by the conservatory*). I haven't done much painting this while back.

MRS ALVING. Even an artist needs to rest now and again.

MANDERS. I can well imagine. Yes, he needs to prepare himself, muster up his strength for some great work.

OSVALD. Yes . . . Mother, will lunch be ready soon?

MRS ALVING. In about half an hour. He's still got a good appetite, thank heavens.

MANDERS. And a taste for tobacco, too.

OSVALD. I found father's pipe upstairs in the bedroom.

MANDERS. Ah! So that explains it!

MRS ALVING. Explains what?

MANDERS. When Osvald was standing in the doorway there, with that pipe in his mouth, it was his father all over again, large as life.

OSVALD. Really?

MRS ALVING. Oh, how can you say that? Osvald takes after me.

MANDERS. Yes, but there's something about the corners of his mouth, something about his lips, that exactly recalls Captain Alving – at any rate, when he's smoking.

MRS ALVING. Not at all. If anything, Osvald has more of a clergyman's mouth, I'd say.

MANDERS. Yes, yes, I suppose so. A good many of my colleagues have the same expression.

MRS ALVING. Put that pipe away now, my dear. I don't like smoke in here.

OSVALD (*does so*). Yes, of course. I just wanted to try it. I smoked it once when I was a child.

MRS ALVING. You did?

OSVALD. Yes. I was quite small at the time. And I remember going up to father's room one evening, when he was in a good mood.

MRS ALVING. Oh, you can't remember anything from those days.

OSVALD. Yes, I can. I remember quite clearly he sat me on his knee and let me smoke his pipe. 'Go on, lad,' he said, 'Have a good puff!' And I puffed with all my might, till I felt myself going quite pale, and great beads of sweat stood out on my forehead. And then he roared with laughter.

MANDERS. That's most peculiar.

MRS ALVING. Oh, that's just something Osvald has dreamed.

OSVALD. No, mother, that was no dream. You must remember, surely – you came in and carried me off to the nursery. Then I was sick, and I could see you were crying . . . Did father often play tricks like that?

MANDERS. He had a great zest for life, in his young days.

OSVALD. And yet he managed to achieve so much – so much that was good and useful, brief though that life was.

MANDERS. Yes indeed, you've inherited the name of a fine, enterprising man, my dear Osvald Alving. Let's hope it spurs you on to greater things.

OSVALD. It should do, shouldn't it.

MANDERS. At any rate, it was good of you to come home in time to honour his memory.

OSVALD. It's the least I could do for father.

MRS ALVING. And the fact that I can keep him here for a while – that's the best thing of all.

MANDERS. Yes, you're going to be at home over the winter, I hear.

OSVALD. I'll be staying indefinitely, Pastor – oh, it's wonderful to be back home again!

MRS ALVING (*beaming*). Yes, isn't it, Osvald.

MANDERS (*looks at him sympathetically*). You went out into the world very early, my dear Osvald.

OSVALD. I did indeed. I sometimes wonder if it wasn't *too* early.

MRS ALVING. Not at all. It's the best thing for a lively young lad. Especially an only child. Far better than staying at home with his mother and father, getting spoilt.

MANDERS. That's a debatable point, Mrs Alving. I mean, the parental home is, and always will be, a child's proper place.

OSVALD. I'm afraid I'm at one with the Pastor there.

MANDERS. You only have to look at your own son. I daresay we can talk about this in front of him. What's been the outcome in his case? Here he is, twenty-six or twenty-seven, and he's never had the opportunity to learn what a real home is like.

OSVALD. I beg your pardon, Pastor, but you couldn't be more wrong.

MANDERS. Really? I thought you'd been moving more or less exclusively in artistic circles?

OSVALD. Yes, I have.

MANDERS. And generally among younger artists.

OSVALD. That's true.

MANDERS. And I thought most of those people couldn't afford to set up home, or support a family?

OSVALD. A lot of them can't afford to get married, Pastor.

MANDERS. Yes, that's what I'm trying to say.

OSVALD. But they can still have a home. And quite a few of them do. Real homes, comfortable homes, besides.

MRS ALVING *listens to him intently, nods, but says nothing.*

MANDERS. I'm not talking about bachelor apartments. By a home, I mean a *family* home, where a man lives with his wife and children.

OSVALD. Yes, or with his children and the mother of his children.

MANDERS (*starts, claps his hands together*). Mercy on us!

OSVALD. What?

MANDERS. Lives with the mother of his children!

OSVALD. Well, would you rather he abandoned her? The mother of his children?

MANDERS. These are unlawful relationships you're talking about – these so-called 'free marriages'.

OSVALD. Well, I can't say I've ever noticed anything particularly 'free' about the way these people live.

MANDERS. But how can any reasonably well brought up young man or woman bring themselves to live like that – openly, in full view of the world?

OSVALD. What else can they do? A struggling artist . . . a poor young girl – it costs money to get married. So what else can they do?

MANDERS. What else can they do? I'll tell you, Mr Alving, what else they can do – they can keep away from each other in the first place, that's what they can do!

OSVALD. Well, that kind of talk won't get you very far with young, hot-blooded people – people in love.

MRS ALVING. No, it *won't* get you very far!

MANDERS (*persistently*). And to think that the authorities tolerate such things! That they're allowed to go on quite openly! (*Turns to* MRS ALVING.) Hadn't I good reason to be so concerned about your son? Moving in circles where immorality is practised quite blatantly, where it's even become the norm . . .

OSVALD. I'll tell you this much, Pastor Manders. I've been a regular Sunday guest in one or two of these unconventional homes . . .

MANDERS. On a Sunday, no less!

OSVALD. Yes, of course – that's when people enjoy themselves. And I've never heard a single offensive word, still less seen anything that could be called immoral. No, indeed. But do you know when and where I *have* encountered immorality among artists?

MANDERS. No, thank God, I don't!

OSVALD. Well, let me enlighten you. I've encountered it more than once, when some of our exemplary husbands and fathers arrived in town for a spree on their own, and did the artists the honour of looking them up in their humble little cafés. By God, they could tell us a thing or two! Yes, those gentlemen knew about places and things we'd never so much as dreamt of.

MANDERS. What? Are you suggesting that respectable men from this country would . . . ?

OSVALD. Haven't you heard these selfsame respectable men when they get back home? Haven't you heard them holding forth on the topic of rampant immorality in foreign countries?

MANDERS. Yes, of course . . .

MRS ALVING. I've heard them too.

OSVALD. Yes, well, you can take their word for it. Some of those people are connoisseurs. (*Clutching his head.*) Oh God, when I think of the wonderful free life over there – that it should be defiled in this way.

MRS ALVING. You mustn't get worked up, Osvald. It's not good for you.

OSVALD. No, you're right, mother. It's not good for my health. It's this damned tiredness, that's what it is. I think I'll go for a little walk before lunch. I'm sorry, Pastor. I know you can't see it from my point of view, but that's just how I feel. (*Goes out through the second door, right.*)

MRS ALVING. My poor boy . . .

MANDERS. Yes, you may well say that. So this is what it's come to.

MRS ALVING *looks at him, but says nothing.* MANDERS *paces up and down.*

He called himself the Prodigal Son. That's only too true, unfortunately.

She continues to look at him.

And what have you to say to all this?

MRS ALVING. I say Osvald was right, every single word of it.

MANDERS (*stops in his tracks*). Right? Right? To have principles like that?

MRS ALVING. Living on my own here, I've come round to much the same way of thinking, Pastor. But I've never dared to say so out loud. Well, no matter – my boy will speak for me now.

MANDERS. You're greatly to be pitied, Mrs Alving. But I must give you a word of warning. No longer as your financial adviser, or your and your late husband's lifelong friend – no, I stand before you now as your priest, as that same priest once stood before you at the most confused time in your life.

MRS ALVING. And what does the priest have to say to me?

MANDERS. Let me first refresh your memory, Mrs Alving. This is a particularly apt moment. Tomorrow will be the tenth anniversary of your husband's death. Tomorrow, a memorial will be unveiled in honour of the departed. Tomorrow, I shall make a speech to the assembled flock. Today, however, I shall speak to you alone.

MRS ALVING. Very well, Pastor Manders. Speak.

MANDERS. Do you remember how, after barely a year of marriage, you stood on the very edge of the abyss? How you walked out of house and home? How you ran away from your husband? Yes, Mrs Alving – ran away. Ran away and refused go back to him, even though he begged and pleaded with you.

MRS ALVING. Have you forgotten how desperately unhappy I was that first year?

MANDERS. Yes, that's it exactly – this rebellious spirit, this craving for happiness in life. What right have we human beings to happiness? No, Mrs Alving, we have our duty to do. And your duty was to remain with the man you had chosen, and to whom you were bound by sacred ties.

MRS ALVING. You know perfectly well what kind of life my husband led in those days – the excesses he committed.

MANDERS. I'm well aware of the rumours that were going round about him, yes. And I should be the very last person to approve of his conduct as a young man, assuming there were any substance to those rumours. But it isn't a wife's place to sit in judgment on her husband. Your duty was to bear, with humility, that cross which a higher power had seen fit to lay upon you. But instead you defiantly fling that cross aside, abandon that wayward

soul you should have supported, put your own reputation
at risk – and almost ruin other people's good names into
the bargain.

MRS ALVING. Other people's? One other person's, don't
you mean?

MANDERS. It was extremely thoughtless of you to seek
refuge with me.

MRS ALVING. What, with our priest? Our family friend?

MANDERS. All the more reason. Yes, you should thank
God I had the necessary strength of mind – that I was
able to dissuade you from carrying out your neurotic
intentions, and that it was granted to me to lead you back
to the path of duty, and home to your lawful husband.

MRS ALVING. Yes, Pastor Manders, that was certainly your
doing.

MANDERS. I was merely the humble instrument of a
higher power. And the fact that I returned you to the
path of duty and obedience, hasn't that proved a blessing
ever since, all the days of your life? Didn't I prophesy all
this? Didn't Alving turn his back on his dissolute years, as
any decent man should? And from then on, didn't he live
a loving and blameless life with you, the rest of his days?
Didn't he go on to become a benefactor to the whole
district? And didn't he raise you up with him, so that
you eventually became his trusted collaborator, in all his
undertakings? And a thoroughly capable helpmeet you
were – oh, I know that, Mrs Alving. Credit where it's
due. However, I come now to the second serious mistake
you've made in your life.

MRS ALVING. What do you mean by that?

MANDERS. Well, just as you once denied your duty as a
wife, so you've gone on to deny it as a mother.

MRS ALVING. Ah!

MANDERS. You've spent your entire life in the grip of a
dangerous spirit of self-will. You've always been drawn to
the idea of emancipation and lawlessness. You've never

been able to bear any kind of restraint. Anything you've
ever found inconvenient in life, you've selfishly cast aside
without a thought, as if it were a burden you could
dispose of at will. You got tired of being a wife, so you
walked out on your husband. It was hard work being a
mother, so you put your child out to strangers.

MRS ALVING. Yes, that's true. That's what I did.

MANDERS. And that's why you've become a stranger to
him yourself.

MRS ALVING. No, no, I'm not!

MANDERS. You are. You must be. And just how have you
got him back? Think, Mrs Alving, think hard. You've
done your husband a great wrong – the very fact that
you're raising this memorial to him is a clear admission of
that. But you should also admit to the wrong you've done
your son. There may yet be time to lead him back from
the paths of error. Turn back from them yourself, and
save what can still be saved in him. (*With raised forefinger.*)
For in truth, Mrs Alving, you are a guilty mother! I
consider it my duty to say these things to you.

   A silence.

MRS ALVING (*slowly, and with restraint*). Well, you've said
your piece, Pastor Manders. And tomorrow you'll make a
speech in public, in memory of my husband. I won't be
speaking tomorrow. But I will speak to you now, the way
you have spoken to me.

MANDERS. Well, of course – you want to make excuses for
your actions . . .

MRS ALVING. No. I just want to tell you something.

MANDERS. Oh?

MRS ALVING. You know, everything you said just now
about me and my husband, and our life together, after
you returned me to the path of duty, as you put it – not
one word of it comes from first-hand knowledge. You used
to visit us every day, but from that moment on, you never
once set foot in the house.

MANDERS. Well, you and your husband moved out of town not long after.

MRS ALVING. Yes, and you never once came out here to see us either, while my husband was alive. You were eventually forced to come here on business, in connection with the Orphanage.

MANDERS (*quietly, unsure of himself*). Helene, if this is meant as a reproach, I can only ask you to bear in mind . . .

MRS ALVING. The respect you owed to your position, yes. And the fact that I was a runaway wife. One can't be too careful about getting involved with such wanton women.

MANDERS. My dear . . . Mrs Alving, that is a gross exaggeration . . .

MRS ALVING. Yes, yes, let that be. All I wanted to say is that when you pass judgment on my married life, you're basing it on nothing more than popular opinion at the time.

MANDERS. Well? So?

MRS ALVING. Well, Pastor Manders, I'm now going to tell you the truth. I swore to myself that you'd know it one day – you, and you alone!

MANDERS. And what is the truth?

MRS ALVING. The truth is that my husband died just as depraved as he had been all his life.

MANDERS (*groping for a chair*). What did you say?

MRS ALVING. After nineteen years of marriage, every bit as dissolute – in his desires at any rate – as he had been before you married us.

MANDERS. Those youthful indiscretions, those improprieties – excesses, if you will . . . you call that a dissolute life?

MRS ALVING. That was the expression our doctor used.

MANDERS. I don't understand you.

MRS ALVING. You don't need to.

MANDERS. I feel quite dizzy. You mean your entire married life – all those years together with your husband – was nothing but a façade?

MRS ALVING. Nothing more. And now you know.

MANDERS. This is . . . I find this very hard to accept. I don't understand. I can't take it in. I mean, how was it possible? How could such a thing be kept hidden?

MRS ALVING. That was my constant struggle, day in, day out. After we had Osvald, I thought I could see a slight improvement. But that didn't last long. I had to fight twice as hard, a desperate battle to keep people from finding out what sort of man my child had for a father. And of course you know how charming my husband could be. Nobody could believe anything but good of him. Alving was one of those people whose real life seems to have no impact on their reputation. But then, Pastor Manders – and this is something else you should know – then came the most abominable thing of all.

MANDERS. What, worse than this?

MRS ALVING. I'd managed to put up with it, though I knew perfectly well what was going on outside this house. But when he brought the scandal within these four walls . . .

MANDERS. What are you saying? Here?

MRS ALVING. Yes, here, in our own home. In there . . . (She points to the near door at right.) It was in the dining-room I first found out about it. I was busy doing something in there, and the door was open. I heard our maid coming up from the garden, with some water for the flowers.

MANDERS. And?

MRS ALVING. A short while after, I heard my husband come in. He said something to her in a low voice. Then I heard . . . (A short laugh.) Oh, it rings in my ears even now, heart-breaking, but at the same time so ridiculous . . . I heard my own servant whispering: 'Let me go, Mr Alving, please! Leave me alone!'

MANDERS. Well, that's most unseemly behaviour, a foolish indiscretion. But I'm sure it was no more than an indiscretion, Mrs Alving. You must believe me.

MRS ALVING. I knew soon enough what to believe. My husband had his way with the girl – and that affair had its consequences, Pastor Manders.

MANDERS (*stunned*). And all that in this house? In this house!

MRS ALVING. I've suffered a great deal in this house. To keep him at home in the evenings, and at nights, I had to join him in secret drinking bouts up in his room. I had to sit there with him, just the two of us, drinking, listening to his obscene, mindless talk, then end up wrestling with him, dragging him into his bed.

MANDERS (*moved*). And you were able to endure all that?

MRS ALVING. I had to, for my little boy's sake. Then came the crowning insult, when my own servant-girl . . . I swore then it would have to end! So now I seized power in my own house – absolute power. Power over him, and everything else besides. I had a weapon to use against him, you see, and he didn't dare say a word. That was when Osvald was sent away. He was going on for seven then, beginning to notice things and ask questions, the way children do. I couldn't bear that, Pastor Manders. I felt as if the child would be poisoned, just breathing the air of this polluted house. That's why I sent him away. You can understand too, why he was never allowed to set foot in this house, while his father was still alive. And what that cost me, no one knows.

MANDERS. You've suffered terribly, indeed.

MRS ALVING. I'd never have borne it if I hadn't had my work. Yes, I can safely say I've worked hard – all those additions to the property, all the improvements, all the innovations, for which Alving got the credit, of course – do you honestly think he had the initiative for these things? A man who used to lounge around on the sofa the whole day, reading an old Court gazette? No, and I'll tell you something else – it was I who drove him on, during his more lucid intervals. And I had to bear the whole burden when he took to his debauched ways again, or lapsed into abject self-pity.

MANDERS. And you're putting up a memorial to this man.

MRS ALVING. Well, there you see the power of a bad conscience.

MANDERS. A bad . . . ? What do you mean?

MRS ALVING. I've always had the fear that the truth must come out one day, and people would believe it. So the Orphanage is meant to kill off the rumours, as it were, and remove any doubts.

MANDERS. Well, you certainly haven't failed in your intention, Mrs Alving.

MRS ALVING. There was one other reason. I didn't want Osvald, my son, to inherit anything whatsoever from his father.

MANDERS. So it's actually Alving's money, that . . .

MRS ALVING. Yes, it is. The money I've given towards this Orphanage, year after year, comes to exactly the same amount – I've calculated it very precisely – the same amount which in his day made Lieutenant Alving such a good catch.

MANDERS. I understand.

MRS ALVING. That was my bride price. And I don't want any of that money to pass to Osvald. Everything my son inherits will be from me – from me.

OSVALD *enters through the second door, right. He has taken off his hat and coat outside.* MRS ALVING *goes towards him.*

Back so soon? My dear, dear boy!

OSVALD. Yes, what can you do outside in this interminable rain? Still, I hear lunch is ready – that's splendid!

REGINE (*enters from the dining-room, with a parcel*). There's a parcel come for you, Mrs Alving. (*Hands it to her.*)

MRS ALVING (*with a glance at* PASTOR MANDERS). The songs for tomorrow's ceremony, I suppose.

MANDERS. Hm . . .

REGINE. Lunch is served, ma'am.

MRS ALVING. Good. We'll be in in a minute. I just want to . . . (*Begins unwrapping the parcel.*)

REGINE (*to* OSVALD). Would Mr Alving like red or white wine?

OSVALD. Both, please, Miss Engstrand.

REGINE. *Bien* . . . very well, Mr Alving. (*Goes into the dining-room.*)

OSVALD. I'd better give you a hand with the corks . . . (*Follows her into the dining-room; the door swings half-open behind him.*)

MRS ALVING (*who has now unwrapped the parcel*). Yes, as I thought. The song-sheets are here, Pastor Manders.

MANDERS (*clasping his hands*). How am I ever going to make my speech tomorrow with a clear conscience?

MRS ALVING. Oh, I'm sure you'll manage.

MANDERS (*in a low voice, so as not to be heard in the dining-room*). Yes, we mustn't cause any offence.

MRS ALVING (*quietly, but firmly*). No. And then this long, hateful farce will be at an end. After tomorrow, it'll be as if that man had never lived in this house. There'll be no one here but my son and his mother.

From the dining-room comes the noise of a chair being overturned. At the same time, REGINE'*s voice is heard, an urgent whisper.*

REGINE. Osvald! Are you mad? Let me go!

MRS ALVING (*starts in terror*). Ah!

She stares wildly at the half-open door. OSVALD *coughs, then begins humming a tune. A bottle is uncorked.*

MANDERS (*agitated*). What on earth was that? What *was* it, Mrs Alving?

MRS ALVING (*hoarsely*). Ghosts. The two in the conservatory
. . . they've returned.

MANDERS. What are you saying? Regine . . . ? Is *she*
the . . . ?

MRS ALVING. Yes. Come. Not a word . . . !

Grips MANDERS *by the arm and walks unsteadily towards the
dining-room.*

Curtain.

ACT TWO

The same room. A dense mist still hangs over the landscape.
MANDERS *and* MRS ALVING *emerge from the dining-room.*

MRS ALVING *(from the doorway).* You're very welcome, Pastor. *(Calls into the dining-room.)* Aren't you joining us, Osvald?

OSVALD *(offstage).* No, thank you. I think I'll go out for a bit.

MRS ALVING. Yes, do. It's clearing up a little now. *(Closes the dining-room door, crosses to the hall door and calls.)* Regine!

REGINE *(offstage).* Yes, ma'am?

MRS ALVING. Go down to the laundry, and give them a hand with the bunting.

REGINE. Yes, ma'am.

MRS ALVING *makes sure that* REGINE *is going, then closes the door.*

MANDERS. I don't suppose he can hear in there, can he?

MRS ALVING. Not when the door's closed. Anyway, he's going out.

MANDERS. Actually, I'm still quite dazed. I don't know how I managed to swallow a single mouthful of that excellent meal.

MRS ALVING *(trying to control herself, pacing up and down).* Nor I. But what are we going to do?

MANDERS. Yes, what *are* we going to do? I've honestly no idea. I have absolutely no experience in this sort of thing.

MRS ALVING. I'm pretty sure there's been no harm done as yet.

MANDERS. No, God forbid! But it's a rather unseemly business, all the same.

MRS ALVING. It's just a silly notion of Osvald's – you can be sure of that.

MANDERS. Yes, well, as I said – I know very little about these things, but I can't help feeling that . . .

MRS ALVING. Of course, she'll have to leave the house. Immediately. That's clear as daylight.

MANDERS. Yes, obviously.

MRS ALVING. But where to? We can't simply . . .

MANDERS. Where to? Why, home to her father, of course.

MRS ALVING. To whom, did you say?

MANDERS. To her . . . Oh no, of course – Engstrand isn't her . . . Good Lord, Mrs Alving, how can this be possible? You must be mistaken, surely?

MRS ALVING. Unfortunately, no. There's no mistake. Johanne eventually had to confess everything to me, and Alving couldn't deny it. So, there was nothing we could do except hush the whole business up.

MANDERS. No, you couldn't do anything else.

MRS ALVING. The girl left at once, after receiving a tidy sum to keep her mouth shut. The rest she managed for herself, when she got to town. She took up where she'd left off with Engstrand, dropped a few hints, no doubt, about how much money she had, and spun him a yarn about some foreigner who'd put in here with his yacht that summer. So she and Engstrand got married, in a great hurry. Why, you married them yourself.

MANDERS. But how am I supposed to make sense of . . . ? I distinctly recall Engstrand coming to see me about the wedding. He was full of apologies, bitterly unhappy, blaming himself for the foolish thing he and his fiancée had done.

MRS ALVING. Well, of course, he had to take the blame.

MANDERS. But the sheer duplicity of the man! To me, of all people. I'd honestly never have believed it of Jakob Engstrand. Well, I'll give him a serious talking-to, he can be sure of that. And the immorality of that sort of match besides – for money! How much did the girl receive?

MRS ALVING. Three hundred dollars.

MANDERS. Hm, just think – for a paltry three hundred dollars, agreeing to marry a fallen woman!

MRS ALVING. And what would you say about me – agreeing to marry a fallen man?

MANDERS. Good heavens, Mrs Alving – what are you talking about? A fallen man?

MRS ALVING. What, do you imagine my husband was any purer, when I went to the altar with him, than Johanne was when Engstrand married her?

MANDERS. Oh come, there's a world of difference.

MRS ALVING. No, not that much. There was a big difference in the price, certainly – a paltry three hundred dollars against an entire fortune.

MANDERS. But how can you compare two totally different things? I mean, you had listened to the promptings of your heart, the advice of your own family.

MRS ALVING (*without looking at him*). I thought you understood where my heart, as you put it, had strayed to at that time.

MANDERS (*distantly*). If I had understood anything of the kind, I wouldn't have continued to be a daily guest in your husband's house.

MRS ALVING. Yes, well, the fact remains, I didn't listen to myself at all.

MANDERS. To your closest relatives, then – as was your duty. To your mother, and both your aunts.

MRS ALVING. Yes, that's true. The three of them did the arithmetic for me. It's incredible how neatly they had it all worked out, proving it would be sheer madness to turn down an offer like that. If only my mother could look down now, and see what's become of all that splendour.

MANDERS. Nobody can be held responsible for the way things have turned out. At least one thing's certain – your marriage was conducted in strict accordance with the law.

MRS ALVING. Oh yes, the law. Law and order! I sometimes think that's the cause of all the unhappiness in the world.

MANDERS. That's a sinful way to talk, Mrs Alving.

MRS ALVING. Well, maybe so. But I won't be tied down by all these conventions any longer. I can't stand it! I've got to work my way out to freedom.

MANDERS. What do you mean by that?

MRS ALVING (*drumming her fingers on the window-sill*). I should never have kept it hidden, the kind of life Alving led. But at the time I didn't dare do otherwise – for my own sake, as much as anything. I was such a coward.

MANDERS. A coward?

MRS ALVING. If people had got to know, they'd have said, 'Oh, the poor man, no wonder he goes astray now and again, with a wife that runs out on him'.

MANDERS. And they'd have had a certain amount of justice on their side.

MRS ALVING (*looks hard at him*). If I were the woman I should be, I'd go up to Osvald and say, 'Listen, my boy, your father was an old lecher' . . .

MANDERS. Good God!

MRS ALVING. And then I'd tell him everything I've just told you – down to the last detail.

MANDERS. I'm frankly rather shocked at you, Mrs Alving.

MRS ALVING. Yes, I know, I'm well aware of that. I find the idea rather shocking myself. (*Walks away from the window.*) I'm such a coward.

MANDERS. And you call it cowardice, to do what is clearly your bounden duty? Have you forgotten that a child should love and honour its father and mother?

MRS ALVING. Don't let's go into generalities. The question is, should Osvald love and honour Captain Alving?

MANDERS. Don't you feel your mother's heart urging you not to destroy your son's ideals?

MRS ALVING. What about the truth?

MANDERS. What about his ideals?

MRS ALVING. Oh, ideals, ideals! If only I weren't such a coward!

MANDERS. Don't despise ideals, Mrs Alving. They may come back to haunt you. Take Osvald's own case, now. Osvald hasn't too many ideals, more's the pity. But I've seen enough to realise that his father does represent something of an ideal to him.

MRS ALVING. Yes, you're right there.

MANDERS. And it was you yourself who awakened and nurtured those ideas in him, through your letters.

MRS ALVING. Yes, doing my duty, doing the right thing. That's why I lied to my son, year after year. Oh, what a coward . . . what a coward I've been!

MANDERS. Mrs Alving, you have established a beautiful illusion in your son's mind – and that's something you shouldn't undervalue.

MRS ALVING. Hm. Who knows if it's a good thing or not? But I absolutely won't tolerate any messing around with Regine. He's not going to ruin that poor girl's life.

MANDERS. Good Lord, no – that would be dreadful!

MRS ALVING. If I thought he was serious, and that it would make him happy . . .

MANDERS. Yes? What then?

MRS ALVING. But it wouldn't work. Regine's not that type, unfortunately.

MANDERS. So? What do you mean?

MRS ALVING. If only I weren't such a pathetic coward, I'd say to him: 'Marry her, or come to some arrangement between you – just don't do anything on the sly.'

MANDERS. Merciful Heaven! You're not suggesting a legal marriage? But that's frightful! Absolutely unheard-of!

MRS ALVING. Unheard-of, you call it? Hand on heart, Pastor Manders – don't you think there are plenty of married couples out here in the country, just as closely related as they are?

MANDERS. I don't understand you at all.

MRS ALVING. Oh yes, you do.

MANDERS. Well, I suppose you're thinking of cases where it's possible that . . . Yes, unfortunately, family life isn't always as pure as it should be. But the sort of thing you're hinting at, you can't ever know, not with any certainty. And in this case . . . ! How could you, a mother, be willing to allow your own . . .

MRS ALVING. I'm *not* willing! I wouldn't allow it, not at any price. That's just what I'm saying.

MANDERS. Yes, because you're a coward, as you put it. But supposing you weren't a coward? Good God, a relationship like that, it's outrageous!

MRS ALVING. Well, we're all sprung from relationships like that, so they say. And just who was it that ordered things so in this world, Pastor Manders?

MANDERS. I'm not going to dispute such matters with you, Mrs Alving. You aren't exactly in the right frame of mind. But how you can dare to call yourself cowardly . . . !

MRS ALVING. Yes, well, I'll tell you what I mean by that. I'm timid and fearful, yes, and it's because I can't ever get free of all the ghosts that haunt me.

MANDERS. What did you call them?

MRS ALVING. Ghosts. Ghostly presences. When I heard Regine and Osvald in there, it was as if I was seeing ghosts. I'm half inclined to think we're all ghosts, Pastor Manders. It's not just what we inherit from our mother and father that lives on in us. It's all kinds of old, dead ideas, all kinds of old, dead beliefs and suchlike. They're not actually *alive* in us, they're just stuck there, and we can't get rid of them. I've only to pick up a newspaper, and I seem to see ghosts lurking between the lines. There must be ghosts the whole country over. Packed tighter than grains of sand. And we're so desperately afraid of the light, every one of us.

MANDERS. Aha! So there we see the fruits of your reading. And fine fruits they are, indeed. Oh, these freethinkers, and their vile, seditious writings!

MRS ALVING. You're quite wrong, my dear Pastor. It was you who first prodded me into thinking. And you have my eternal gratitude for that.

MANDERS. *Me?*

MRS ALVING. Yes, when you forced me to submit to what you called my bounden duty. When you held up as right and proper what my whole being revolted against, as against something abominable. It was then I began to take a close look at your teachings. I only wanted to pick at a single knot, but as soon as I'd loosened that, the whole thing unravelled. I realised then it was all just machine-sewn.

MANDERS (*quietly, moved*). And that was the outcome of the hardest battle of my life?

MRS ALVING. Call it rather your most crushing defeat.

MANDERS. It was my life's greatest victory, Helene – victory over myself.

MRS ALVING. It was a crime against both of us.

MANDERS. A crime? That I begged you, saying, 'Woman, go back to your lawful husband!' when you came to me half-distracted and shouting, 'Here I am! Take me!' Was *that* a crime?

MRS ALVING. Yes, I think it was.

MANDERS. We two don't understand each other.

MRS ALVING. No. Not any longer.

MANDERS. Never once – not even in my most secret thoughts – have I looked on you as anything but another man's wife.

MRS ALVING. Really?

MANDERS. Helene!

MRS ALVING. We forget what we were like so easily.

MANDERS. Not me. I'm the same as I always was.

MRS ALVING (*changing the subject*). Yes, well – let's not talk any more about the old days. You're now up to your ears in committee work and administration, and I sit here doing battle with ghosts, both within and without.

MANDERS. Well, I can at least help you to overcome the ghosts without. After all the frightful things I've heard from you today, for the sake of my own conscience, I can't allow a defenceless young girl to remain in your house.

MRS ALVING. It would be best if we could get her settled, don't you think? Suitably married, I mean.

MANDERS. Undoubtedly. I think it would be desirable for her in every respect. Regine is now at an age when . . . Well, I know nothing about these things, really, but . . .

MRS ALVING. Regine matured very early.

MANDERS. Yes, didn't she. As I recall, she was strikingly well developed, in a physical sense, when I was preparing her for confirmation. Anyway, she'd better go home for the time being, in her father's care . . . But of course, Engstrand isn't her . . . Honestly, to think that he, of all people, could conceal the truth from me like that!

There is a knock at the hall door.

MRS ALVING. Who can *that* be? Come in!

ENGSTRAND (*in his Sunday suit, in the doorway*). I beg your pardon, ma'am, but . . .

MANDERS. Aha! Hm . . .

MRS ALVING. It's you then, Engstrand?

ENGSTRAND. There wasn't any of the girls around, so I took the liberty of knocking.

MRS ALVING. Oh, all right. Come in. Was there something you wanted to see me about?

ENGSTRAND (*comes in*). No, thanks all the same, ma'am. It was really the pastor I wanted a word with.

MANDERS (*pacing up and down*). Hm, do you now? You want to speak with me? Is that so?

ENGSTRAND. Yes, sir, I'd be really grateful . . .

MANDERS (*stops in front of him*). Well, now. May I ask what it is about?

ENGSTRAND. Well, the thing is, Pastor, we're being paid off now down there – oh, and many thanks, ma'am – now that the work's finished. And I was thinking it would only be right and proper, if all of us that's worked so hard together this while back . . . well, I was thinking we should maybe have a few prayers there this evening.

MANDERS. Prayers? Down at the Orphanage?

ENGSTRAND. Well, of course, if you don't think it's right, Pastor . . .

MANDERS. No no, I do, but . . . Hm . . .

ENGSTRAND. I've got into the habit of saying a few prayers down there myself of an evening . . .

MRS ALVING. Have you?

ENGSTRAND. Oh yes, now and again. A little bit of uplift, as you might say. But I'm just an ordinary bloke, I've no real gift for it, God knows. So anyway I thought, being as Pastor Manders was out this way . . .

MANDERS. Yes, but look here, Engstrand, I really must ask you something first. Are you in the right frame of mind for such a meeting? Do you feel your conscience is clear?

ENGSTRAND. Oh, God help us, Pastor, there's no point talking about consciences.

MANDERS. Ah, but there is – and that's just what we're going to talk about. Now, then – what's your answer?

ENGSTRAND. Oh well, conscience – it can be pretty bad, at times.

MANDERS. Well, at least you admit it. But I want you to be straight with me. What's all this I hear about Regine?

MRS ALVING (*hastily*). Pastor Manders!

MANDERS (*reassuringly*). Leave this to me . . .

ENGSTRAND. About Regine? Lord, you didn't half give me a turn there! (*Looks at* MRS ALVING.) There's nothing the matter with Regine, surely?

MANDERS. Well, let's hope not. No, what I mean is, what's the position between you and Regine? You're supposed to be her father, isn't that so? Eh?

ENGSTRAND (*uncertainly*). Well . . . hm . . . the Pastor knows what happened with me and my poor Johanne . . .

MANDERS. Now, let's have no more distortions of the truth. Your late wife confessed everything to Mrs Alving before she left her service.

ENGSTRAND. Well, I'll be . . . ! She didn't, did she?

MANDERS. So you've been found out, Engstrand.

ENGSTRAND. And she promised, she swore her Bible oath . . .

MANDERS. She took an oath?

ENGSTRAND. Well, she didn't actually swear, but she gave me her solemn word.

MANDERS. And you've kept the truth hidden from me all these years. Kept it from *me*, and I've given you my absolute trust.

ENGSTRAND. I'm sorry to say I have, sir.

MANDERS. And have I deserved this of you, Engstrand? Haven't I always been ready to help you, in word or deed, to the best of my ability? Answer me! Haven't I?

ENGSTRAND. I'd have had a pretty rough time of it more than once, if it hadn't been for Pastor Manders.

MANDERS. And this is how you repay me. You get me to make false entries in the parish register, and then for years afterwards you withhold information which you owe not just to me, but to truth. Your conduct has been quite inexcusable, Engstrand. From now on we're finished.

ENGSTRAND (*with a sigh*). Well, that's that, I suppose.

MANDERS. I don't see how you could justify it at all.

ENGSTRAND. Well, she couldn't go around making the scandal worse by talking about it, could she? I mean, you imagine how you'd feel, Pastor, if you were in poor Johanne's situation?

MANDERS. Me?

ENGSTRAND. Oh, Lord, Lord, I don't mean in her situation exactly. But supposing the Pastor had something to be ashamed of in the eyes of the world, as they say. We men shouldn't judge a poor woman too harshly, Pastor.

MANDERS. But that's not what I'm doing. My reproach is directed at you.

ENGSTRAND. Well, do you mind if I ask you one little question, Pastor?

MANDERS. No, go ahead.

ENGSTRAND. Isn't it right and proper for a man to raise up the fallen?

MANDERS. Yes, of course.

ENGSTRAND. And isn't a man bound to keep his solemn word?

MANDERS. Indeed he is. But . . .

ENGSTRAND. Well, when Johanne got into trouble that time, through that Englishman – or it might've been an American or a Russian, whatever they're called – well, she came back into town. Poor creature, she'd already turned me down once or twice – she couldn't see beyond handsome, that one, and of course I had this bad leg. I mean, you'll remember, Pastor, how I took a risk going into one of them dance-halls, where seafaring men were getting drunk and disorderly, as they say. And I started calling on them to mend their evil ways . . .

MRS ALVING (*beside the window*). Hm . . .

MANDERS. Yes, I know, Engstrand. The ruffians threw you downstairs. You've told me about that before. Your injury is a badge of honour.

ENGSTRAND. I'm not one to brag about it, Pastor. But what I wanted to say was that she came and confided everything to me, weeping and wailing and gnashing her teeth. It fair broke my heart to hear it, Pastor, I can tell you.

MANDERS. Did it indeed, Engstrand? Well, what then?

ENGSTRAND. Anyway, I says to her: this American, well, he's off sailing the seven seas. And as for you, Johanne, I says, you've committed a sin, you're a fallen woman. But Jakob Engstrand, I says, he can stand on his own two feet . . . Of course, I meant that as a figure of speech, Pastor.

MANDERS. Yes, I quite understand. Go on.

ENGSTRAND. Anyway, that was how I raised her up, you see, made her my lawful wife so's people wouldn't find out she'd been messing around with foreigners.

MANDERS. That was very noble of you. But what I can't fathom is how you could bring yourself to accept money . . .

ENGSTRAND. Money? Me? No, not a penny.

MANDERS (looks questioningly at MRS ALVING). But . . . ?

ENGSTRAND. Oh, wait a minute . . . yes, I remember now. Johanne did have a few shillings. But I wouldn't touch that. Ugh, that's Mammon, I says, that's the wages of sin. Let's just take that rotten gold, or notes, or whatever it was, and fling it right back at that American, I says. But he'd already cleared off, Pastor, over the stormy seas.

MANDERS. Had he indeed, my dear Engstrand?

ENGSTRAND. Yes, sir. Anyway, Johanne and me decided the money should go to bring up the child. So that's what happened. And I can account for every last shilling of that money.

MANDERS. That puts a very different light on the matter.

ENGSTRAND. So that's how it was, Pastor. And I think I can say I've been a good father to Regine, as far as lay in my power. I'm only a poor sinner, God knows.

MANDERS. Oh come, my dear Engstrand . . .

ENGSTRAND. But I can safely say I brought up that child, and was a loving husband to poor Johanne. I kept a decent home, sir, as the Bible tells us. But it would never have entered my head to go bragging about it to Pastor Manders, just because I'd done a good deed for once in my life. No, when something like that happens to Jakob Engstrand, he keeps quiet about it. Not that it happens all that often, I'm sad to say. Whenever I *do* go and see Pastor Manders, I've enough to talk about, with all my faults and weaknesses. As I've just said, and I'll say again – a man's conscience can be in pretty bad shape at times.

MANDERS. Give me your hand, Jakob Engstrand.

ENGSTRAND. Oh Lord, Pastor . . .

MANDERS. No nonsense, now. (*Shakes his hand.*) There!

ENGSTRAND. And if I might humbly beg your forgiveness, Pastor . . .

MANDERS. You? No, quite the contrary. It's I who should be asking you for your forgiveness.

ENGSTRAND. Heavens, no, sir.

MANDERS. Yes, absolutely. And I do so with all my heart. Please forgive me for misjudging you like that. And if there's any way I can show you some proof of my sincere regret, and my goodwill towards you . . .

ENGSTRAND. Do you mean that, Pastor?

MANDERS. It would give me the greatest pleasure.

ENGSTRAND. Well, actually there is something you could do right now. I've put aside a decent bit of money from this job here, and I was thinking of starting up a kind of seamen's hostel in the town.

MRS ALVING. You what?

ENGSTRAND. Yes, it would be a sort of refuge, so to speak. I mean, there are so many temptations, lying in wait for sailors, as they wander about on shore. But in this place of mine, well, I was thinking they'd be under a fatherly eye, as it were.

MANDERS. Now, what do you say to that, Mrs Alving!

ENGSTRAND. Lord knows, I haven't got much to start with, but if someone was to reach out a helping hand, well . . .

MANDERS. Yes, yes, let's discuss the matter in more detail. This project of yours seems immensely attractive. But you go on ahead now, see that everything's in order, and light the candles, make it a bit more festive-looking. Then we'll spend an uplifting hour or so together, my dear Engstrand – for I really do think you're in the right frame of mind now.

ENGSTRAND. Yes, I believe I am, sir. Goodbye then, Mrs Alving, and thanks for everything. Take good care of Regine for me. (*Wipes a tear from his eye.*) Poor Johanne's little girl . . . you know, it's a funny thing, but it's as if she's put down roots, right into my heart. It's really strange. (*He bows, and goes out through the hall.*)

MANDERS. Well, Mrs Alving, what have you to say about this man now? That puts an entirely different light on the matter.

MRS ALVING. It does that, certainly.

MANDERS. You see now how extremely careful we have to be before condemning our fellow-men. Then again, what a great joy it is to discover that we've been wrong about them all along. What do *you* say?

MRS ALVING. I say you're a big baby, Manders, and you always will be.

MANDERS. Me?

MRS ALVING (*places both hands on his shoulders*). And I say I've half a mind to fling my arms round your neck and kiss you.

MANDERS (*hastily withdraws*). No no no – good heavens! What an idea!

MRS ALVING (*with a smile*). Oh, you needn't be afraid of me.

MANDERS (*by the table*). You have such an extravagant way of expressing yourself at times. Anyway, I'll just gather up these papers now and put them in my bag. (*Does so.*) There we are. So, goodbye for the moment. Keep your eyes open when Osvald comes back. I'll look in on you again later.

He picks up his hat and goes out through the hall door. MRS ALVING sighs, looks out of the window for a moment, then briefly tidies up the room. She turns to go into the dining-room, suddenly stops in the doorway, and lets out a muffled cry.

MRS ALVING. Osvald, are you still at table!

OSVALD (*from the dining-room*). I'm just finishing my cigar.

MRS ALVING. I thought you'd gone out for a walk.

OSVALD. In this weather?

A glass clinks. MRS ALVING leaves the door open and sits down with her knitting on the sofa beside the window.

Wasn't that Pastor Manders who went out just now?

MRS ALVING. Yes, he's gone down to the Orphanage.

OSVALD. Hm. (*The glass and decanter clink again.*)

MRS ALVING (*with a worried look*). Osvald dear, you should go easy with that liqueur. It's very strong.

OSVALD. It keeps out the damp.

MRS ALVING. Wouldn't you rather come in here with me?

OSVALD. I can't smoke in there.

MRS ALVING. I don't mind cigars, you know that.

OSVALD. All right, I'll come in. Just another little drop . . . There we are . . .

He enters, smoking a cigar, and closes the door behind him. A brief silence.

So, where's the pastor gone?

MRS ALVING. I told you, he's gone down to the Orphanage.

OSVALD. Oh yes, that's right.

MRS ALVING. You shouldn't sit so long after dinner, Osvald.

OSVALD (*holding his cigar behind his back*). But I find it such a comfort, mother. (*Strokes and pats her affectionately.*) Just think – to come home, to sit at my mother's own table, in my mother's own dining-room, savouring my mother's delicious food.

MRS ALVING. Oh, my dear, dear boy!

OSVALD (*impatiently, pacing up and down, smoking*). I mean, what else is there for me to do here? I can't get started on anything.

MRS ALVING. You can't?

OSVALD. In this foul weather? Without a blink of sunlight the entire day? (*Walks across the room.*) And not being able to work – oh!

MRS ALVING. Maybe it wasn't such a good idea to come home after all.

OSVALD. No, mother, I had to.

MRS ALVING. Because I'd ten times rather forgo the happiness of having you at home, than that you should . . .

OSVALD (*stops by the table*). But tell me, mother – does it really make you so very happy to have me at home?

MRS ALVING. Does it make me happy?

OSVALD (*crumples up a newspaper*). I shouldn't think it much mattered to you, whether I was dead or alive.

MRS ALVING. I don't know how you have the heart to say that to your mother, Osvald.

OSVALD. Well, you've got along quite happily without me before.

MRS ALVING. Yes, I've managed to live without you. That's true.

A silence. Dusk slowly begins to fall. OSVALD *paces up and down the room. He has put down his cigar.*

OSVALD (*stops beside* MRS ALVING). Mother, may I sit down on the sofa beside you?

MRS ALVING (*makes room for him*). Yes, of course, my dear boy.

OSVALD (*sits down*). I've got something to tell you, mother.

MRS ALVING (*strained*). Yes?

OSVALD (*staring straight ahead of him*). Because I can't stand it any longer.

MRS ALVING. Can't stand what? What is it?

OSVALD (*as before*). I couldn't bring myself to write to you about it – and since I've come home . . .

MRS ALVING (*grips his arm*). Osvald, what is it?

OSVALD. Yesterday and today I've tried to put these thoughts out of my mind – to break free of them. But it's no use.

MRS ALVING (*stands up*). Osvald, you must tell me what's wrong!

OSVALD (*pulls her back down onto the sofa*). Sit down, mother, and I'll try and tell you. I've been complaining of tiredness after my journey . . .

MRS ALVING. Yes, so you have. Well?

OSVALD. But that's not what's the matter with me. This isn't any ordinary tiredness . . .

MRS ALVING (*makes to jump up*). Osvald, you're not ill!

OSVALD (*pulls her down again*). Mother, sit still. Calm down. I'm not really ill either – not what people generally call 'ill'. (*Clasps his head in his hands.*) It's my spirit that's broken – my mind's gone – I'll never be able to work again!

He covers his face with his hands, and buries his head in her lap, sobbing bitterly.

MRS ALVING (*pale and trembling*). Osvald! Look at me! No, no, it isn't true!

OSVALD (*looks up with despair in his eyes*). Never able to work again! Never – never! Like a living death! Mother, can you imagine anything more horrible?

MRS ALVING. Oh, my poor, unhappy boy! How did this dreadful thing happen to you?

OSVALD (*sits upright again*). That's just what I can't understand. I've never lived recklessly. Not in any sense. You've got to believe me, mother! I've never done that.

MRS ALVING. No, Osvald, I'm sure you haven't.

OSVALD. And yet this happens to me just the same! This terrible disaster!

MRS ALVING. But it'll get better, my dear, darling boy. It's overwork, nothing more, believe me.

OSVALD. Yes, that's what I believed at first. But it isn't.

MRS ALVING. Tell me the whole story, from beginning to end.

OSVALD. All right, I will.

MRS ALVING. When did you first notice it?

OSVALD. It was just after I'd been home last time, and had got back to Paris again. I began to have the most violent pains in my head – mostly here, at the back, I think. It felt as if there was an iron ring clamped tightly round my neck, and just above it.

MRS ALVING. And then?

OSVALD. Well, at first I thought it was just the sort of headaches I used to suffer from when I was growing up.

MRS ALVING. Yes, yes . . .

OSVALD. But it wasn't. I soon realised that. I couldn't work any longer. I wanted to make a start on a big new painting, but my powers seemed to have deserted me. It was as if I was paralyzed. I couldn't form any clear impressions, everything was swimming before my eyes,

round and round. It was a horrible experience! In the end
I sent for the doctor – and it was from him I learned the
truth.

MRS ALVING. What do you mean?

OSVALD. He was one of the best doctors in Paris. I had
to tell him how I felt, and he started asking me a whole
series of questions, which I thought had nothing to do
with the matter. I couldn't understand what the man was
driving at . . .

MRS ALVING. And?

OSVALD. Well, in the end he said: 'You've been worm-
eaten from birth'. That was his exact expression – *vermoulu*
– worm-eaten.

MRS ALVING (*tensely*). What did he mean by that?

OSVALD. I couldn't understand him either, and asked him
to explain more clearly. So then the old cynic . . . Oh!
(*Clenches his fists.*)

MRS ALVING. What did he say?

OSVALD. He said: 'The sins of the fathers are visited upon
the children.'

MRS ALVING (*slowly rises*). The sins of the fathers . . . !

OSVALD. I very nearly punched him in the face . . .

MRS ALVING (*walks across the floor*). The sins of the
fathers . . .

OSVALD (*smiles sadly*). Yes, what do you think of that?
Well, of course I assured him that was absolutely out of
the question. But d'you think he would give in? No, he
stuck to his guns, and it was only when I brought out
your letters, and translated all those bits about father for
him . . .

MRS ALVING. And then?

OSVALD. Well, of course he had to admit he was on the
wrong track. And so I got to know the truth. The
incomprehensible truth! That blissfully happy young life
I had enjoyed with my comrades – I should have stayed

clear of it. It had all been too much for my strength. So it was my own fault!

MRS ALVING. Osvald, no! Don't think that ever!

OSVALD. There was no other possible explanation, he said. That's what's so terrible about it. An incurable cripple for the rest of my life, and all because of my own stupidity. All the things I wanted to do in life – I don't dare even think of them now – I *can't* think of them! Oh, if only I could have my life over again – undo it all!

He flings himself face-down on the sofa. MRS ALVING *paces up and down, wringing her hands, struggling with her emotions. After a while,* OSVALD *looks up, and remains resting on his elbow.*

If it had only been something I'd inherited – something that couldn't be helped. But this! It's so shameful. So carelessly, without a thought – to have thrown away health, happiness, everything – my future, my very life!

MRS ALVING. No, no, my dear, darling boy! (*Bends over him.*) It's not as desperate as you think.

OSVALD. Oh, you don't know . . . (*Jumps up.*) And look at the worry I'm giving you, mother. Many a time I've almost wished you really didn't care about me at all.

MRS ALVING. Me, Osvald? My only boy? The only thing I possess in all the world – the only thing I do care about.

OSVALD (*seizes both her hands and kisses them*). Yes, yes, I can see that well enough. When I'm at home, I do see it. And that makes it even harder for me. Anyway, now you know. Don't let's talk any more about it today. I can't bear to think about it for too long. (*Walks across the room.*) Get me something to drink, mother.

MRS ALVING. To drink? What do you want to drink now?

OSVALD. Oh, anything at all. If you've some of that cold punch left . . .

MRS ALVING. Yes, but Osvald, dear . . .

OSVALD. Now, don't refuse me, mother. Be nice. I really must have something to drown out all these nagging thoughts. (*Goes into the conservatory.*) And it's so . . . it's so *dark* here! (MRS ALVING *pulls the bell-rope, right.*) And this incessant rain! It can go on week after week, for months on end. Not so much as a glimpse of the sun. You know, the times I've been home, I don't recall ever once having seen the sun.

MRS ALVING. Osvald, you're thinking of leaving me!

OSVALD. Hm . . . (*Sighs deeply.*) I'm not thinking about anything. I *can't* think about anything! (*In a low voice.*) I've had enough of that.

REGINE (*enters from the dining-room*). Did you ring, ma'am?

MRS ALVING. Yes, let's have the lamp in, please.

REGINE. Right away, ma'am. It's already lit. (*Goes out.*)

MRS ALVING (*crosses to* OSVALD). Osvald, you're not keeping anything back from me?

OSVALD. I'm not, mother. (*Goes over to the table.*) I think I've told you rather a lot.

REGINE *brings in the lamp and sets it down on the table.*

MRS ALVING. Oh, and Regine, you might bring us in a half-bottle of champagne.

REGINE. Yes, ma'am. (*Goes out again.*)

OSVALD (*puts his arm round* MRS ALVING's *neck*). That's more like it. I knew my mother wouldn't let her boy go thirsty.

MRS ALVING. Oh, my poor, dear Osvald – how could I possibly refuse you anything now?

OSVALD. Is that true, mother? Do you really mean that?

MRS ALVING. What? Mean what?

OSVALD. That you couldn't refuse me anything?

MRS ALVING. Osvald, my dear . . .

OSVALD. Ssshh!

REGINE *brings in a tray with a half-bottle of champagne and two glasses, which she puts down on the table.*

REGINE. Shall I open . . .

OSVALD. No, thanks – I'll do it.

REGINE *goes out again.*

MRS ALVING (*sits down at the table*). What was it you meant – I mustn't refuse you?

OSVALD (*busy opening the bottle*). First, let's have a glass – or two.

The cork pops, he fills one glass and is about to fill the other. MRS ALVING *covers it with her hand.*

MRS ALVING. No, thanks. Not for me.

OSVALD. Really? Well, I will!

He empties his glass, re-fills it and empties it again, then sits down at the table.

MRS ALVING (*expectantly*). Well?

OSVALD (*without looking at her*). Tell me . . . you and Pastor Manders . . . I thought you were a bit strange . . . hm, a bit subdued, at lunch today.

MRS ALVING. Did you notice?

OSVALD. Yes. Hm . . . (*After a brief silence.*) So tell me – what do you think of Regine?

MRS ALVING. What do I think of her?

OSVALD. Yes – isn't she lovely?

MRS ALVING. Osvald dear, you don't know her as well as I do . . .

OSVALD. So?

MRS ALVING. Regine stayed too long at home, unfortunately. I should have taken her under my wing sooner.

OSVALD. Yes, but she's really beautiful, isn't she, mother. (*Fills his glass.*)

MRS ALVING. Regine has a number of serious faults . . .

OSVALD. So, what does that matter? (*Drinks again.*)

MRS ALVING. But I'm fond of her all the same. And I'm responsible for her. I wouldn't want anything to happen to her, not for the world.

OSVALD (*jumps up*). Mother, Regine is my only hope!

MRS ALVING (*rising*). What do you mean by that?

OSVALD. I can't go on bearing all this torment alone.

MRS ALVING. Haven't you got your mother to bear it with you?

OSVALD. Yes, that's what I thought. That's why I came home to you. But it's no use. I can see it's no use. I can't bear this life!

MRS ALVING. Osvald!

OSVALD. I've got to live differently, mother. That's why I have to leave you. I don't want you watching me.

MRS ALVING. Oh, my poor boy! But, Osvald, while you're so unwell . . .

OSVALD. If it was just the illness, I'd willingly stay with you, mother. You're my best friend in all the world.

MRS ALVING. Yes, Osvald, that's true, isn't it.

OSVALD (*pacing restlessly up and down*). But it's the mental agony, the bitterness, the remorse – and above all, the monstrous, deathly fear. Oh, this terrible feeling of fear!

MRS ALVING (*following him*). Fear? Fear of what? What do you mean?

OSVALD. Oh, don't ask me any more, I don't know. I can't put it into words.

MRS ALVING *goes over and pulls the bell-rope, right.*

What is it you want?

MRS ALVING. I want my boy to be happy, that's what I want. He mustn't sit here brooding. (*To* REGINE, *who appears in the doorway.*) More champagne. A full bottle. (REGINE *goes out.*)

OSVALD. Mother!

MRS ALVING. D'you think we don't know how to live out here in the country?

OSVALD. And isn't she so beautiful? What a figure! And the very picture of health.

MRS ALVING (*sits down at the table*). Sit down, Osvald – let's have a quiet talk.

OSVALD (*sits down*). I don't suppose you know, mother, but I've got something to put right with Regine.

MRS ALVING. You?

OSVALD. Oh, just a little thoughtlessness, I suppose you might call it. All very innocent, anyhow. Last time I was home . . .

MRS ALVING. Yes?

OSVALD. Well, she kept asking me about Paris, and I told her a bit about the life over there. Anyway, I remember saying to her one day: 'Wouldn't you like to go there yourself?'

MRS ALVING. And?

OSVALD. Well, she blushed bright red, and said: 'Oh yes, I'd really love that.' 'Fine,' I said, 'We'll see what we can do,' or something like that.

MRS ALVING. So?

OSVALD. Well, naturally, I forgot all about it. But when I asked her a few days ago if she was pleased I was going to be at home so long . . .

MRS ALVING. Yes?

OSVALD. She gave me an odd sort of look, and asked: 'But what's to happen about my trip to Paris?'

MRS ALVING. Her trip to Paris!

OSVALD. So then I got out of her that she'd taken the whole thing seriously – that she'd been going around here thinking about me the whole time, that she'd even started learning French . . .

MRS ALVING. So that's why!

OSVALD. Mother, when I saw that lovely, radiant, fresh-faced girl standing there – I'd never paid her that much attention before – standing there, as if with open arms, ready to receive me . . .

MRS ALVING. Osvald!

OSVALD. I realised then that she was my salvation. Because I could see she was filled with the joy of life.

MRS ALVING (*taken aback*). The joy of life? Can there be salvation in *that*?

REGINE *enters from the dining-room with a bottle of champagne.*

REGINE. I'm sorry I've taken so long. I had to go down to the cellar . . . (*Puts the bottle on the table.*)

OSVALD. And fetch another glass, please.

REGINE (*looks at him in surprise*). Mrs Alving has a glass, sir.

OSVALD. Yes, but one for yourself, Regine. (REGINE *starts, flashes a nervous, sidelong glance towards* MRS ALVING.) Well?

REGINE (*quietly, hesitant*). Is that all right, ma'am?

MRS ALVING. Bring another glass, Regine.

REGINE *goes out to the dining-room.*

OSVALD (*watching her*). Have you noticed the way she walks? So firm and resolute.

MRS ALVING. Osvald, this won't work!

OSVALD. Mother, it's already decided. You must see that. There's no point in arguing. (REGINE *enters with an empty glass, which she keeps in her hand.*) Sit down, Regine. (REGINE *looks questioningly at* MRS ALVING.)

MRS ALVING. Sit down. (REGINE *sits down on a chair near the dining-room door, still holding the empty glass in her hand.*) So, Osvald – what was that you were saying about the joy of life?

OSVALD. Oh yes, mother, the joy of life – people round here don't know much about that. I never feel it here.

MRS ALVING. Not even when you're with me?

OSVALD. No, never when I'm at home. But you wouldn't understand.

MRS ALVING. Yes, yes – I think I'm beginning to understand . . . now.

OSVALD. Well, that – and the joy of work too. Basically it's the same thing. But people here know nothing about that either.

MRS ALVING. You may be right. Tell me more about this, Osvald.

OSVALD. Well, all I mean is that people here are brought up to believe that work is a curse, a punishment for sin – that life is a miserable sort of business altogether, and the sooner it's over and done with, the better.

MRS ALVING. A vale of tears, that's right. And we do our level best to make it so.

OSVALD. But people elsewhere don't see it that way. Nobody accepts those sort of doctrines any longer. Over there, they're blissfully happy, just to be alive. Haven't you noticed, mother, how everything I've ever painted has centred on this joy of life? Always the joy of life, incessantly. Filled with light, and sunshine – an air of festival, people's faces radiant with happiness. That's why I'm afraid to stay here with you.

MRS ALVING. Afraid? What are you afraid of, here with me?

OSVALD. I'm afraid that everything inside me will degenerate into ugliness.

MRS ALVING (looks steadily at him). Do you think that's what will happen?

OSVALD. I'm sure of it. Even if we lived here the way they do abroad, it still wouldn't be the same life.

MRS ALVING (who has been listening intently, rises, deep in thought). Now I see the connection.

OSVALD. What is it you see?

MRS ALVING. I see it for the first time now. And now I can speak.

OSVALD (*rises*). Mother, I don't understand you.

REGINE (*who has also stood up*). Perhaps I should go?

MRS ALVING. No, stay. Now I can speak. Now, my son, you shall know the whole truth. And then you can choose. Osvald! Regine!

OSVALD. Ssshh! The pastor . . .

MANDERS (*entering by the hall door*). Well now, we've had a most illuminating time down there.

OSVALD. So have we.

MANDERS. Engstrand really needs help with that seamen's hostel of his. Regine should move in with him and lend a hand.

REGINE. No, thank you, Pastor.

MANDERS (*noticing her for the first time*). What? You're here – and with a glass in your hand?

REGINE (*hastily puts the glass down*). *Pardon!*

OSVALD. Regine's leaving with me, Pastor.

MANDERS. Leaving with you?

OSVALD. Yes. As my wife – if that's what she wants.

MANDERS. Good God!

REGINE. This has nothing to do with me, Pastor.

OSVALD. Or else she's staying here, if I stay.

REGINE (*spontaneously*). Here!

MANDERS. Mrs Alving, I'm astonished at you.

MRS ALVING. They'll do neither of these things. Because now I can speak out.

MANDERS. No, you can't do that! No, no, no!

MRS ALVING. Yes, I can, and I will. And without destroying anyone's ideals.

OSVALD. Mother, you're keeping something from me – what is it!

REGINE (*listening*). Ma'am! Listen! There are people shouting outside. (*Goes into the conservatory and looks out.*)

OSVALD (*over by the window, left*). What's going on? Where's that glow coming from?

REGINE. The Orphanage is on fire!

MRS ALVING (*goes to the window*). On fire!

MANDERS. On fire? That's impossible – I've just come from there.

OSVALD. Where's my hat? Oh, never mind . . . Father's Orphanage! (*Runs out through the garden door.*)

MRS ALVING. My shawl, Regine! The whole place is in flames!

MANDERS. Dreadful! Mrs Alving, that fire is a judgment on this house of sin!

MRS ALVING. Yes, quite. Come on, Regine. (*She and REGINE hurry out through the hall.*)

MANDERS (*clasps his hands*). And no insurance! (*Follows them out.*)

Curtain.

ACT THREE

The room as before. All the doors are standing open. The lamp is still burning on the table. It is dark outside, except for a faint glow from the fire, visible in the background, left. MRS ALVING *has a shawl over her head, and is standing in the conservatory, looking out.* REGINE, *also wrapped in a shawl, is standing a little behind her.*

MRS ALVING. It's all burnt down. Burnt to the ground.

REGINE. It's still on fire in the basement.

MRS ALVING. Why doesn't Osvald come home? There's nothing to be saved.

REGINE. Maybe I should take him his hat?

MRS ALVING. Hasn't he even got his hat?

REGINE (*pointing into the hall*). No, it's hanging there.

MRS ALVING. Oh, never mind. He ought to be here soon. I'll go and look for him myself.

She goes out by the garden door. PASTOR MANDERS *enters from the hall.*

MANDERS. Isn't Mrs Alving here?

REGINE. She's just this minute gone down into the garden.

MANDERS. This is the most dreadful night I've ever experienced.

REGINE. It's a terrible misfortune, isn't it, Pastor.

MANDERS. Oh, don't talk about it. I hardly dare even think about it.

REGINE. But how could it have happened?

MANDERS. Don't ask me, Miss Engstrand, I've no idea. You're not suggesting that . . . ? Isn't it bad enough that your father . . . ?

REGINE. What about him?

MANDERS. Oh, he's driving me crazy.

ENGSTRAND (*enters from the hall*). Pastor Manders!

MANDERS (*turns round, startled*). Are you *still* chasing after me?

ENGSTRAND. Well, God help me, I've got to! Oh, Lord! This is a dreadful business, Pastor.

MANDERS (*pacing up and down*). Yes, yes, I'm afraid so.

REGINE. What do you mean?

ENGSTRAND. It was that prayer meeting that started it, you see. (*Aside.*) We've caught him now, my girl! (*Aloud.*) And to think it's all my fault that Pastor Manders is at fault for something like this!

MANDERS. But I assure you, Engstrand . . .

ENGSTRAND. I mean, nobody else down there touched the candles, apart from yourself, Pastor.

MANDERS (*comes to a halt*). Yes, so you say. But I have absolutely no recollection of ever having a candle in my hand.

ENGSTRAND. Well, I saw you quite distinctly picking up a candle and snuffing it with your fingers, then tossing it into a pile of shavings.

MANDERS. And you saw that?

ENGSTRAND. As plain as day, yes.

MANDERS. I can't understand that at all. Anyway, I'm not in the habit of snuffing out candles with my fingers.

ENGSTRAND. Yes, I thought it looked a mite careless. But it can't be as bad as all that, can it, Pastor?

MANDERS (*pacing restlessly up and down*). Oh, don't ask!

ENGSTRAND (*following him*). And you hadn't insured it either, had you?

MANDERS (*still pacing up and down*). No no no! I've told you already.

ENGSTRAND (*following him still*). Not insured. And then to go right off and set the whole place on fire. God, how's that for bad luck!

MANDERS (*wiping the sweat from his brow*). You can say that again.

ENGSTRAND. I mean, a thing like that happening to a charitable institution, that was going to be an asset to town and country alike, as they say. I'm afraid the papers won't let you off lightly, Pastor.

MANDERS. No, that's just what I've been thinking. That's almost the worst part of the whole business. All those spiteful attacks and accusations – terrible, it doesn't bear thinking about!

MRS ALVING (*entering from the garden*). I can't get him to come away from the fire.

MANDERS. Ah, there you are, Mrs Alving.

MRS ALVING. Well, at least you won't have to make your speech now, Pastor Manders.

MANDERS. Oh, that would have been a pleasure . . .

MRS ALVING (*subdued*). It's just as well it's turned out this way. That Orphanage would have done nobody any good.

MANDERS. You think not?

MRS ALVING. Don't you?

MANDERS. Well, it was a terrible tragedy, nonetheless.

MRS ALVING. We'll discuss it strictly as a business matter . . . Are you waiting to see Pastor Manders, Engstrand?

ENGSTRAND (*by the hall door*). Yes, I am actually.

MRS ALVING. Well, have a seat, then.

ENGSTRAND. Thanks, I'm quite happy to stand.

MRS ALVING (*to MANDERS*). You'll be catching the steamer back, I suppose?

MANDERS. Yes. It leaves in about an hour.

MRS ALVING. Please take all these documents away with you. I don't want to hear another word on this affair. I've got other things to think about.

MANDERS. Mrs Alving . . .

MRS ALVING. I'll send you a power of attorney later, so you can deal with it however you wish.

MANDERS. I shall be only too pleased to undertake that. Unfortunately, the original terms of the bequest will have to be entirely revised now.

MRS ALVING. Of course.

MANDERS. Anyway, my thought at the moment is that we should arrange to transfer the Solvik estate to the parish. I mean, the land can't be described as entirely worthless, indeed no. It can always be turned to account for something or other. And there's the interest on the capital in the bank – perhaps the most appropriate use of that would be to support some enterprise that might be of benefit to the town.

MRS ALVING. Do whatever you like. It's a matter of complete indifference to me.

ENGSTRAND. You'll bear my seamen's hostel in mind, won't you, Pastor?

MANDERS. Yes, absolutely – you may have a point there. It's worth careful consideration.

ENGSTRAND. Oh, to hell with consideration – oh, Lord!

MANDERS (*with a sigh*). Unfortunately, I don't know how much longer I'll have a say in these matters. Or if public opinion might not force me to resign. That'll all depend on the result of the enquiry into the fire.

MRS ALVING. What's that you're saying?

MANDERS. It's impossible to predict the outcome of these things.

ENGSTRAND (*approaches*). Oh no, it isn't. Because I'm standing here, and I'm Jakob Engstrand.

MANDERS. Yes, but . . .

ENGSTRAND (*lowering his voice*). And Jakob Engstrand isn't the sort of man to desert a worthy benefactor in his hour of need, as the saying goes.

MANDERS. But, my dear sir . . . how . . . ?

ENGSTRAND. Jakob Engstrand's a sort of angel of mercy, Pastor, as you might say.

MANDERS. No no, I couldn't possibly allow that.

ENGSTRAND. Oh, that's how it'll be, just the same. It wouldn't be the first time somebody's taken the blame for somebody else, I know that much.

MANDERS. Jakob! (*Shakes his hand.*) You're truly an exceptional person! Well, you'll get some help with your seamen's hostel, you can rest assured.

ENGSTRAND *tries to thank him, but is overcome by emotion.* MANDERS *slings his travel-bag over his shoulder.*

Let's go now. We can travel together.

ENGSTRAND (*by the dining-room door, sotto voce to* REGINE). You stick with me, girl. You'll be snug as a bug in a rug.

REGINE (*tossing her head*). *Merci!*

She goes out into the hall to fetch MANDERS's *things.*

MANDERS. Goodbye, Mrs Alving. Let's hope some sense of order and propriety will soon descend upon this house.

MRS ALVING. Goodbye, Manders!

She goes towards the conservatory, having seen OSVALD *entering through the garden door.* ENGSTRAND *and* REGINE *help* MANDERS *on with his overcoat.*

ENGSTRAND. Goodbye, my girl. And if you're ever in any trouble, you know where to find Jakob Engstrand. (*Lowering his voice.*) Little Harbour Street – hm? (*To* MRS ALVING *and* OSVALD.) And this house for seafaring men, yes, it's going to be called the 'Captain Alving Home'. And if I'm allowed to run it the way I have in mind, I think I can promise it'll be a credit to the Captain's memory, bless him.

MANDERS (*in the doorway*). Hm . . . hm! Come along, my
   dear Engstrand. Goodbye, goodbye! (*He and*
   ENGSTRAND *go out through the hall.*)

OSVALD (*goes over to the table*). What house was he talking
   about?

MRS ALVING. It's a sort of hostel he and Pastor Manders
   are planning to start up.

OSVALD. It'll burn down the same as this one.

MRS ALVING. What makes you say that?

OSVALD. It'll all burn. There'll be nothing left to remind
   people of father. I'm burning up too.

   REGINE *looks at him, alarmed.*

MRS ALVING. Osvald! My poor boy – you shouldn't have
   stayed so long down there.

OSVALD (*sits down at the table*). I think you're probably right.

MRS ALVING. Here, let me dry your face, Osvald, you're
   dripping wet. (*She dries him with her handkerchief.*)

OSVALD (*looking straight ahead, expressionless*). Thank you,
   mother.

MRS ALVING. Aren't you tired, Osvald? You wouldn't
   want to have a sleep?

OSVALD (*uneasily*). No, no – not sleep! I never sleep, I only
   pretend to. (*Gloomily.*) That'll come soon enough.

MRS ALVING (*looks at him anxiously*). Yes, my darling boy,
   you really are ill.

REGINE (*strained*). Is Mr Alving ill?

OSVALD (*impatiently*). And close all the doors! This deathly
   fear . . .

MRS ALVING. Close them, Regine.

   REGINE *does so, and remains standing by the hall door.* MRS
   ALVING *takes off her shawl, and* REGINE *does likewise.*
   MRS ALVING *then pulls up a chair and sits down beside*
   OSVALD.

There now – I'll sit down beside you.

OSVALD. Yes, do that. And Regine has to stay too. I want Regine near me always. You'll give me a helping hand, Regine, you will, won't you?

REGINE. I don't understand.

MRS ALVING. A helping hand?

OSVALD. Yes – when it becomes necessary.

MRS ALVING. Osvald, haven't you got your mother to give you a helping hand?

OSVALD. You? (*Smiles.*) No, mother, you can't give me that kind of help. (*Laughs sardonically.*) You? Ha-ha! (*Looks gravely at her.*) Though you've got most right, just the same. (*Suddenly angry.*) Why don't you call me by my first name, Regine? Why don't you call me Osvald?

REGINE (*quietly*). I don't think Mrs Alving would like it.

MRS ALVING. You'll soon have the right to do that. Come over and sit beside us.

REGINE *sits down meekly, after some hesitation, at the other side of the table.*

And now, my poor, tormented boy, I'm going to lift a great burden from your mind . . .

OSVALD. You, mother?

MRS ALVING. . . . All that bitterness and remorse, as you called it . . .

OSVALD. And you think you can?

MRS ALVING. Yes, I can now, Osvald. You were talking earlier about the joy of life, and it was as if I could see the whole of my own life, and everything in it, in a new light.

OSVALD (*shakes his head*). I don't understand any of this.

MRS ALVING. You should have known your father when he was just a young lieutenant. *He* had the joy of life, I can tell you!

OSVALD. Yes, I know.

MRS ALVING. It did your heart good just to look at him – the tremendous energy he had, all that vitality!

OSVALD. So?

MRS ALVING. So here was this happy, carefree boy – he was still very much a boy, in those days – stuck in a small provincial town, which had no real joy to offer him, only shallow entertainments. Stuck out here with no real purpose in life, only an official position. Nothing he could throw himself into, heart and soul – no real work, only business. And he hadn't a single friend capable of appreciating what the joy of life means – only layabouts and drinking companions.

OSVALD. Mother!

MRS ALVING. So the inevitable happened.

OSVALD. What do you mean, the inevitable?

MRS ALVING. Well, you told me yourself this evening what would happen to you if you stayed at home.

OSVALD. Are you trying to say that father . . . ?

MRS ALVING. Your poor father couldn't find any outlet for this overwhelming joy that was in him. And I didn't bring any sunshine into his life either.

OSVALD. You didn't?

MRS ALVING. Oh, they'd taught me plenty about duty and suchlike, all the things I went on believing for so long. Everything came down to duty in the end – *my* duty, and *his* duty, and . . . Anyway, I'm afraid I made this house unbearable for your poor father, Osvald.

OSVALD. Why didn't you ever write to me about this?

MRS ALVING. Well, up till now, I've never looked on this as something I could discuss with you – you being his son.

OSVALD. And how did you look on it then?

MRS ALVING (*slowly*). I could see only one thing: that your father was a lost soul even before you were born.

OSVALD (*subdued*). Ah! (*He stands up and goes over to the window.*)

MRS ALVING. And day in, day out, one thought occupied my mind – that Regine belonged here, in this house . . . just as much as my own son.

OSVALD (*turns round sharply*). Regine?

REGINE (*leaps to her feet, then asks softly*). Me?

MRS ALVING. Yes. Now you both know.

OSVALD. Regine!

REGINE (*to herself*). So that's what my mother was like.

MRS ALVING. Your mother had many fine qualities, Regine.

REGINE. Yes, but she was one of that kind, just the same. Well, I've had my suspicions about that. Anyway, Mrs Alving, if you don't mind I'll leave right now.

MRS ALVING. Is that what you really want, Regine?

REGINE. Yes, it is indeed.

MRS ALVING. Well, of course you can do as you please, but . . .

OSVALD (*goes over to* REGINE). What, leave now? But you belong here.

REGINE. *Merci*, Mr Alving. Actually, I suppose I am allowed to say 'Osvald' now. But this is certainly not what I had in mind.

MRS ALVING. Regine, I'm afraid I haven't been open with you . . .

REGINE. No, I should think you haven't! If I'd known Osvald was so ill . . . Anyway, now that there can't be anything serious between us – well, I'm not going to be stuck out here in the wilds, wearing myself out running after sick people.

OSVALD. Not even somebody so close to you?

REGINE. Not on your life. A poor girl's got to make the most of things, while she's still young. Either that or before you know it, you end up on the shelf. And I've got the joy of life in me too, Mrs Alving!

MRS ALVING. Yes, unfortunately you have. But don't go throwing yourself away, Regine.

REGINE. Well, whatever's going to happen will happen. The way I see it, if Osvald takes after his father, then I'll most likely take after my mother. Mrs Alving, may I ask if Pastor Manders knows all this about me?

MRS ALVING. Pastor Manders knows everything.

REGINE (*putting on her shawl*). Well, the best thing I can do is get down to that steamer as fast as I can. The Pastor's an easy man to get along with. And I reckon I've as much right to some of that money as him – that nasty carpenter.

MRS ALVING. You're very welcome to it, Regine.

REGINE (*stares fixedly at her*). You know, you could've brought me up as a gentleman's daughter, Mrs Alving. That would've been more appropriate. (*Tosses her head.*) Oh, what the hell? (*With a bitter glance at the unopened bottle.*) I'll be drinking champagne with the toffs yet, you'll see.

MRS ALVING. And if you ever need a home, Regine, come to me.

REGINE. No, thanks all the same, Mrs Alving. Pastor Manders will look after me. And if things don't pan out, well, I know a place where I'll fit right in.

MRS ALVING. Where?

REGINE. The Captain Alving Home.

MRS ALVING. Regine . . . I can see it now – you're going to your ruin!

REGINE. Oh, rubbish! *Adieu* . . . (*Nods and goes out through the hall.*)

OSVALD (*stands at the window looking out*). Has she gone?

MRS ALVING. Yes.

OSVALD (*mutters to himself*). I think this is a terrible mistake.

MRS ALVING *goes and stands behind him, and puts her hands on his shoulders.*

MRS ALVING. Osvald, my dear – has it upset you so much?

OSVALD (*turns round to face her*). All this about father, you mean?

MRS ALVING. Yes, your poor unhappy father. I'm afraid it's all been too much for you.

OSVALD. What makes you think that? It came as a great surprise, of course, but deep down, it doesn't really matter to me.

MRS ALVING (*takes her hands away*). Doesn't matter! That your father was so desperately unhappy!

OSVALD. Well, of course I feel sorry for him, yes, same as I would for anybody, but . . .

MRS ALVING. Is that all! For your own father!

OSVALD (*impatiently*). Oh yes, my father. I never knew anything about my father. All I remember about him is that he made me throw up once.

MRS ALVING. That's a dreadful thing to say. Surely a child should feel some affection for its father, no matter what?

OSVALD. What, when the child has nothing to thank its father for? When it's never even known him? Do you really still cling to that old superstition? And you're supposed to be so enlightened?

MRS ALVING. That's superstition, is it?

OSVALD. Yes, surely you can see that, mother? It's just one of these ideas that get into circulation, and eventually . . .

MRS ALVING (*shaken*). Ghosts!

OSVALD (*walks across the room*). Yes, you may well call them ghosts.

MRS ALVING (*cries out*). Osvald! So you don't love *me* either!

OSVALD. Well, at least I know you.

MRS ALVING. Yes, you know me – but is that all!

OSVALD. I also know how fond you are of me. And that's something I have to be grateful for. Besides which, you can be extremely useful to me, now that I'm ill.

MRS ALVING. Yes, I can, Osvald, can't I! Oh, I could almost bless this sickness of yours, for driving you home to me. But I can see well enough, you're not *mine* yet – I still have to win you.

OSVALD (*impatiently*). Yes, yes – these are all just empty words. You must remember I'm a sick man, mother. I can't be too concerned with other people – I've enough to think about with myself.

MRS ALVING (*meekly*). I shall be patient and easily satisfied.

OSVALD. And cheerful too, mother!

MRS ALVING. Yes, my dear boy, you're right, of course. (*She goes over to him.*) Now, have I taken away all that bitterness and remorse?

OSVALD. Yes, you have. But who'll take away the feeling of dread?

MRS ALVING. Dread?

OSVALD (*walks across the room*). Regine would have done it, for a kind word.

MRS ALVING. I don't understand. What's all this about dread – and what's Regine got to do with it?

OSVALD. Is it very late, mother?

MRS ALVING. It's early morning. (*Looks out through the conservatory.*) The dawn's already breaking on the mountains. And it's a clear sky, Osvald! You'll be able to see the sun in a little while.

OSVALD. I'm looking forward to that. Oh, there could be so much still to take pleasure in, and to live for.

MRS ALVING. I should think so, indeed!

OSVALD. Even if I can't work, I can . . .

MRS ALVING. You'll soon be able to work again, my dear. Now you've no longer got all those depressing thoughts nagging away at you.

OSVALD. Yes, you've managed to stop me having delusions, and that's good. And if I could just overcome this one thing . . . (*Sits down on the sofa.*) Mother, we need to talk.

MRS ALVING. Yes, let's.

She pushes an armchair over to the sofa, and sits close beside him.

OSVALD. And while we do, the sun will come up. And then you'll know. And I won't have this feeling of dread any longer.

MRS ALVING. What will I know?

OSVALD (*not listening to her*). Mother, didn't you say this evening that there was nothing in the world you wouldn't do for me, if I asked?

MRS ALVING. Yes, I certainly did say that.

OSVALD. And you'll keep your promise, mother?

MRS ALVING. Rest assured I will, my darling boy. I've nothing to live for, except you.

OSVALD. Yes, yes. All right, then, I'll tell you . . . You're very strongminded, mother, I know that. So you must sit quite still when you hear what it is.

MRS ALVING. But what is this terrible thing?

OSVALD. You mustn't scream. Do you hear? Promise me? We'll sit and talk about it quite calmly? Promise me, mother?

MRS ALVING. Yes, yes, I promise. Just tell me!

OSVALD. All right. What you have to know is that this tiredness – this not being able even to think of work – none of that's the real illness.

MRS ALVING. Then what is the real illness?

OSVALD. The sickness I've inherited . . . (*Points to his forehead and adds quietly.*) . . . is lodged here.

MRS ALVING (*almost speechless*). Osvald! No! No!

OSVALD. Don't scream. I can't stand it. Yes, mother, it sits in here, just waiting. And it can break out any day, at any moment.

MRS ALVING. Oh, that's horrible!

OSVALD. Now, calm down. That's just how things are with me –

MRS ALVING (*leaps to her feet*). No, that's not true, Osvald! It's not possible! It can't be!

OSVALD. I've already had one attack over there. It passed off quite quickly. But when I was told what I'd been like, well, that's when this ghastly feeling of dread began to haunt me. And I came home to you as quickly as I could.

MRS ALVING. So this is the feeling of dread?

OSVALD. Yes, because it's so disgusting, you see, it's indescribable. If it were just some ordinary kind of fatal illness . . . I mean, I'm not afraid to die, although I'd obviously like to live as long as I can.

MRS ALVING. Yes, yes, Osvald, you must!

OSVALD. But this is disgusting, it's horrible. It's like becoming a helpless child all over again – to have to be fed, to have to be . . . Oh, God, it's unspeakable!

MRS ALVING. The child has its mother to look after it.

OSVALD (*jumps up*). No, never! That's just what I don't want! I can't bear the thought of hanging on like that, for years maybe – till I'm old and grey. And in the meantime you might die and leave me. (*Sits down on* MRS ALVING*'s chair.*) Because it wouldn't necessarily prove fatal right away, so the doctor said. He called it a sort of softening of the brain – something like that. (*Smiles gloomily.*) I think that's such a lovely expression. Makes me think of cherry-red velvet curtains – something soft and luxurious to the touch.

MRS ALVING (*screams*). Osvald!

OSVALD (*leaps up again and walks across the room*). And now you've taken Regine away from me! If I'd only had her. She'd have given me the help I need, for sure.

MRS ALVING (*walks over to him*). What do you mean, my darling? Is there anything in this world I wouldn't do to help you?

OSVALD. You know, when I came round after that last attack over there, the doctor said that when it happened again – and it *will* happen again – there'd be no more hope.

MRS ALVING. And he was heartless enough to . . .

OSVALD. I forced it from him. I told him I had some things to take care of . . . (*Smiles cunningly.*) And so I had. (*Brings a little box out of his breast-pocket.*) You see this, mother?

MRS ALVING. What is it?

OSVALD. Morphine.

MRS ALVING (*looks at him in horror*). Osvald . . . my child!

OSVALD. I've managed to save up twelve tablets . . .

MRS ALVING (*snatches at it*). Osvald, give me that box!

OSVALD. Not yet, mother! (*Returns the box to his pocket.*)

MRS ALVING. I'll never get over this!

OSVALD. You'll have to. If I had Regine here now, I'd have told her the state I'm in. I'd have asked her to do me this last service. She'd have helped me, I know she would.

MRS ALVING. Never!

OSVALD. If this horrible thing came over me – if she saw me lying there like a helpless infant, lost and beyond all hope – no possibility of recovery . . .

MRS ALVING. Regine would never have done it!

OSVALD. Regine would have. Regine was so wonderfully carefree. And she'd have soon got bored looking after an invalid like me.

MRS ALVING. Then thank God Regine isn't here!

OSVALD. All right then – you'll have to do me this service, mother.

MRS ALVING (*shrieks*). Me!

OSVALD. Who has a better right than you?

MRS ALVING. Me! Your own mother!

OSVALD. Precisely.

MRS ALVING. Who gave you life!

OSVALD. I never asked you for life. And what sort of life is this you've given me? I don't want it. You can take it back!

MRS ALVING. Help! Help! (*She runs out into the hall.*)

OSVALD (*runs after her*). No, don't leave me! Where are you going?

MRS ALVING (*in the hall*). To fetch the doctor, Osvald! Let me out!

OSVALD (*also in the hall*). No, you're not getting out! And nobody's getting in, either! (*A key is turned in the lock.*)

MRS ALVING (*re-enters*). Osvald! Osvald – my child!

OSVALD (*follows her in*). You have a mother's love for me – yet you can still let me suffer this unspeakable terror!

MRS ALVING (*after a moment's silence, in a controlled voice*). Here's my hand on it.

OSVALD. You'll do it?

MRS ALVING. If it becomes necessary. But it won't *be* necessary. No, no, that's quite impossible.

OSVALD. Well, let's hope so. And let's go on living together, as long as we can. Thank you, mother.

He sits down in the armchair which MRS ALVING *had moved beside the sofa. Day is dawning; the lamp is still burning on the table.*

MRS ALVING (*tentatively approaching*). Do you feel calmer now?

OSVALD. Yes.

MRS ALVING (*bends over him*). These dreadful things, Osvald, you've just imagined them. It's all in your imagination. All this excitement's been too much for you. But you'll be able to have a rest now. At home with your own mother, my dear, darling boy. You'll be able to have anything you want, just like when you were a little boy. There, now . . . The attack's over. You see how quickly it passed? Oh yes, I knew it would. And you see, Osvald, what a beautiful day it's going to be? Brilliant sunshine. You'll be able to see the place properly now.

She walks across to the table and puts out the lamp. Sunrise. The glacier and snow-capped peaks in the background are bathed in dazzling morning light.

OSVALD (*sitting motionless in the armchair with his back to the view, suddenly speaks*). Mother, give me the sun.

MRS ALVING (*by the table, looks at him in astonishment*). What did you say?

OSVALD (*repeats, in a dull, toneless voice*). The sun. The sun.

MRS ALVING (*goes over to him*). Osvald, what's the matter with you?

OSVALD *seems to shrink in his chair; all his muscles go limp; his face is expressionless; his eyes are staring into space.*

MRS ALVING (*trembling with fear*). What is it? (*Screams.*) Osvald! What's the matter with you! (*Throws herself on her knees beside him and shakes him.*) Osvald! Osvald! Look at me! Don't you know me?

OSVALD (*expressionlessly as before*). The sun . . . The sun.

MRS ALVING (*leaps up, tearing at her hair with both hands and screams*). I can't bear it! (*Then whispers as though petrified with fear.*) I can't bear it! Never! (*Suddenly.*) Where did he put them? (*Fumbles hastily in his coat.*) They're here! (*Recoils a few paces and screams.*) No, no, no! . . . Yes! No, no!

She stands back from him a little way, with her hands thrust into her hair, staring at him in wordless horror.

OSVALD (*sitting motionless as before*). The sun . . . The sun.

Curtain.

HEDDA GABLER

translated by Kenneth McLeish

Characters

JØRGEN TESMAN, *a cultural historian*

HEDDA TESMAN, *née Hedda Gabler, his wife*

MISS JULIA TESMAN, *his aunt (Norwegian: Juliane)*

MRS ELVSTED

BRACK, *a circuit judge*

EJLERT LØVBORG

BERTA, *the maid (Norwegian: Berthe)*

The action takes place in Tesman's house in the western part of town. There are four acts.

Pronunciation of Proper Names

Jørgen – like the English word 'Yearn'

Ejlert – EYE-lert ('eye' as in 'eyesight')

Løvborg – LE(R)V-bor (silent 'R')

ACT ONE

A smart, spacious living room, stylishly decorated in dark colours.
Upstage, a wide double-doorway, with its curtains drawn back, leads
into a smaller room, decorated in the same style. Right, exit to the hall.
Opposite left, through a glass screen door with its curtains also drawn
back, can be seen part of a raised verandah and a garden. It is
autumn. Centre stage, dining chairs and an oval table covered with a
cloth. Downstage right, against the wall, a dark tiled stove, a wing
chair, an upholstered footstool and two stools. Upstage right, a corner
seat and a small table. Downstage left, a little out from the wall, a
sofa. Upstage of the screen door, a piano. On either side of the main
double-doorway, whatnots displaying artefacts of terracotta and majolica.
In the inner room can be seen a sofa, a table and two chairs. Over the
sofa hangs the portrait of a handsome elderly man in general's uniform.
Over the table, a hanging lamp with a pearled glass shade. All round
the main room are vases and glass containers full of cut flowers; other
bouquets lie on the tables. Thick carpets in both rooms. Sunlight streams
in through the screen door.

Enter MISS JULIA TESMAN *and* BERTA *from the hall.*
BERTA *is carrying a bouquet.* MISS TESMAN *is a placid-looking*
woman of about 65. Her grey outdoor clothes are plain but well-made.
BERTA *is a simple countrywoman, getting on in years.* MISS
TESMAN *stops in the doorway and listens.*

MISS TESMAN (*in a low voice*). They *aren't* up yet!

BERTA (*in a low voice*). I told you, Miss Tesman. The boat
came in very late last night. And even then, mercy!, the
things the young lady had to unpack before she'd go to
bed.

MISS TESMAN. We won't disturb them. But we *will* let
some air in for when they do get up.

She opens the screen door, wide. BERTA, *at the table, is not sure*
what to do with her flowers.

BERTA. There's no room anywhere. I'll put them over here.

She props them on the piano.

MISS TESMAN. Just fancy, Berta – you, and a new mistress. I don't know how I brought myself to part with you.

BERTA (*close to tears*). It was hard for me too, Miss Tesman. After all these years, with you and Miss Rina.

MISS TESMAN. Now, Berta, what else could we do? Jørgen needs you here. Needs you. Ever since he was a little boy, he's relied on you.

BERTA. Oh Miss Tesman, I keep thinking of that poor lady lying at home. Can't do a thing for herself, poor soul. And a new maid now. That one won't learn how to look after an invalid.

MISS TESMAN. I'll show her. And I'll do much more myself. Dear Berta, for my poor sister's sake, don't worry so.

BERTA. There's something else, Miss Tesman. The new mistress . . . I'm afraid . . . I won't give satisfaction.

MISS TESMAN. Don't be silly. There may be a few small difficulties, at first –

BERTA. She's such a particular lady.

MISS TESMAN. Of course she is. General Gabler's daughter. The style she had, when her father was alive! D'you remember her riding beside him, down the road? In that long black skirt? With the feather in her hat?

BERTA. Oh yes, Miss Tesman. I'd never have dreamed, back then, that one day she'd marry Mr Jørgen.

MISS TESMAN. We none of us dreamed it, Berta. But so she did. Oh and Berta, you mustn't call Jørgen 'Mister' any more. He's 'Doctor Tesman' now.

BERTA. The young lady told me that as well, as soon as they got in last night.

MISS TESMAN. Just fancy, Berta, they made him a doctor while he was away. On honeymoon. I didn't know a thing about it, till he told me at the pier last night.

BERTA. Such a clever man. He can do anything he sets his mind to. But even so . . . curing people!

MISS TESMAN. Not that kind of doctor. (*With meaning.*) In any case, before long you may be calling him something else.

BERTA. Miss Tesman, what do you mean?

MISS TESMAN (*with a smile*). Ah! Wait and see. (*With emotion.*) If poor dear Jochum could only come back, and see what's become of his little boy! (*Looking round.*) Berta, what have you . . . ? Why ever have you . . . ? You've uncovered all the furniture.

BERTA. Madam told me. She won't have covers on chairs, she said.

MISS TESMAN. So they'll be using this room, making this their sitting room?

BERTA. So madam said. Mr Jørgen . . . Doctor Tesman . . . he said nothing.

Enter TESMAN *from the inner room, right. He is humming, and carrying an empty, unlocked suitcase. He is 33, fresh-faced, medium height, stoutish. Blonde hair and beard; round, open, happy face. Glasses; casual, almost rumpled clothes.*

MISS TESMAN. Good morning, Jørgen.

TESMAN (*in the doorway*). Aunt Julia! Aunt Julia! (*Shaking her hand.*) Fancy coming all this way, so early. All this way.

MISS TESMAN. I had to see you both, take a good look at you.

TESMAN. You've hardly had time to sleep.

MISS TESMAN. That doesn't matter.

TESMAN. You got home from the pier all right?

MISS TESMAN. Judge Brack was very kind, took me right to the door.

TESMAN. We were so sorry we couldn't give you a lift. But you saw for yourself. The carriage was full. All Hedda's luggage.

MISS TESMAN. Hedda's luggage. Yes.

BERTA (*to* TESMAN). Shall I go and ask madam if she needs any help?

TESMAN. No, Berta. Thank you. There's no need. She says she'll ring if she wants you.

BERTA (*about to go*). Yes.

TESMAN. Oh Berta, take this suitcase.

BERTA (*taking it*). I'll put it in the attic.

Exit through the hall, right.

TESMAN. It was wonderful, Aunt Julia. That whole case, full of notes. You wouldn't believe what I found, going round the museums. Old documents, artefacts, things no one's bothered with before.

MISS TESMAN. Dear Jørgen! You made good use of your honeymoon?

TESMAN. I certainly did. But take your hat off, auntie. Here, I'll unpin it for you.

MISS TESMAN (*while he does so*). It's as if you were still at home with us.

TESMAN (*turning the hat over*). What a wonderful hat! Is it new?

MISS TESMAN. I bought it because of Hedda.

TESMAN. Pardon?

MISS TESMAN. So that she won't be embarrassed when we go for walks together.

TESMAN (*patting her cheek*). Aunt Julia, how thoughtful you are!

He puts the hat on a chair by the table.

Sit down, here on the sofa, next to me. Let's have a gossip, till Hedda comes.

They sit. She rests her parasol in the corner of the sofa. She takes his hands and gazes at him.

MISS TESMAN. It's so good to have you home again. Dear
Jørgen. Poor Jochum's own little boy.

TESMAN. Dear Aunt Julia. You've been father and mother
to me, all these years.

MISS TESMAN. Promise you won't forget your poor old
aunties.

TESMAN. How is Aunt Rina? No better?

MISS TESMAN. Oh Jørgen, you know she'll never get
better. She's lying there, as she's lain there all this time.
Every day I pray the good Lord to spare her for a few
years more. If she died, I don't know what I'd do.
Especially now, Jørgen, now I don't have you to look
after.

TESMAN (*patting her back*). Now, now, now.

MISS TESMAN (*brightening*). Just imagine, we never expected
to see Jørgen Tesman married. And to Hedda Gabler,
too. Imagine. You, and Hedda. She had so many beaux.

TESMAN (*smiling, humming a little tune*). You're right. Some of
my friends must be quite green-eyed. No doubt of it. No
doubt.

MISS TESMAN. And such a long honeymoon! Five . . . six
months.

TESMAN. I made it a field trip. All those museums. All
those books to read.

MISS TESMAN. That's right. (*Lower, more confiding.*) You . . .
haven't any other news?

TESMAN. From the honeymoon?

MISS TESMAN. Exactly.

TESMAN. I don't think so. It was all in my letters. My
doctorate – I told you that yesterday.

MISS TESMAN. Of course you did. I'm talking about . . .
other prospects.

TESMAN. Prospects?

MISS TESMAN. Oh Jørgen, I am your aunt.

TESMAN. Well, of course I've other prospects.

MISS TESMAN. I thought so!

TESMAN. For example, I'm pretty sure that one day I'll be . . . a professor.

MISS TESMAN. A professor.

TESMAN. In fact, not 'pretty sure': really sure. But you know that already, auntie.

MISS TESMAN (*with a light laugh*). That's right. (*Changed tone.*) But we were talking about the honeymoon. It must have cost a fortune.

TESMAN. I did have that grant.

MISS TESMAN. Enough for two? I don't believe it.

TESMAN. Not entirely.

MISS TESMAN. Of course not. Two never travel as cheaply as one. Especially when one of them's a lady. That's what people say.

TESMAN. It's true. But Hedda needed that trip. No question. Needed it.

MISS TESMAN. A honeymoon abroad. That's essential nowadays. Or so they say. Well now, Jørgen, have you had time to look round the house?

TESMAN. I've been up since dawn, exploring.

MISS TESMAN. And what d'you think?

TESMAN. Wonderful! Won-derful! The only thing I can't imagine . . . What will we do with those two empty rooms, between the hall there and Hedda's bedroom?

MISS TESMAN (*with a light laugh*). Oh Jørgen, you'll find a use for them soon. You'll see.

TESMAN. You're right, auntie. After all, I'll need somewhere for my books.

MISS TESMAN. Just what I meant: your books.

TESMAN. I'm pleased most of all for Hedda. Before we were married, she often said she'd never be happy unless she could live in the old Falk villa.

MISS TESMAN. And then it came on the market. While you were away.

TESMAN. So lucky, aunt Julia, so lucky.

MISS TESMAN. But expensive, Jørgen. This will all cost money.

TESMAN (*looking at her, a little downcast*). You think so?

MISS TESMAN. Well, of course it will!

TESMAN. How much do you think? About.

MISS TESMAN. Who knows, till the bills come in?

TESMAN. Thank heavens Judge Brack saw to everything. Made a wonderful bargain. He explained it all to Hedda, in a letter.

MISS TESMAN. No need to worry on that account. And I gave security for the furniture, the carpets.

TESMAN. Aunt Julia, what possible security could you put down?

MISS TESMAN. I mortgaged the annuities.

TESMAN (*jumping up*). Your annuities? Yours and aunt Rina's?

MISS TESMAN. There aren't any others.

TESMAN (*facing her*). Auntie, you're crazy. Those annuities – they're all you and Aunt Rina have to live on.

MISS TESMAN. Don't worry. It was just a formality. His Honour said so. He arranged everything. He told me: a formality.

TESMAN. Maybe. Maybe. But even so . . .

MISS TESMAN. And now you've an income of your own to rely on. In any case, why shouldn't we spend a little . . . to give you a start . . . ? It's a pleasure, Jørgen, a pleasure.

TESMAN. Oh auntie, you're always sacrificing yourself for me.

MISS TESMAN *stands and puts her hands on his shoulders.*

MISS TESMAN. In all the world, what matters more to me than smoothing the path for my darling boy? All these years you've had no mother, no father. And now it's all right. We've reached harbour. Once or twice, the skies looked black. But you managed, Jørgen, you succeeded.

TESMAN. Things certainly have gone well.

MISS TESMAN. Your rivals, the people who blocked your path – you've passed them. They've fallen, Jørgen. And he's fallen furthest of all, the one you'd most to fear. The poor man's made his bed, and now he must lie on it.

TESMAN. How is Ejlert? Have you heard any news? I mean since I went away.

MISS TESMAN. I don't think so. He's published a book.

TESMAN. Ejlert? Recently?

MISS TESMAN. So they say. It's nothing important. Now, when your book comes out, Jørgen, that'll really be something. What's it about?

TESMAN. Domestic crafts in fourteenth-century Brabant.

MISS TESMAN. Fancy being able to write about things like that!

TESMAN. It may take some time. All this new research. I've that to catalogue before I start.

MISS TESMAN. Cataloguing. Research. You're so good at that. You're not Jochum's son for nothing.

TESMAN. I can't wait to start. Especially with such a comfortable home to work in.

MISS TESMAN. Ah Jørgen – and especially now you've the wife you set your heart on.

TESMAN (*hugging her*). Yes, auntie! Hedda. She's the best thing of all.

He looks towards the door.

I think she's coming.

Enter HEDDA *from the inner room left. She is 29, a woman of style and character. Her complexion is smooth and pale; her grey eyes are cold, clear and calm. Attractive, light-brown hair, not particularly full. A modish, loose-fitting morning dress.* MISS TESMAN *goes to greet her.*

MISS TESMAN. Good morning, my dear, good morning.

HEDDA (*shaking her hand*). Miss Tesman, good morning. How kind of you to call so early.

MISS TESMAN (*seeming a little flustered*). I hope you slept well, in your new home.

HEDDA. Fairly well, thank you.

TESMAN (*with a laugh*). Oh Hedda, fairly well! You were sleeping like a log when I got up. A log!

HEDDA. Wasn't that amazing? One gets used to new experiences all the time, Miss Tesman. Gradually. (*Glancing left.*) Look, the maid's left the verandah door wide open. There's a *sea* of sun.

MISS TESMAN (*going to the door*). Why don't we close it, then?

HEDDA. No, no. Tesman, please draw the blinds. A softer light.

TESMAN (*at the door*). There. There. Now you've shade *and* fresh air.

HEDDA. Fresh air, thank goodness. These dreadful flowers. Do sit down, Miss Tesman.

MISS TESMAN. I just came to see that everything's as it should be – and it is, it is. Now I really must hurry. She'll be waiting, lying there, poor soul.

TESMAN. Kiss her from me. Tell her I'll pop round this afternoon.

MISS TESMAN. I'll tell her. Oh, Jørgen, I nearly forgot . . .

She rummages in her bag.

I've something for you.

TESMAN. What, auntie?

MISS TESMAN *gives him a flat wrapped package.*

MISS TESMAN. What d'you say to this?

TESMAN (*opening it*). You kept them! Look, Hedda. Isn't this wonderful?

HEDDA (*at the whatnot upstage right*). Yes. What?

TESMAN. My slippers. Look!

HEDDA. The ones you kept talking about while we were away.

TESMAN. I really missed them.

He goes to her.

Now you can see them in person!

HEDDA *crosses to the stove.*

HEDDA. There's really no need.

TESMAN (*going after her*). Aunt Rina embroidered them with her own hands. Lying there. That poor invalid. You can imagine the memories in every stitch.

HEDDA (*by the table*). No memories for me.

MISS TESMAN. Hedda's right, Jørgen.

TESMAN. But now she's one of the family –

HEDDA (*interrupting*). We're going to have problems with that maid.

MISS TESMAN. With Berta? Problems?

TESMAN. What d'you mean, darling?

HEDDA (*pointing*). Look. Here on this chair. She's left her old hat.

TESMAN *drops the slippers in his agitation.*

TESMAN. Hedda . . .

HEDDA. Suppose someone came, and saw?

TESMAN. Hedda, that's aunt Julia's hat.

HEDDA. Really?

MISS TESMAN (*taking the hat*). Yes, Hedda, mine. And it's certainly not old.

HEDDA. I didn't look closely.

MISS TESMAN (*pinning on the hat*). As it happens, this is the first time I've worn it. The very first time.

TESMAN. It's a wonderful hat. Magnificent.

MISS TESMAN. Now, Jørgen, it's nothing of the kind.

She searches.

My parasol . . . ? Yes, here. (*Taking it.*) This is mine too. (*Tightly.*) Not Berta's.

TESMAN. New hat and parasol! Eh, Hedda?

HEDDA. Very nice.

TESMAN. Of course. Of course. Now, auntie, before you go, take a proper look at Hedda. Isn't she beautiful? Isn't she a picture?

MISS TESMAN. Well, of course she is. She's been special all her life.

She nods and crosses right. TESMAN *follows.*

TESMAN. But don't you think she looks well? Don't you think she's filled out on our travels, rounded out?

HEDDA (*crossing the room*). That's enough.

MISS TESMAN (*turning*). Rounded out?

TESMAN. Yes, auntie. You can't see it. That dress . . . But I can, I'm privileged –

HEDDA (*by the screen door; shortly*). Privileged!

TESMAN. It's the Alpine air, the mountain air.

HEDDA (*interrupting curtly*). I haven't changed since the day we left.

TESMAN. So you keep saying. But you have. You have. Hasn't she, auntie?

MISS TESMAN *has clasped her hands and is gazing at* HEDDA.

MISS TESMAN. Special. That's what Hedda is.

She goes to her, puts her hands round her head to bend it forwards, and kisses her hair.

God bless and protect Mrs Hedda Tesman. For Jørgen's sake.

HEDDA (*gently breaking free*). Do let go.

MISS TESMAN (*with quiet force*). I'll come every day to see you both.

TESMAN. Yes, auntie, please.

MISS TESMAN. Goodbye for now. Goodbye.

She goes out through the hall, accompanied by TESMAN. *They leave the door ajar, and* TESMAN *can be heard thanking her for the slippers and sending Aunt Rina his love. Meanwhile,* HEDDA *paces the room, arms folded, as if beside herself. She flings aside the curtains from the screen door and looks out. Almost at once,* TESMAN *returns, closing the door after him. He picks up his slippers, and starts wrapping them to put on the table.*

TESMAN. What are you looking at, Hedda?

HEDDA (*calm once again*). I was looking at the leaves. So yellow, so withered.

TESMAN. We are in September.

HEDDA (*edgy again*). So we are. So soon. September.

TESMAN. Aunt Julia was a little odd, didn't you think? Almost like a stranger. You've no idea why, have you?

HEDDA. I hardly know her. Isn't that what she's usually like?

TESMAN. Not like today.

HEDDA (*moving from the screen door*). D'you think that hat business offended her?

TESMAN. No. A little perhaps. At first. Just for a moment.

HEDDA. Such extraordinary behaviour, throwing it down in the sitting room like that. No one does that.

TESMAN. She won't do it again.

HEDDA. I'll sort things out with her.

TESMAN. Darling, if only you would.

HEDDA. When you go there this afternoon, invite her over this evening.

TESMAN. Of course I will. And Hedda, there's something you could do which would give her so much pleasure.

HEDDA. What?

TESMAN. Call her Auntie. For my sake. Hedda . . . ?

HEDDA. No, Tesman. I told you when you asked before. Miss Tesman she is, and Miss Tesman she stays.

TESMAN. It's just . . . now you're one of the family . . .

HEDDA (*moving upstage*). I wonder . . .

TESMAN (*following*). What is it, Hedda?

HEDDA. My old piano. It doesn't look right, in here.

TESMAN. When my first month's salary comes, we'll change it.

HEDDA. I don't want to change it. I don't want rid of it. We'll put it in the back room, and get another one in here. As soon as we can, I mean.

TESMAN (*subdued*). As soon as we can. Of course.

HEDDA (*picking up the flowers from the piano*). These flowers weren't here last night.

TESMAN. Aunt Julia must have brought them.

HEDDA (*looking inside the bouquet*). A visiting card. (*Reading.*) 'Will call later.' You'll never guess who it's from.

TESMAN. I can't imagine.

HEDDA. Mrs Elvsted. Look.

TESMAN. Mrs Elvsted! The solicitor's wife. She used to be Miss Rysing.

HEDDA. And she kept flaunting that confounded hair. An old flame of yours, they said.

TESMAN (*with a laugh*). Hedda, that was years ago. Before I met you. Fancy her coming into town.

HEDDA. And coming here. A social call. I remember her vaguely from high school.

TESMAN. I haven't seen her for – goodness knows how long. How can she stand it so far from town, in that poky little place?

HEDDA (*suddenly*). Tesman, wasn't it there, out of town, somewhere . . . ? Didn't Ejlert Løvborg –

TESMAN. He did! Out of town. That's right.

Enter BERTA *from the hall.*

BERTA. She's here again, madam, the lady who left the flowers. (*Pointing.*) Those flowers, madam.

HEDDA. Please show her in.

BERTA *opens the door to admit* MRS ELVSTED, *and then goes out.* MRS ELVSTED *is slim, with a soft, pretty face. Large blue eyes, slightly prominent; a nervous manner. Blonde, almost yellow hair, unusually luxuriant and curly. She is some two years younger than* HEDDA. *Her formal wear is dark and well cut, but not in the latest style. She is agitated, struggling for self-control.* HEDDA *goes to welcome her in a friendly way.*

Mrs Elvsted, good morning. How nice to meet you again.

MRS ELVSTED. It was a long time ago.

TESMAN (*shaking hands*). I remember you too.

HEDDA. Thank you for the flowers. Delightful.

MRS ELVSTED. I'd have come at once, yesterday afternoon. But they said you were away.

TESMAN. You've just arrived in town?

MRS ELVSTED. Yesterday lunchtime. When they told me you were away, I didn't know what to do.

HEDDA. How, what to do?

TESMAN. My dear Miss Rysing . . . Mrs Elvsted, I beg your pardon . . .

HEDDA. Is something wrong?

MRS ELVSTED. Yes. And I don't know anyone else. I've no one else to turn to.

HEDDA *puts the flowers down on the table.*

HEDDA. Sit on the sofa, here with me.

MRS ELVSTED. How can I sit? I haven't . . . I can't . . .

HEDDA. It's all right. Sit down.

She pulls MRS ELVSTED *to the sofa, and sits beside her.*

TESMAN. Now, dear lady, how can we help?

HEDDA. Is something wrong at home?

MRS ELVSTED. Yes. No. Both. I don't want you to misunderstand.

HEDDA. In that case, best say it, say it right out.

TESMAN. That's why you came.

MRS ELVSTED. That's why I came. In case . . . in case you don't know . . . Ejlert Løvborg's here in town.

HEDDA. Løvborg!

TESMAN. Ejlert Løvborg back. Amazing! Hedda –

HEDDA. I heard.

MRS ELVSTED. He's been here a week now. A whole week. Alone in this dreadful place. So many temptations.

HEDDA. But, dear Mrs Elvsted, why should you be so concerned?

MRS ELVSTED (*with a frightened glance at her*). He was the children's tutor.

HEDDA. Your children?

MRS ELVSTED. My husband's. I've none of my own.

HEDDA. Your stepchildren.

MRS ELVSTED. Yes.

TESMAN (*carefully*). Was he . . . how shall I put this? . . . was he *fit* for that?

MRS ELVSTED. No one's said a word against him these last two years.

TESMAN. Two years. Did you hear that, Hedda?

HEDDA. I heard.

MRS ELVSTED. Not a breath of scandal. Nothing. But now, when I know he's here, in the city, with money in his pockets, I'm afraid for him.

TESMAN. Why didn't he stay where he was? With you and your husband?

MRS ELVSTED. As soon as his book came out, he was so restless. So on edge. He couldn't stay with us.

TESMAN. That's right. Aunt Julia said he'd a new book out.

MRS ELVSTED. A big new book. *The Story of Civilisation.* Two weeks ago. And when it began to sell so well, and caused all that interest . . .

TESMAN. He wrote it some time ago . . . ? When he was . . . ?

MRS ELVSTED. Before, you mean.

TESMAN. Well, yes.

MRS ELVSTED. He wrote it while he was with us. All of it. In the last twelve months.

TESMAN. That's wonderful! Isn't that wonderful, Hedda?

MRS ELVSTED. If only it lasts.

HEDDA. Have you found him yet?

MRS ELVSTED. Not yet. It was hard getting hold of his address. But I found it at last, this morning.

HEDDA (*with a sharp look*). I'm surprised your husband –

MRS ELVSTED (*startled*). What d'you mean?

HEDDA. – should send you to town, on that kind of errand. Why didn't he come himself, or send one of his friends?

MRS ELVSTED. He hasn't time. In any case, I . . . I had some shopping.

HEDDA (*smiling*). Of course.

MRS ELVSTED (*jumping up nervously*). Mr Tesman, please, if Ejlert Løvborg comes here, be nice to him. He will come, he will. You were such good friends before. Both studying the same subject . . . the same approach . . .

TESMAN. In those days, yes.

MRS ELVSTED. So please . . . Mr Tesman, Mrs Tesman . . . please be kind to him. Oh Mr Tesman, will you promise?

TESMAN. Of course, my dear Mrs Rysing.

HEDDA. Elvsted.

TESMAN. I'll do everything I can. Everything.

MRS ELVSTED. You're so kind, so generous . . . (*Shaking his hand.*) Thank you, thank you. (*Timidly.*) My husband thinks so much of him.

HEDDA (*getting up*). Tesman, write him a note. If you leave it up to him, he may not come.

TESMAN. Good idea, Hedda. Good idea.

HEDDA. Do it now. Right now.

MRS ELVSTED (*begging*). Oh please.

TESMAN. This very minute. Have you his address, Mrs . . . Mrs Elvsted?

MRS ELVSTED. Yes.

She gives him a piece of paper from her bag.

There.

TESMAN. Wonderful. I'll go in there. (*Looking round.*) Slippers, slippers. Ah.

He picks up the package.

HEDDA. Write a friendly letter . . . long . . .

TESMAN. I certainly will.

MRS ELVSTED. But don't tell him I asked. Please don't.

TESMAN. Of course not. No question. Now . . .

Exit right, through the inner room.

HEDDA (*quietly, close to* MRS ELVSTED). There! Two birds with one stone.

MRS ELVSTED. What d'you mean?

HEDDA. Couldn't you see I wanted him to go?

MRS ELVSTED. To write the letter –

HEDDA. And so that we could talk, alone.

MRS ELVSTED (*bewildered*). About all this.

HEDDA. Yes.

MRS ELVSTED (*alarmed*). Mrs Tesman, there isn't any more. There isn't.

HEDDA. Of course there is. That's obvious. There's a lot more. Come and sit down. Let's make ourselves comfortable.

She propels MRS ELVSTED *to the chair beside the stove, and herself sits on one of the stools.*

MRS ELVSTED (*looking nervously at her watch*). I didn't mean to stay.

HEDDA. There's no rush. Is there? Tell me a little: how are things are at home?

MRS ELVSTED. That's just what I didn't want to talk about.

HEDDA. Not even to me? We were at school together.

MRS ELVSTED. You were in a higher class. You terrified me.

HEDDA. How, terrified?

MRS ELVSTED. When we met on the stairs, you pulled my hair.

HEDDA. I did?

MRS ELVSTED. You said, once, you'd burn it off.

HEDDA. Just talk.

MRS ELVSTED. I know that now. But in those days, I believed everything. And over the years, we've moved so far apart. Our friends, our social lives . . .

HEDDA. Well, now we can move back again. D'you remember, at school, we called each other by our Christian names?

MRS ELVSTED. We didn't.

HEDDA. I remember clearly. We'll be such friends again, just like before.

She moves the stool closer.

I mean it.

She kisses her cheek.

You must call me Hedda.

MRS ELVSTED *clasps* HEDDA's *hands and pats them.*

MRS ELVSTED. You're so kind, so friendly. I'm not used to it.

HEDDA. Well. I'll do the same: I'll call you . . . Thora.

MRS ELVSTED. My name's Thea.

HEDDA. Of course it is. Thea. (*With a tender look.*) Poor Thea. Not much kindness, not much companionship at home?

MRS ELVSTED. I don't have a home. I never have.

HEDDA (*after a short pause, gazing at her*). I thought that might be it.

MRS ELVSTED (*staring dully ahead*). Never.

HEDDA. I don't remember the details . . . When you first went out of town, to the solicitor's, wasn't it as housekeeper?

MRS ELVSTED. Governess. But his wife – his late wife – was an invalid . . . bedridden. I ran the house.

HEDDA. And you ended up . . . its mistress.

MRS ELVSTED (*dully*). That's right.

HEDDA. And now . . . how long is it now?

MRS ELVSTED. Since I married him?

HEDDA. Yes.

MRS ELVSTED. Five years.

HEDDA. Of course.

MRS ELVSTED. Five years! And the last two or three . . .
Oh Mrs Tesman, if you only knew –

HEDDA (*lightly slapping her wrist*). Thea! Mrs Tesman . . . ?

MRS ELVSTED. I'm sorry. I will try. Oh . . . Hedda . . . if
you only knew . . .

HEDDA (*offhand*). Wasn't it three years ago that Ejlert
Løvborg moved out there?

MRS ELVSTED (*looking enquiringly at her*). Ejlert Løvborg?
I suppose so.

HEDDA. Didn't you know him before? From the old days,
here?

MRS ELVSTED. I knew his name, of course.

HEDDA. And when he moved out there . . . he visited you
and your husband?

MRS ELVSTED. Every day. He gave the children lessons.
By then, I couldn't manage everything myself.

HEDDA. Of course not. And your husband's . . . often away
on business?

MRS ELVSTED. Mrs – Hedda – you understand. It's his
work . . . he has to go . . .

HEDDA *leans on the arm of the chair.*

HEDDA. Poor little Thea, what is it? Tell me everything.

MRS ELVSTED. Ask what you want to know. I'll answer.

HEDDA. What sort of man is your husband, Thea? What's
he like – at home, with you? Is he . . . kind to you?

MRS ELVSTED (*evasively*). He . . . thinks so.

HEDDA. He must be older than you. Much older. Twelve years, at least.

MRS ELVSTED (*breaking out*). That too. One thing and another. I can't bear him. We've nothing in common, nothing at all.

HEDDA. But doesn't he care for you? In his own way?

MRS ELVSTED. I don't know if he cares or not. I'm useful to him. And I don't cost much. I'm cheap.

HEDDA. Silly.

MRS ELVSTED (*shaking her head*). It'll never change. He'll never change. He cares for no one but himself. And the children, perhaps, a little.

HEDDA. And Ejlert Løvborg.

MRS ELVSTED (*staring*). Ejlert Løvborg! What d'you mean?

HEDDA. Oh Thea . . . when he sends you here to find him. (*With an almost imperceptible smile.*) You told Tesman so yourself.

MRS ELVSTED (*uncomfortably*). Oh. Yes, I did. (*All at once, low.*) I might as well tell you. Now, not later. It'll come out anyway.

HEDDA. Thea. Tell me what?

MRS ELVSTED. The truth. My husband knows nothing about this.

HEDDA. Really?

MRS ELVSTED. How could he? He was away on business. I couldn't stand it any longer, Hedda. I'd have been alone up there. Alone.

HEDDA. So you –

MRS ELVSTED. I packed my things . . . just the essentials. Secretly. And I . . . left.

HEDDA. Without a second thought?

MRS ELVSTED. I took the train, here to town.

HEDDA. Thea, how could you dare?

MRS ELVSTED *gets up and goes to the table.*

MRS ELVSTED. What else could I do? What else was left?

HEDDA. But what will he say, your husband, when you go back home?

MRS ELVSTED (*staring*). Back home – to him?

HEDDA. That's right.

MRS ELVSTED. I'm not going back.

HEDDA *goes to her.*

HEDDA. You mean you've left him? Forever?

MRS ELVSTED. What else could I do?

HEDDA. But to go like that. So . . . openly.

MRS ELVSTED. You can't hide such things.

HEDDA. But Thea, what will people say?

MRS ELVSTED. Good heavens, let them say what they like.

Sadly, heavily, she sits on the sofa.

What else could I do?

HEDDA (*after a short pause*). And what will you do now? What kind of job – ?

MRS ELVSTED. All I can say is, I have to live here, where Ejlert Løvborg lives. If I'm to live at all.

HEDDA *moves a chair from the table, sits beside her and strokes her hands.*

HEDDA. Thea, Thea, how did it start, this . . . friendship between you and Ejlert Løvborg?

MRS ELVSTED. It . . . happened. Little by little. It was as if I'd some kind of power over him.

HEDDA. Power?

MRS ELVSTED. He gave up his old ways. I didn't ask him. I didn't dare. But he could see I disapproved. So he . . . gave up.

HEDDA (*hiding involuntary scorn*). You 'saved' him, Thea. That's what you mean. Isn't that what it's called?

MRS ELVSTED. He called it that himself. At the end. But he, too . . . He made me a real person, Hedda. He taught me how to think. To understand . . . one thing . . . and then another.

HEDDA. He gave you lessons?

MRS ELVSTED. Not proper lessons. He talked to me. About anything, everything. Then came the special, wonderful day when I was able to help with his work. He let me help him.

HEDDA. And you did?

MRS ELVSTED. Oh yes. When he wrote, we worked at everything together. The two of us.

HEDDA. Comrades in arms.

MRS ELVSTED (*eagerly*). Oh Hedda, that's what he said. I ought to be so happy. But I'm not. I don't know how long it'll last.

HEDDA. Don't you trust him?

MRS ELVSTED (*dully*). There's a shadow between us. A woman's shadow.

HEDDA (*looking narrowly at her*). D'you know whose?

MRS ELVSTED. Some woman . . . from his past. He's never forgotten her.

HEDDA. He's talked about it?

MRS ELVSTED. Once. Nothing specific.

HEDDA. What did he say?

MRS ELVSTED. When they parted, he said, she wanted to shoot him with a pistol.

HEDDA (*icily calm*). Amazing. No one does that.

MRS ELVSTED. I thought it must be that singer, that redhaired creature he –

HEDDA. It must have been.

MRS ELVSTED. People said she always carried a loaded gun.

HEDDA. That proves it was her.

MRS ELVSTED (*wringing her hands*). Oh Hedda, they say she's . . . she's here. What can I do?

HEDDA (*glancing towards the inner room*). Shh! Tesman.

She gets up and whispers.

This is our secret, Thea.

MRS ELVSTED (*jumping up*). In God's name, yes.

Enter TESMAN *from the inner room right, with a letter in his hand.*

TESMAN. There. Written and ready.

HEDDA. Good. Now Mrs Elvsted really has to go. You stay here. I'll go to the gate with her.

TESMAN. Would you ask Berta to see to this?

HEDDA (*taking the letter*). I'll tell her.

Enter BERTA *from the hall.*

BERTA. Madam, His Honour Judge Brack is here.

HEDDA. Ask the gentleman in. Oh, and post this letter, will you?

BERTA (*taking the letter*). Yes, madam.

She holds the door for BRACK, *then goes out.* BRACK *is 45, stockily built but light in his movements. His face is round but fine-boned. Short, well-groomed hair, still mostly black. Bushy eyebrows; bright, sharp eyes. Full moustache, with shaped tips. He wears a fashionable morning suit, a little young for him. He uses an eyeglass, which he now and then lets fall. Hat in hand, he greets the company.*

BRACK. Not too early in the day?

HEDDA. Of course not.

TESMAN (*shaking hands*). You're welcome any time. (*Introducing them.*) Judge Brack, Miss Rysing . . .

HEDDA. Tst!

BRACK (*bowing*). Charmed.

HEDDA (*bantering*). How odd to see you in daylight for a change.

BRACK. Do I look so different?

HEDDA. A little younger.

BRACK. How kind.

TESMAN. And what d'you think of Hedda? Doesn't she look well? Doesn't she look –

HEDDA. Enough about me. Thank His Honour for all his hard work –

BRACK. Believe me, a pleasure.

HEDDA. Such a good friend. But here's my other friend standing, burning to be off. Excuse me, Your Honour. I won't be a moment.

A round of goodbyes, then she and MRS ELVSTED *go out through the hall.*

BRACK. Well. Is she pleased, your lady wife?

TESMAN. We can't thank you enough. A few changes here and there, I gather. One or two things still needed.

BRACK. Really?

TESMAN. But don't you trouble yourself. Hedda said she'd see to them herself. Do sit down. Sit down.

BRACK. Thank you.

He sits at the table.

My dear Tesman, there is one thing we ought to discuss.

TESMAN. Ah!

He sits.

The spectre at the feast? Go on.

BRACK. The money side's fine. Moving more slowly than I'd like, and a touch extravagant . . .

TESMAN. My dear man, this is for Hedda. I couldn't ask Hedda to live in one of those little suburban boxes.

BRACK. No, no, no.

TESMAN. In any case, it won't be long now, God willing, till I get my professorship.

BRACK. These things can take their time.

TESMAN. You've still heard nothing?

BRACK. Nothing certain. (*Sudden change of tone.*) There is one thing I have to tell you.

TESMAN. What?

BRACK. Your old friend Ejlert Løvborg's back. Here, in town.

TESMAN. She told us, the lady who went out with Hedda.

BRACK. What was her name? I didn't quite catch it.

TESMAN. Mrs Elvsted.

BRACK. Of course. Her husband's a solicitor. Løvborg's been out there, staying with them.

TESMAN. And have you heard? Wonderful news! He's back on the rails again.

BRACK. So people say.

TESMAN. He's even published a book.

BRACK. That's right.

TESMAN. And made quite a stir.

BRACK. I believe so.

TESMAN. Well that's wonderful! So talented . . . I was afraid he'd gone astray for good.

BRACK. Everyone thought so.

TESMAN. But what on Earth will he do now? What on Earth will he live on?

During this, HEDDA *comes back through the hall.*

HEDDA (*to* BRACK). He's always the same. Always wondering what people are going to live on.

TESMAN. Oh Hedda. We were talking about that poor man Ejlert Løvborg.

HEDDA *gives him a sharp look.*

HEDDA. Really. (*Lightly.*) Why d'you call him poor?

TESMAN. He must have run through his inheritance years ago. And he can't produce a new book every year. So I was wondering, what's he going to do?

BRACK. I may have news about that.

TESMAN. Really?

BRACK. He's well-connected. Influential relatives.

TESMAN. Relatives who want nothing to do with him, unfortunately.

BRACK. They used to call him their golden boy.

TESMAN. Until he spoiled it, spoiled everything.

HEDDA. One never knows. (*With a light laugh.*) After all, they 'saved' him at the Elvsteds'.

BRACK. And there is this book of his.

TESMAN. Let's hope it leads him somewhere. I've just sent him a letter. Hedda, I invited him here this evening.

BRACK. Oh Tesman. My dinner-party tonight. Bachelors and husbands only. You promised yesterday, on the pier.

HEDDA. Tesman, you'd forgotten.

TESMAN. So I had.

BRACK. Well, it doesn't matter. He won't turn up.

TESMAN. Why ever not?

With some reluctance, BRACK *gets up and stands with his hands on the chair-back.*

BRACK. Tesman . . . Mrs Tesman . . . I think you really should be told. It's something −

TESMAN. To do with Ejlert Løvborg?

BRACK. With him and with you.

TESMAN. My dear Brack, what is it?

BRACK. Your professorship . . . may not come through as quickly as you'd like, as you'd expect . . .

TESMAN (*jumping up in alarm*). There's a problem. What is it?

BRACK. There may be . . . competition.

TESMAN. Competition! Did you hear that, Hedda?

HEDDA (*leaning back in the chair*). I heard.

TESMAN. But who with? Surely not with –

BRACK. Exactly. Ejlert Løvborg.

TESMAN (*clasping his hands*). I don't believe it. It's impossible.

BRACK. It may still happen.

TESMAN. But Brack, this is hardly fair. To me.

He gestures.

I'm a married man. Hedda and I . . . We married because of my prospects. We plunged into debt, even borrowed from Aunt Julia. I was as good as promised that professorship.

BRACK. Now, now. It's yours, no question. But first there'll be a competition.

HEDDA (*at ease in the chair*). Ha, Tesman, it's like a tournament.

TESMAN. Hedda, darling, how can you make a joke of it?

HEDDA (*as before*). I'm hanging on the outcome.

BRACK. Whatever the outcome, Mrs Tesman, I thought you ought to know. The way things are. Especially since I hear you're planning . . . purchases.

HEDDA. This makes no difference.

BRACK. In that case . . . please excuse me. (*To* TESMAN.) When I go for my constitutional this afternoon, I'll call for you.

TESMAN. I . . . I don't know what to . . .

HEDDA (*lying back, stretching out her hand*). Goodbye, Your Honour. Come again soon.

BRACK. Thank you. Goodbye. Goodbye.

TESMAN (*accompanying him to the door*). Goodbye, old man. I do apologise . . .

Exit BRACK *through the hall.* TESMAN *paces.*

TESMAN. Oh Hedda, people should never live in fairy tales.

HEDDA (*looking at him and smiling*). Is that what you do?

TESMAN. That's what we did. Getting married, setting up house on nothing but my prospects . . . a fairy tale.

HEDDA. If you say so.

TESMAN. Well, at least we have our home. Our beautiful home. The home we dreamed of, swooned over, almost. Both of us.

HEDDA (*getting up slowly, heavily*). We agreed on a certain style . . . a certain standard of living.

TESMAN. Of course we did. And I really looked forward to it: seeing you at the heart of things, in a house of your own, with a throng of guests. Wonderful! It's just that . . . for the moment, it'll have to be just the two of us, Hedda. We can invite Aunt Julia now and then. Oh, this was never for you. Things should have been so different.

HEDDA. No footman, yet.

TESMAN. I'm afraid not. Out of the question.

HEDDA. And the horse I hoped for? −

TESMAN (*startled*). Horse?

HEDDA. I mustn't even think about riding now.

TESMAN. Good heavens, no.

HEDDA (*crossing the room*). Thank goodness I've one thing left. I can still amuse myself.

TESMAN (*overjoyed*). Wonderful. What is it, Hedda? What is it you have?

From the rear door, HEDDA *looks at him with scorn.*

HEDDA. My pistols . . . Jørgen.

TESMAN *(horrified).* Pistols!

HEDDA *(cold-eyed).* General Gabler's pistols.

Exit. TESMAN *runs to the door and shouts after her.*

TESMAN. No, Hedda! For God's sake! They're dangerous. Please, Hedda! I beg you. No!

Curtain.

ACT TWO

The scene is the same as in Act One, except that the piano has been replaced by an elegant little writing-desk and bookcase. A side-table stands beside the sofa left. Most of the flowers have gone, though MRS ELVSTED*'s bouquet is on the large table centre stage. It is afternoon.* HEDDA *is alone in the room. She wears afternoon dress. She stands by the open screen door, loading a pistol. The gun's twin is in an open pistol-case on the writing-desk.*

HEDDA (*calling into the garden*). Your Honour. Hello again.

BRACK (*in the distance, off*). Mrs Tesman, hello.

   HEDDA *lifts the pistol and takes aim.*

HEDDA. Your Honour, I'm going to shoot you.

BRACK (*shouting from below*). Don't point that thing at me.

HEDDA. If you will use the back way in.

   She fires.

BRACK (*nearer*). Are you out of your mind?

HEDDA. I didn't hit you. Did I?

BRACK (*still outside*). Don't play the fool.

HEDDA. Come in, Your Honour. Come in.

   BRACK *comes in by the screen door. He is dressed for his party, with a light coat over his arm.*

BRACK. What on Earth are you doing? This isn't the first time. What are you shooting at?

HEDDA. The sky. I stand and shoot the sky.

   BRACK *takes the pistol gently.*

BRACK. Excuse me . . . (*Examining it.*) I remember this one. (*Looking round.*) Where's the case? Ah, here.

He puts the pistol in its case and shuts it.

No more games today.

HEDDA. What else am I to do, in Heaven's name?

BRACK. Has no one called?

HEDDA (*closing the screen door*). Not a soul. Everyone we know must still be in the country.

BRACK. Isn't Tesman back yet?

HEDDA (*putting the pistol-case in the drawer of the writing-desk*). No. Straight after lunch, off he ran to his aunties. He wasn't expecting you so soon.

BRACK. I should have thought of that. Silly of me.

HEDDA (*turning and looking at him*). Silly?

BRACK. If I had thought, I'd have come – even earlier.

HEDDA (*crossing the room*). There'd have been no one at home at all. I was in my room, changing after lunch.

BRACK. And no cracks in the door, for making conversation.

HEDDA. One arrangement you forgot.

BRACK. Silly again.

HEDDA. We'd better sit down here, and wait. Tesman won't be long. He'll be home any minute.

BRACK. I'll possess my soul in patience.

HEDDA *sits at one end of the sofa.* BRACK *lays his coat over the back of the nearest chair and sits down, still holding his hat. Short pause. They look at each other.*

HEDDA. Well now.

BRACK (*same tone*). Well now.

HEDDA. I said it first.

BRACK (*leaning forward*). Let's make polite conversation, Mrs Tesman.

HEDDA (*leaning back in the sofa*). It does seem an age since you and I last talked. A few pleasantries last night, this morning – I don't count those.

BRACK. The two of us. Alone, you mean?

HEDDA. Something like that.

BRACK. I called every single day, praying you were home from your travels.

HEDDA. I prayed the same thing, every single day.

BRACK. Dear Mrs Tesman, I thought you were having such a wonderful time.

HEDDA. You can't imagine.

BRACK. That's what Tesman wrote.

HEDDA. Oh, he did. Rooting about in libraries. Copying ancient manuscripts. Wonderful!

BRACK (*with a touch of malice*). It's what he was put in the world to do. Most of the time.

HEDDA. Exactly. Always busy. But I wasn't, Brack! I was bored. So . . . bored.

BRACK (*sympathetically*). You're serious. You really mean it.

HEDDA. Of course I mean it. Six months without meeting anyone from . . . from our circle. Shared interests. Someone to talk to.

BRACK. I know what you mean.

HEDDA. And hardest of all —

BRACK. What?

HEDDA. To be with the same individual, every second, day after day after day —

BRACK (*nodding agreement*). Day and night . . .

HEDDA. I said: every second.

BRACK. But Tesman, dear Tesman . . . Surely . . .

HEDDA. For Heaven's sake! He's a . . . a scholar.

BRACK. True.

HEDDA. And scholars are not good company on journeys. Not day after day after day.

BRACK. Not even . . . scholars one loves?

HEDDA. Don't be silly.

BRACK (*surprised*). Pardon, Hedda?

HEDDA (*half joking, half cross*). You should try it. The history of civilisation, day and night.

BRACK. Every second.

HEDDA. Domestic crafts in the fourteenth century. What could be worse?

BRACK (*looking narrowly at her*). Are you saying . . . ? D'you really mean . . . ?

HEDDA. That Tesman and I can't make a match of it?

BRACK. If you like.

HEDDA. Good lord, does it surprise you?

BRACK. Yes. And no.

HEDDA. I'd danced myself out. That was all. My time was up. (*Checking herself.*) No, I mustn't say that. Not even think it.

BRACK. You've really no cause –

HEDDA. Oh, cause. (*Looking carefully at him.*) In any case, Jørgen Tesman . . . such a model husband.

BRACK. And such a good soul. No doubt of it.

HEDDA. I don't think he's a fool. Do you?

BRACK. Not exactly –

HEDDA. So . . . tireless. Bound to get there in the end.

BRACK (*looking at her quizzically*). I assumed you were like everyone else: thought he was on his way.

HEDDA (*wearily*). Yes. I did. And he was so determined . . . so sure he'd be able to support me . . . Why should I turn him down?

BRACK. What other choice had you?

HEDDA. Your Honour, I don't remember any of my other admirers making a similar offer.

BRACK (*with a laugh*). I can't answer for all the others, Mrs Tesman. But me: you know what enormous respect I've always had for . . . the marriage tie. In theory.

HEDDA (*mocking*). Oh, I never had hopes of you.

BRACK. All I ask of life is a circle of close friends . . . people I can help and advise, places I can come and go as I please, as a trusted friend of −

HEDDA. − the husband.

BRACK (*leaning forward*). Well, frankly, I'd prefer the wife. But the husband will do. I tell you, this kind of . . . triangular relationship . . . can be highly satisfying for all three parties.

HEDDA. I often longed for a third party on that trip. To sit in a carriage side by side with just one man −

BRACK. But the honeymoon journey's over now.

HEDDA (*shaking her head*). There's still the marriage journey. On and on. This is just a temporary stop.

BRACK. Exactly. One jumps out . . . one stretches one's legs . . .

HEDDA. I won't jump out.

BRACK. You won't?

HEDDA. Some of us −

BRACK (*laughing*). Watch our step.

HEDDA. Exactly.

BRACK. You're joking.

HEDDA (*gesturing 'No'*). I don't want that. I prefer to stay where I am. Sitting side by side.

BRACK. But suppose a third person did join the party?

HEDDA. That's different.

BRACK. A trusted friend. A soul-mate.

HEDDA. Making interesting conversation about all kinds of things.

BRACK. And a total stranger to scholarship.

HEDDA (*sighing audibly*). A change indeed.

The hall door is heard opening and closing.

BRACK. The triangle is complete.

HEDDA (*low*). And the train goes on.

Enter TESMAN *from the hall. He is wearing a grey outdoor suit and a trilby. He is carrying an armful of journals and magazines, and his pockets are stuffed with more of them. He goes to put them down on the table by the corner sofa.*

TESMAN. Phew. Far too hot to be carting all these around.

He puts them down.

Look, Hedda, I'm sweating like a pig. Ah, Brack, you're here. Why didn't Berta say?

BRACK (*getting up*). I came through the garden.

HEDDA. Magazines. What are they?

TESMAN (*turning them over*). Not magazines, journals. Learned journals. New issues I had to have.

HEDDA. Learned journals.

BRACK. Learned journals, Mrs Tesman.

They smile pointedly at one another.

HEDDA. You need more learned journals?

TESMAN. It's not a case of more. One has to have them all. One has to keep up.

HEDDA. Ah. So one does.

TESMAN (*rooting in the pile*). I managed to get Ejlert Løvborg's new book too.

He finds it.

You'd like a look at that, Hedda. Wouldn't you?

HEDDA. No thanks. Yes. Some other time.

TESMAN. I dipped into it on the way.

BRACK. And how does it seem to you . . . a colleague?

TESMAN. Remarkable. Rational. Objective. It's like nothing else he's ever written.

He gathers the magazines.

I'll take these in. I can't wait to cut the pages! And I really must change. (*To* BRACK.) We're not rushing off this minute, are we?

BRACK. Take as long as you like.

TESMAN. As long as I like. Right. (*With the magazines, at the door.*) Oh, Hedda, Aunt Julia won't be coming this evening.

HEDDA. Not that business with the hat . . . ?

TESMAN. How can you think such a thing? Aunt Julia? No no. Aunt Rina's poorly.

HEDDA. She always is.

TESMAN. Poor soul, she's really bad today.

HEDDA. Then of course the other one must stay. I understand.

TESMAN. She was so delighted, Aunt Julia, to see how you've put on weight while we were away.

HEDDA (*to herself, getting up*). Never-ending aunts!

TESMAN. Pardon?

HEDDA (*crossing to the screen door*). Nothing.

TESMAN. Well . . . excuse me . . .

Exit right through the inner room.

BRACK. What business with the hat?

HEDDA. Just something with Miss Tesman this morning. She left her hat on a chair. (*Grinning at him.*) I pretended I thought it was Berta's.

BRACK (*shaking his head*). Mrs Tesman, how could you? Such a sweet old lady . . . !

HEDDA (*edgy, crossing the room*). I . . . it's . . .

She sits heavily in the chair by the stove.

Sometimes I just have to. I can't explain.

BRACK (*behind the chair*). You're unhappy. That's all it is.

HEDDA (*gazing into the distance*). And tell me. Why should I be . . . happy?

BRACK. Among other things . . . you've got the house you longed for.

HEDDA (*mocking him*). Just like a fairy tale. You believe that?

BRACK. Not true?

HEDDA. Not entirely.

BRACK. Ha!

HEDDA. This is what's true. Last summer I used Tesman to escort me home after evening parties.

BRACK. Unfortunately I went a different way.

HEDDA. Yes. You went a different way last summer.

BRACK (*laughing*). Mrs Tesman! Go on. You and Tesman . . .

HEDDA. One evening we came this way. Tesman was . . . wriggling and writhing. He'd run out of conversation.
I took pity on him –

BRACK (*smiling in disbelief*). Really?

HEDDA. To help him out, I said, just for something to say, that I wouldn't mind living here one day.

BRACK. Nothing else?

HEDDA. Not then.

BRACK. But later?

HEDDA. I should have known. One should think before one speaks.

BRACK. One never does.

HEDDA. Thanks. It was passion for this villa, the widow Falk's villa, that brought us together. Tesman and me. Engagement, marriage, honeymoon – all of it. I should have known. I nearly said: As you make your bed, so you're bound to lie on it.

BRACK. So you didn't really like the house?

HEDDA. Not at all.

BRACK. But now? Now we've made it . . . cosy for you.

HEDDA. I can smell nothing but lavender, dried roses, in every room. I blame Aunt Julia.

BRACK (*laughing*). More likely the late widow Falk.

HEDDA. 'Late' is right. Or the flowers from yesterday's ball.

She clasps her hands behind her head, leans back in the chair and looks at him.

Dear Brack, you can't imagine how bored I'm going to be here.

BRACK. Oh surely, Mrs Tesman, life will find something to offer you.

HEDDA. Something . . . absorbing?

BRACK. If you're lucky.

HEDDA. What will it be? What could it be? I sometimes wonder . . . (*Interrupting herself.*) Out of the question.

BRACK. What is?

HEDDA. Just: I wonder if I could persuade Tesman to go into politics.

BRACK (*laughing*). You're joking. Tesman! Politics! Not his style at all.

HEDDA. All the same, if I could persuade him . . .

BRACK. But why should you want to? If he's not cut out for it . . . Why should you want to?

HEDDA. I told you. Because I'm bored.

Short pause.

You really think it's out of the question? Tesman . . . in parliament?

BRACK. You don't understand. If he'd been rich to start with . . .

HEDDA (*jumping up*). Genteel poverty! Again! I married it!

She paces.

It makes everything mean, ridiculous. It does. It does.

BRACK. I think there's something else.

HEDDA. What?

BRACK. In your whole life, you've never had anything really . . . serious to think about.

HEDDA. What d'you mean?

BRACK. But now, things may change.

HEDDA (*tossing her head*). You mean this wretched professorship. That's Tesman's affair. Entirely. I won't waste my brain on that.

BRACK. Hmhm. I didn't mean that. I meant . . . how can I put it . . . something vital . . . vitally dependent. On you. (*Smiling.*) Dependent on you, Mrs Tesman.

HEDDA (*furious*). No! Don't even think such things.

BRACK (*carefully*). We'll see. In a very few months. We'll see.

HEDDA (*curtly*). I've no talent for that, Your Honour. No talent for . . . things that depend on me.

BRACK. You're a woman. It's a woman's . . . talent. Her calling.

HEDDA (*at the screen door*). I said: no! I've only one talent. I decided that long ago.

BRACK (*going towards her*). For what? If you don't mind me asking.

HEDDA (*standing there, looking out*). For boring myself to death.

She turns, glances into the inner room and laughs.

Ah! Here he comes . . . the professor.

BRACK (*quietly, warning*). Mrs Tesman . . .

Enter TESMAN, *from the inner room right. He is dressed for the dinner-party, and carries his hat and gloves.*

TESMAN. Hedda, we've not had Eilert's answer yet? That he isn't coming?

HEDDA. No.

TESMAN. He'll be here any minute then. You'll see.

BRACK. You really think he'll come?

TESMAN. I'm sure he will. Almost. That was all just gossip, what you told us this morning.

BRACK. Ah.

TESMAN. Aunt Julia said she was certain he wouldn't stand in my way again. Certain.

BRACK. That's fine, then.

TESMAN *puts his hat and gloves down on a chair, right.*

TESMAN. I really ought to wait for him, as long as possible.

BRACK. We've time. There'll be no one there till seven . . . half past . . .

TESMAN. We can keep Hedda company till then. Pass the time.

HEDDA *lays* BRACK's *coat and hat on the corner sofa.*

HEDDA. If all else fails, Mr Løvborg can stay here with me.

BRACK (*trying to take his coat and hat*). Dear lady! What d'you mean, if all else fails?

HEDDA. If he doesn't want to go with you and Tesman.

TESMAN (*looking at her doubtfully*). Hedda, darling . . . D'you think it's all right, for him to be here with you? I mean, Aunt Julia can't come.

HEDDA. Mrs Elvsted's coming. We'll take tea together. The three of us.

TESMAN. Of course!

BRACK (*with a smile*). In any case, that might be best for him.

HEDDA. What d'you mean?

BRACK. Good gracious, dear lady, haven't you heard about my dinner-parties? They're only for men of iron self-discipline.

HEDDA. But that's what Mr Løvborg is these days. One sinner who repented . . .

Enter BERTA *from the hall.*

BERTA. Madam, there's a gentleman –

HEDDA. Show him in.

TESMAN (*quietly*). It's him. I knew!

Enter LØVBORG *from the hall. He is the same age as* TESMAN, *but looks older and worse preserved. He is slight and gaunt. Dark brown hair and beard. Long, pale face, with patches of colour on the cheekbones. Stylish, almost new, afternoon clothes, dark gloves, a stovepipe hat. He stops by the door and bows awkwardly, seemingly embarrassed.* TESMAN *goes and shakes his hand.*

TESMAN. My dear Ejlert. How good to see you again.

LØVBORG (*in a low voice*). Jørgen, thanks for your note.

He goes to HEDDA.

Mrs Tesman.

HEDDA (*shaking his hand*). Mr Løvborg. (*Gesturing.*) Do you two gentlemen . . . ?

LØVBORG (*bowing slightly*). Judge Brack, isn't it?

BRACK (*the same*). Of course we know each other. A year ago, I think.

TESMAN (*putting his hands on* LØVBORG'*s shoulders*). My dear Ejlert, from now on you must treat this house as your own. Isn't that right, Hedda? You are coming back to town?

LØVBORG. That's right.

TESMAN. Wonderful! D'you know, I've just bought your book. Mind, I haven't had time to read it yet.

LØVBORG. I shouldn't bother.

TESMAN. Why ever not?

LØVBORG. It's a potboiler.

TESMAN. What d'you mean?

BRACK. Everyone admires it.

LØVBORG. I meant them to admire it. There isn't a word to disagree with.

BRACK. Sensible.

TESMAN. But Ejlert —

LØVBORG. I have to build my reputation up again. That's the whole point. From scratch.

TESMAN (*slightly embarrassed*). Yes. That's right.

LØVBORG smiles, puts down his hat and takes a large brown envelope from his pocket.

LØVBORG. But when this comes out, Jørgen, you'd better read it. A real piece of work. The real me.

TESMAN. What's it about?

LØVBORG. It's a continuation.

TESMAN. What of?

LØVBORG. The book.

TESMAN. The new one?

LØVBORG. Exactly.

TESMAN. But Ejlert, that comes right to the present day.

LØVBORG. This is about the future.

TESMAN. The future? We've no information.

LØVBORG. But we can speculate.

He opens the envelope.

Look —

TESMAN. This isn't your writing.

LØVBORG. Dictated.

He turns the pages.

Two sections. Part One: Cultural Determinants in the Future. Part Two . . .

He finds it.

. . . Cultural Directions in the Future.

TESMAN. Amazing! I'd never have imagined such a subject.

HEDDA *is drumming her fingers on the screen door.*

HEDDA. Never.

LØVBORG *slides the manuscript back in the envelope, and puts it on the table.*

LØVBORG. I brought it with me because . . . I thought I might read you some this evening.

TESMAN. Very kind. But . . . this evening?

He glances at BRACK.

I don't see how . . .

LØVBORG. It's all right. Some other time. No hurry.

BRACK. The thing is, Mr Løvborg, I'm giving a dinner-party this evening. In Tesman's honour, as it happens . . .

LØVBORG (*reaching for his hat*). In that case . . .

BRACK. Look here, why don't you come too?

LØVBORG (*short and sharp*). No. Thank you, no.

BRACK. No, come. Just a few close friends. We'll be really quite 'jolly', as Hed – Mrs Tesman – puts it.

LØVBORG. I'm sure. But all the same I –

BRACK. You could bring your manuscript and read it to Tesman there. I've plenty of rooms.

TESMAN. Ejlert. It's not a bad idea . . .

HEDDA (*breaking in*). My dear man, if Mr Løvborg really doesn't want to . . . I'm sure he'd rather dine here, with me.

LØVBORG (*staring*). With you?

HEDDA. And Mrs Elvsted.

LØVBORG. Ah. (*Offhand.*) I ran into her this morning.

HEDDA. She'll be here tonight. So it's essential that you come. Otherwise, who'll see her safely home?

LØVBORG. That's true. Yes. Thank you, Mrs Tesman. I'll be glad to come.

HEDDA. I'll tell Berta.

She goes to the hall door and rings. BERTA *comes in, and* HEDDA *talks quietly to her, pointing to the inner room.* BERTA *nods and exit.*

TESMAN (*meanwhile, to* LØVBORG). Listen, Ejlert, this new stuff . . . the future . . . is that what your lectures are to be about?

LØVBORG. Yes.

TESMAN. They said in the bookshop that you're giving a course this autumn.

LØVBORG. Yes. I'm sorry, Jørgen.

TESMAN. No, no, no. I . . .

LØVBORG. I can see how annoying it must be for you.

TESMAN (*weakly*). Oh, I couldn't expect you to . . . for my sake . . .

LØVBORG. I am waiting till you've got your professorship.

TESMAN. Waiting! But you . . . You're not competing?

LØVBORG. You take the professorship; I'll take fame.

TESMAN. So Aunt Julia was right! I knew it. Hedda, Ejlert won't stand in our way at all.

HEDDA (*curtly*). Our way? Leave me out of it.

She goes to the inner room, where BERTA *is setting glassware on the table.* HEDDA *nods approvingly and comes in again. Exit* BERTA.

TESMAN (*meanwhile*). Brack, you heard this. What do you think?

BRACK. Reputation . . . fame . . . they're very attractive . . .

TESMAN. Attractive. But not . . . not . . .

HEDDA (*smiling icily at him*). You look as if you've been struck by lightning.

TESMAN. I . . . something like that . . .

BRACK. There were thunderclouds, Mrs Tesman. But they've passed, they've passed.

HEDDA (*gesturing towards the inner room*). Would you gentlemen care for a glass of cold punch?

BRACK (*looking at his watch*). A stirrup-cup? Not a bad idea.

TESMAN. Wonderful, Hedda. Wonderful. I feel so relieved, such a burden's been –

HEDDA. Mr Løvborg?

LØVBORG (*gesturing 'No'*). Not for me, thanks.

BRACK. For Heaven's sake, man. Cold punch is hardly poison.

LØVBORG. Not for everyone, perhaps.

HEDDA (*to* BRACK *and* TESMAN). You go in. I'll keep Mr Løvborg company.

TESMAN. Wonderful, Hedda. Yes.

During what follows, he and BRACK *go into the inner room, sit down, drink punch, smoke and talk animatedly.* HEDDA *goes to the writing-desk.* LØVBORG *stays by the stove.*

HEDDA (*loudly*). If you like, I'll show you some photographs. Tesman and I have just come back . . . from the Tyrol . . . our honeymoon . . .

She takes an album and puts it on the table by the sofa. She sits at one end of the sofa. LØVBORG *approaches and stands looking down at her. Then he takes a chair and sits to her left with his back to the inner room.*

(*Opening the album.*) D'you see this range of mountains, Mr Løvborg? The Ortler Range. Tesman's written it underneath, look: 'The Ortler Range, from Melan'.

LØVBORG *has been gazing intently at her.*

LØVBORG (*softly and slowly*). Miss . . . Hedda . . . Gabler.

HEDDA (*glancing at him*). Tss!

LØVBORG (*as before*). Miss . . . Hedda . . . Gabler.

HEDDA (*looking through the album*). I was, once. When we knew each other . . . then.

LØVBORG. And never again? Must I make a resolution, never to utter those words again? Miss Hedda Gabler.

HEDDA (*turning the pages*). Make a resolution. Make it now.

LØVBORG (*in an injured tone*). Hedda Gabler, married? And to . . . Jørgen Tesman.

HEDDA. Exactly.

LØVBORG. Oh Hedda, how could you throw yourself away?

HEDDA (*with a sharp glance*). Shh!

LØVBORG. Why?

TESMAN *comes in and goes to the sofa.*

HEDDA (*in a bored voice*). Look, Mr Løvborg. This is the view from Ampezzo. Look at those mountains. (*With an affectionate glance up at* TESMAN.) What do they call these wonderful mountains, Tesman?

TESMAN. Which mountains? Oh, the Dolomites.

HEDDA. Of course. Mr Løvborg, the Dolomites.

TESMAN. Hedda, can't we bring in some punch? At least for you?

HEDDA. Yes please. And some biscuits, perhaps.

TESMAN. Cigarettes?

HEDDA. No.

TESMAN. All right.

He goes into the inner room, and exit right. BRACK *stays in the inner room, looking occasionally at* HEDDA *and* LØVBORG.

LØVBORG (*in a low voice, as before*). Hedda, darling, answer me. How could you . . . do this?

HEDDA (*apparently absorbed in the album*). If you keep calling me darling, I won't talk to you.

LØVBORG. When no one else is there?

HEDDA. You can think it. But you mustn't say it.

LØVBORG. It offends your love . . . for Tesman.

HEDDA (*with a quizzical smile at him*). Love?

LØVBORG. No love!

HEDDA. No . . . disloyalty. I won't have that.

LØVBORG. Hedda, tell me one thing –

HEDDA. Shh!

TESMAN *comes from the inner room with a tray.*

TESMAN. Time to enjoy yourselves!

He puts the tray on the table, and begins filling glasses.

HEDDA. Why did you fetch it?

TESMAN. My dear, I wait on you hand and foot.

HEDDA. You've filled both glasses. You know Mr Løvborg doesn't –

TESMAN. But Mrs Elvsted'll be here any minute.

HEDDA. Mrs Elvsted. Yes.

TESMAN. Had you forgotten?

HEDDA. We were so engrossed. (*Showing him a photo.*) D'you remember this village?

TESMAN. The one at the foot of the Brenner Pass. Where we spent the night –

HEDDA. And met all those jolly tourists.

TESMAN. That's right. You should've been with us, Ejlert! Ha ha!

He goes in again and sits with BRACK.

LØVBORG. Answer me one thing, Hedda.

HEDDA. What?

LØVBORG. Did you feel no love for me? A flicker . . . a spark . . . for me?

HEDDA. It's hard to say. I thought we were close. Close friends. Comrades in arms: no secrets. (*With a smile.*) You always said what was on your mind.

LØVBORG. You didn't mind.

HEDDA. When I think about it now . . . It was beautiful . . . exciting . . . daring. Secrets . . . We were comrades in arms. It was our secret, shared by no other living soul.

LØVBORG. Our secret. I called on your father every afternoon. He sat by the window, the General, reading the paper. His back to us –

HEDDA. We sat on the corner seat –

LØVBORG. Always looking at the same magazine –

HEDDA. Like this album, now.

LØVBORG. And Hedda, the things I told you! Things about myself. No one else knew, then. My drinking . . . days and nights on end. I sat there and told you. Days and nights. Oh Hedda, what gave you such power? To make me tell you . . . things like that?

HEDDA. You think I had power?

LØVBORG. What else would've made me tell you? All those questions . . . things you asked . . . indirectly . . .

HEDDA. You understood.

LØVBORG. The things you asked. Absolute trust.

HEDDA. Asked indirectly.

LØVBORG. Absolute trust. You asked – everything.

HEDDA. And you, Mr Løvborg, answered.

LØVBORG. Looking back, that's what I don't understand. Hedda, are you sure there wasn't love, deep down? When I confessed, didn't you want to absolve me, to wash away my sin?

HEDDA. Not exactly.

LØVBORG. What, then?

HEDDA. You really don't know? A young girl . . . without anyone knowing . . . her chance . . .

LØVBORG. Chance?

HEDDA. To glimpse a world that . . .

LØVBORG. That − ?

HEDDA. That she'd no business to know existed.

LØVBORG. That's all it was?

HEDDA. That's all it was. To me.

LØVBORG. We both longed to discover life. Comrades in arms. But why did it have to stop?

HEDDA. Your fault.

LØVBORG. You stopped it.

HEDDA. Before we grew . . . too close. How could you, Mr Løvborg? Absolute trust. Comrades in arms.

LØVBORG (*clenching his fists*). Oh, why didn't you do as you promised? You said you'd shoot me. Why didn't you?

HEDDA. Simple: the scandal.

LØVBORG. Well, well! Underneath, you're a coward.

HEDDA. Absolutely. (*New tone.*) Lucky for you, though. And you consoled yourself. Look what a time you've been having, at the Elvsteds'.

LØVBORG. I know what Thea's told you.

HEDDA. And have you told her − about us?

LØVBORG. Not a word. She wouldn't understand. She's a fool.

HEDDA. A fool?

LØVBORG. In things like that.

HEDDA. And I'm a coward.

She leans towards him, looks into his eyes, and says gently:

Now I'll confess to you.

LØVBORG (*tense*). What?

HEDDA. When I . . . didn't shoot you −

LØVBORG. Well?

HEDDA. That wasn't my worst cowardice, that evening.

LØVBORG *looks at her a moment, understands, and whispers passionately:*

LØVBORG. Hedda, darling. I see now. Comrades in arms. That was it. You and I. Your longing for life . . .

HEDDA (*in a low voice, and with an angry look*). That's enough. Enough.

It is getting dark. BERTA *opens the hall door.* HEDDA *snaps the album shut and calls out with a smile:*

Thea! So there you are. Come in.

MRS ELVSTED *comes in from the hall. She is wearing formal evening clothes. The door closes behind her.* HEDDA, *on the sofa, holds out her arms.*

You can't believe how glad I am to see you.

MRS ELVSTED, *who has gone to greet the men in the inner room, now comes back to the table, to shake* HEDDA's *hand.* LØVBORG *has stood up. He and* MRS ELVSTED *nod to each other, without speaking.*

MRS ELVSTED. I ought to go in and talk to your husband.

HEDDA. No. Leave them. They're just going out.

MRS ELVSTED. Going out?

HEDDA. Out on the town.

MRS ELVSTED (*quickly, to* LØVBORG). Not you as well?

LØVBORG. No.

HEDDA. Mr Løvborg's staying here with us.

MRS ELVSTED *takes a chair and starts towards* LØVBORG *to sit by him.*

MRS ELVSTED. This is cosy. Cosy.

HEDDA. Not there, Thea. Darling. Over here, by me. I intend to come between you.

MRS ELVSTED. If that's what you want.

She goes round the table and sits on the sofa beside HEDDA. LØVBORG *sits down again.*

LØVBORG (*after a short pause, to* HEDDA). Isn't she wonderful? To sit and look at?

HEDDA (*stroking* MRS ELVSTED*'s hair*). To look at?

LØVBORG. She and I . . . we really are comrades in arms. We sit together, absolute trust, we tell each other everything –

HEDDA. Not indirectly, Mr Løvborg?

LØVBORG. Uh . . .

MRS ELVSTED (*quietly, snuggling to* HEDDA). I'm so lucky, Hedda! Imagine, he calls me his inspiration.

HEDDA (*smiling at her*). Darling. Really?

LØVBORG. She has courage, Mrs Tesman. The courage that gets things done.

MRS ELVSTED. Me? Courage? No.

LØVBORG. The courage to fight. For her comrade in arms.

HEDDA. That courage. Ah. The kind –

LØVBORG. What kind?

HEDDA. – that lets one live. (*Change of tone.*) Thea, dearest, do have a glass of punch.

MRS ELVSTED. No thank you. I never drink alcohol.

HEDDA. Mr Løvborg? Surely.

LØVBORG. Thank you. No.

MRS ELVSTED. He doesn't either.

HEDDA (*looking steadily at him*). Not even for my sake?

LØVBORG. Sorry, no.

HEDDA (*lightly*). Oh dear. I've no power over you at all?

LØVBORG. Not where that's concerned.

HEDDA. I really think you should. For your own sake.

MRS ELVSTED. Hedda!

LØVBORG. What d'you mean?

HEDDA. Or rather, for other people's sake.

LØVBORG. Yes?

HEDDA. In case they think that you . . . can't trust yourself. Absolute trust.

MRS ELVSTED (*quietly*). Hedda. No.

LØVBORG. They can think what they like. They'll see.

MRS ELVSTED (*delighted*). That's right.

HEDDA. I could see, earlier. When Judge Brack -

LØVBORG. What did you see?

HEDDA. I saw how he smiled when you were afraid to go to that party.

LØVBORG. I preferred to stay here with you.

MRS ELVSTED. You see, Hedda.

HEDDA. The Judge couldn't see. I noticed him smiling, glancing at Tesman. Afraid, afraid to go to their harmless little party.

LØVBORG. Don't call me afraid.

HEDDA. Not me. Judge Brack. That's what he thought.

LØVBORG. He can think what he likes.

HEDDA. You're not going?

LØVBORG. I'm staying here with you and Thea.

MRS ELVSTED. He's staying, Hedda.

HEDDA (*smiling and nodding approvingly at* LØVBORG). A rock. A man of principle. Just what a man should be.

She turns to MRS ELVSTED *and pats her.*

Didn't I tell you so this morning, when you were so upset?

LØVBORG (*startled*). Upset?

MRS ELVSTED (*aghast*). Hedda!

HEDDA. Now you see for yourself. There's no need. No need for all this panic. (*Breaking off.*) Never mind. Let's change the subject.

LØVBORG (*insistently*). Mrs Tesman, what is all this?

MRS ELVSTED. Hedda, what are you saying? What are you doing? Oh God.

HEDDA. Shh! That tiresome Judge Brack is watching.

LØVBORG. Panic. About me.

MRS ELVSTED (*quietly, miserably*). Hedda, how could you?

LØVBORG *gazes at her a moment, grim-faced.*

LØVBORG. Comrades in arms. So much for trust.

MRS ELVSTED (*beseeching him*). Please, my dear, please listen.

LØVBORG *snatches up a glass of punch.*

LØVBORG (*quietly, intensely*). Darling, your health.

He drains the glass and takes another.

MRS ELVSTED (*low*). You planned this, Hedda.

HEDDA. You're crazy. Planned?

LØVBORG. Mrs Tesman, your health. Thank you for the truth. To truth!

He drains the glass and refills it. HEDDA *puts a hand on his arm.*

HEDDA. No more for now. Don't forget, you're going out to dinner.

MRS ELVSTED. No, no, no.

HEDDA. Shh! They can see you.

LØVBORG (*putting down the glass*). Your turn, Thea. The truth.

MRS ELVSTED. Yes.

LØVBORG. Does your husband know you followed me?

MRS ELVSTED (*wringing her hands*). Hedda, d'you hear what he's asking me?

LØVBORG. Did you plan this together? You and he? That you'd come after me, spy on me? Was it his idea? Of course it was! He needed me to help in the office. An extra hand at cards!

MRS ELVSTED (*low, anguished*). Ejlert, Ejlert.

LØVBORG *seizes and fills a glass.*

LØVBORG. His health too! His Honour's health!

HEDDA (*checking him*). No more now. Don't forget Tesman. You're going to read him your book.

LØVBORG (*calmly, putting down the glass*). I'm sorry, Thea. I was a fool. Taking it like this. My darling, my comrade in arms, don't worry. Don't be afraid for me. You'll see, they'll all see. I fell before, but now . . . I'm up again. Dearest Thea, all thanks to you.

MRS ELVSTED (*overjoyed*). Thank God, thank God.

BRACK *has meantime looked at his watch, and now he and* TESMAN *come in from the inner room.* BRACK *takes his hat and coat.*

BRACK. Well, Mrs Tesman. It's time.

HEDDA. Yes, time.

LØVBORG (*getting up*). Time for me as well.

MRS ELVSTED (*low, beseeching*). Ejlert, don't.

HEDDA (*pinching her arm*). They can hear you.

MRS ELVSTED (a *little shriek*). Ow.

LØVBORG (*to* BRACK). Your generous invitation.

BRACK. You're coming?

LØVBORG. Please. If I may.

BRACK. Splendid.

LØVBORG *puts his manuscript in his pocket.*

LØVBORG (*to* TESMAN). I've one or two things to show you before I send it off.

TESMAN. Wonderful. Hedda, darling, how will you get Mrs Elvsted home?

HEDDA. We'll find a way.

LØVBORG (*looking at the women*). Mrs Elvsted? I'll fetch her. No question. I'll come and fetch her. (*Going closer.*) Mrs Tesman, about ten o'clock?

HEDDA. Perfect.

TESMAN. Splendid. Excellent. But you mustn't expect me so early, Hedda.

HEDDA. My dear man, stay as long as you like.

MRS ELVSTED (*with forced calm*). Mr Løvborg, I'll wait here till you come.

LØVBORG (*hat in hand*). Mrs Elvsted, excellent.

BRACK. So, gentlemen, the carnival begins! I hope it'll be . . . 'jolly', as a certain charming lady puts it.

HEDDA. I wish a certain charming lady could be there, invisible –

BRACK. Why invisible?

HEDDA. Why Your Honour, to hear some of your . . . jollity uncensored.

BRACK (*laughing*). It's not for charming ladies' ears.

TESMAN (*laughing too*). It certainly isn't, Hedda.

BRACK. Ladies, good afternoon.

LØVBORG (*bowing*). Till ten o'clock.

BRACK, LØVBORG and TESMAN *go out by the hall. At the same time,* BERTA *comes from the inner room with a lighted lamp, puts it on the table and exit as she came in.* MRS ELVSTED *has got up and is pacing restlessly.*

MRS ELVSTED. Hedda, Hedda, what's going to happen?

HEDDA. At ten o'clock, he'll be here. I see him. With vine leaves in his hair. Flushed, confident –

MRS ELVSTED. Oh if only –

HEDDA. He'll have proved himself. In control of himself again. He'll be free, then, forever free.

MRS ELVSTED. God send him so.

HEDDA. He must be. Will be. (*Going to her.*) You doubt him if you like. I believe in him. And now, we'll see.

MRS ELVSTED. Hedda, what is it you want from this?

HEDDA. For once in my life, I want to control another human being's fate.

MRS ELVSTED. But you do.

HEDDA. No I don't.

MRS ELVSTED. Your husband.

HEDDA. If I did . . . You don't know how poor I am. And you, you: promised such riches!

She hugs her affectionately.

I think I'll burn your hair off after all.

MRS ELVSTED. Let me go! Hedda! You're frightening me.

BERTA (*at the door*). Tea's laid in the dining-room, madam.

HEDDA. We're coming.

MRS ELVSTED. No, no! I want to go home. Home, now!

HEDDA. What a goose you are. First, you'll have some tea. Then, at ten o'clock, Ejlert Løvborg will be here . . . with vine leaves in his hair.

She all but drags her into the inner room.

Curtain.

ACT THREE

The scene is the same. The curtains have been drawn over the main doorway and the screen door to the garden. A lighted lamp is on the table, shaded and half turned down. The stove door is open, and the dying embers of a fire can be seen. MRS ELVSTED *is lying back in an armchair next to the stove, with her feet on a stool.* HEDDA *is asleep on the sofa, fully dressed and covered by a rug. After a moment,* MRS ELVSTED *sits up and listens intently. Then she sinks wearily back.*

MRS ELVSTED (*whimpering pitifully*). Still no. Oh God, still no.

> BERTA *tiptoes in through the hall door with a letter.* MRS ELVSTED *turns and whispers eagerly:*

News? Something's happened?

BERTA (*in a low voice*). A servant just came with this.

MRS ELVSTED (*eagerly, holding out her hand*). A letter! Give it to me.

BERTA. I can't, madam. It's for Doctor Tesman.

MRS ELVSTED. Oh.

BERTA. Miss Tesman's maid brought it. I'll leave it on the table.

MRS ELVSTED. Yes.

> BERTA *puts the letter on the table.*

BERTA. The lamp's smoking. I ought to put it out.

MRS ELVSTED. Yes. Please. It'll soon be dawn.

BERTA (*putting out the lamp*). It is dawn, madam.

MRS ELVSTED. Broad daylight! And they're still not home.

BERTA. I expected this.

MRS ELVSTED. Expected it?

BERTA. As soon as I knew that a certain person had
come back to town . . . And then when he went off with
them . . . We all know that gentleman's reputation.

MRS ELVSTED. Not so loud. You'll waken Mrs Tesman.

BERTA (*looking at the sofa and sighing*). Yes. Let the poor soul
sleep. Should I make up the stove?

MRS ELVSTED. Not on my account, thank you.

BERTA. Yes madam.

*She leaves quietly through the hall. The noise of the door closing
wakens* HEDDA.

HEDDA. What's that?

MRS ELVSTED. Just Berta.

HEDDA (*looking round*). Here . . . Oh yes.

She sits up, stretches and rubs her eyes.

What time is it, Thea?

MRS ELVSTED (*looking at her watch*). Just after seven.

HEDDA. When did Tesman come in?

MRS ELVSTED. He didn't.

HEDDA. Didn't?

MRS ELVSTED (*getting up*). No one did.

HEDDA. After we sat up and waited till four o'clock!

MRS ELVSTED (*wringing her hands*). I waited so hard for
him.

HEDDA (*smothering a yawn*). We needn't have bothered.

MRS ELVSTED. Did you sleep at all?

HEDDA. Yes thank you. Very well. Did you?

MRS ELVSTED. Not a wink. I couldn't, Hedda.

HEDDA *gets up and goes to her.*

HEDDA. Don't worry. It's all right. It's perfectly clear what
happened.

MRS ELVSTED. What d'you mean?

HEDDA. It's obvious. They stayed very late at Judge Brack's –

MRS ELVSTED. Oh. Yes. Even so –

HEDDA. – and Jørgen decided not to waken the whole
household, ringing the bell in the middle of the night.
(*With a laugh.*) In any case, perhaps he wasn't fit to be
seen. Rather a heavy night . . .

MRS ELVSTED. But Hedda, where did he go instead?

HEDDA. The aunts, of course. His old room. They keep it
just as it was. He'll have gone there to sleep.

MRS ELVSTED. He can't have done. A note's just come
from Miss Tesman. On the table, there.

HEDDA. Hm.

She looks at the letter.

Aunt Julia's writing. Well, he'll still be at Judge Brack's.
Ejlert Løvborg too. He'll be sitting there, reading his
book to him . . . with vine leaves in his hair.

MRS ELVSTED. You're just saying that, Hedda. You don't
believe it; you're just saying it.

HEDDA. You are a goose.

MRS ELVSTED. I'm sorry.

HEDDA. You look worn out.

MRS ELVSTED. I am.

HEDDA. Well then, do as I say. Go to my room, lie down,
take a nap.

MRS ELVSTED. I won't sleep.

HEDDA. You will if you try.

MRS ELVSTED. Your husband'll be home any minute. And
I've got to know –

HEDDA. As soon as he comes, I'll tell you.

MRS ELVSTED. D'you promise, Hedda?

HEDDA. Cross my heart. Meantime, go in and sleep.

MRS ELVSTED. Yes. Thank you.

She goes in through the inner room. HEDDA goes to the screen door and draws the curtains. Daylight fills the room. She takes a hand mirror from the writing desk and straightens her hair. Then she goes to the bellpull by the hall door and rings. After a short pause, BERTA comes to the door.

BERTA. Yes, madam?

HEDDA. Make up the stove, will you? I'm shivering.

BERTA. Bless you, it'll be warm in no time.

She rakes the stove and puts in fresh wood. Then she stops and listens.

There's someone at the front door, madam.

HEDDA. You answer it. I'll see to the stove.

BERTA. It'll soon burn up.

She goes out through the hall. HEDDA kneels on a footstool and feeds the stove. After a short pause, TESMAN comes in from the hall. He looks exhausted and anxious. He tiptoes across the room to the main door and puts out a hand to draw the curtains.

HEDDA (*at the stove, without looking up*). Good morning.

TESMAN (*turning*). Hedda!

He goes to her.

What on Earth . . . ? You're up early.

HEDDA. So I am.

TESMAN. I was sure you'd be fast asleep.

HEDDA. Not so loud. Mrs Elvsted's asleep in there.

TESMAN. She spent the night here?

HEDDA. No one came to take her home.

TESMAN. No, that's right.

HEDDA closes the stove door and stands up.

HEDDA. How was it at Judge Brack's? Was it . . . jolly?

TESMAN. You were worried about me.

HEDDA. I just asked if it was jolly.

TESMAN. Oh, yes. Especially to begin with, so far as I was concerned. That's when Ejlert read to me. We were an hour too early. Brack had a hundred things to do. So Ejlert read.

HEDDA *sits, right of the table.*

HEDDA. Yes. Tell me –

TESMAN *sits on a stool by the stove.*

TESMAN. Hedda, you can't imagine what it's like, his book. One of the most amazing ever written.

HEDDA. I'm really not interested.

TESMAN. And d'you know, Hedda, when he'd finished . . . I have to admit it . . . I felt awful. Awful.

HEDDA. I don't understand.

TESMAN. I sat there feeling jealous. That Ejlert could write like that. Jealous, Hedda!

HEDDA. I heard you.

TESMAN. And then to think that a man like him . . . so gifted . . . should be so . . . beyond reach.

HEDDA. Beyond reach? Of what – mediocrity?

TESMAN. Of control! Control!

HEDDA. What d'you mean? What happened?

TESMAN. It was . . . well, it was an orgy, Hedda.

HEDDA. Did he have vine leaves in his hair?

TESMAN. I didn't see any. He made a rambling speech about the woman who'd inspired him. His Muse, he called her.

HEDDA. Did he mention her name?

TESMAN. No. But I'm sure he meant Mrs Elvsted. No smoke without fire!

HEDDA. Mm. Where did you leave him?

TESMAN. On the way here. We left the party – the few
that were left – all together. Brack came out with us: he
wanted some fresh air. The end of it was, we all saw
Ejlert home. He was . . . well gone.

HEDDA. Well gone.

TESMAN. But this is the amazing part, Hedda. Or the
depressing part, rather. I'm embarrassed to tell it . . . for
Ejlert's sake.

HEDDA. Tell what?

TESMAN. We were walking along. I was a little behind the
others. A couple of minutes. More or less . . .

HEDDA. For Heaven's sake!

TESMAN. I was hurrying to catch them up – and there, by
the side of the road . . . what d'you think?

HEDDA. I don't know. What?

TESMAN. Hedda, don't breathe a word. To anyone.
Promise. For Ejlert's sake.

He takes a large envelope from his coat pocket.

I found . . . this.

HEDDA. That's the package he brought here yesterday.

TESMAN. His priceless, irreplaceable manuscript. He lost it,
and he didn't even notice. Just think what a tragedy –

HEDDA. Why didn't you give it him right away?

TESMAN. I couldn't. The state he was in.

HEDDA. Did you tell anyone else you'd found it?

TESMAN. I didn't want to. For Ejlert's sake.

HEDDA. So you've got Ejlert Løvborg's book, and no one
knows?

TESMAN. That's right. And no one must know, either.

HEDDA. What did you say to him?

TESMAN. Nothing. I didn't have a chance. By the time we
got to the centre of town, he and one or two others had
vanished. Vanished.

HEDDA. So they must have seen him home.

TESMAN. Exactly. And Brack went home as well.

HEDDA. And since then: what have you been doing?

TESMAN. A few of us took someone else home, someone else who was . . . We had a cup of coffee – Ha! breakfast in the middle of the night! I'll just take a nap . . . I'll wait till poor Ejlert's slept it off . . . then I'll go round and give him this.

HEDDA (*reaching for the envelope*). No, keep it. I mean, for a little longer. Let me read it first.

TESMAN. Darling, I can't. I can't.

HEDDA. Why not?

TESMAN. Think what he'll be like when he wakes up and finds he's lost it. He'll be frantic. This is the only copy. There isn't another.

HEDDA (*with a long look at him*). Can't this sort of thing be written again? A second version?

TESMAN. I shouldn't think so. Inspiration –

HEDDA. Ah well. (*Casually.*) I nearly forgot. There's a letter.

TESMAN. Pardon?

HEDDA (*pointing*). It came earlier.

TESMAN. From Aunt Julia. What can it be?

He puts LØVBORG's *envelope on the other footstool, opens the letter, reads and starts.*

Hedda! She says that poor Aunt Rina's . . . at death's door.

HEDDA. Are you surprised?

TESMAN. And if I want to see her again, I'd better hurry. I'll run –

HEDDA (*lightly*). Run?

TESMAN. Hedda, darling, if only you'd . . . if only you'd come too. Come too.

HEDDA (*getting up; in a weary, dismissive tone*). No. Don't ask. I can't bear sick people, dead people. They're . . . ugly.

TESMAN. Yes. (*Fretting.*) My hat . . . my coat . . . ? In the hall. Oh Hedda, I hope I'm not too late. Too late . . .

HEDDA. You'd better run.

Enter BERTA *from the hall.*

BERTA. His Honour the Judge is here. Shall I show him in?

TESMAN. Now of all times! I can't see him now.

HEDDA. But I can. (*To* BERTA.) Show the gentleman in. (*Urgent whisper, to* TESMAN.) The package!

She takes it from the stool.

TESMAN. Yes. Give it me.

HEDDA. It's all right. I'll keep it for you. Go.

She puts the envelope on one of the shelves of the writing-desk. TESMAN stands there flustered, struggling with his gloves. Enter BRACK from the hall.

HEDDA (*nodding to him*). You are an early bird.

BRACK. You think so? (*To* TESMAN.) You on your way as well?

TESMAN. No choice. My aunts. Poor Aunt Rina, she's at death's door.

BRACK. Good Lord. Don't let me stop you.

TESMAN. Yes, excuse me, I really must . . . Goodbye, goodbye.

Exit through the hall.

HEDDA (*going to* BRACK). Quite a night, last night, Your Honour. Rather more than 'jolly'.

BRACK. Dear Mrs Tesman, I haven't even changed.

HEDDA. You too?

BRACK. Me too. But what's Tesman been telling you?

HEDDA. Nothing very interesting. They went somewhere for coffee.

BRACK. I know about the coffee. Ejlert Løvborg wasn't with them?

HEDDA. They saw him home earlier.

BRACK. Tesman?

HEDDA. A couple of others. Or so he said.

BRACK (*smiling*). Good, honest Tesman.

HEDDA. Absolutely. But what's all this about?

BRACK. You guessed: there's more than meets the eye.

HEDDA. Well, let's sit down. Tell your tale in comfort.

She sits left of the table. BRACK *sits at its long side next to her.*
Go on.

BRACK. It was just as well I checked that my guests got home last night. Or to be exact, some of my guests.

HEDDA. Including, perhaps . . . Ejlert Løvborg?

BRACK. I'm afraid so.

HEDDA. I'm listening.

BRACK. Mrs Tesman, d'you know where he and a couple of the others spent the rest of last night?

HEDDA. Tell me – if it can be told.

BRACK. It can be told. They ended up at a . . . very lively soirée.

HEDDA. Jolly?

BRACK. None jollier.

HEDDA. Go on. Please.

BRACK. Løvborg had been invited. Earlier. I knew that. But he'd refused. Said he'd turned over a new leaf. As you know.

HEDDA. Up at the Elvsteds'. But still he went?

BRACK. Exactly. The idea . . . came to him at my house.

HEDDA. I heard he was 'inspired'.

BRACK. Raging 'inspired'. Whatever it was, he changed his mind about the other invitation. We men aren't always as firm in our resolve as we like to think.

HEDDA. Except for yourself, Your Honour. So Løvborg –

BRACK. To cut it short, he finally reached harbour at Mamzelle Diana's.

HEDDA. Mamzelle Diana's?

BRACK. It was her soirée. For a chosen circle of . . . lady friends and admirers.

HEDDA. She's the one with red hair?

BRACK. Yes.

HEDDA. A kind of . . . singer?

BRACK. Kind of singer, kind of hunter – at least, of men. You've obviously heard of her. Ejlert Løvborg was one of her most devoted followers, in his heyday.

HEDDA. But what happened?

BRACK. A scene. Mamzelle Diana soon moved from hugs to blows.

HEDDA. Against Løvborg?

BRACK. He swore that she or her lady friends had robbed him. His wallet. Other things. He made a spectacular fuss.

HEDDA. Then what?

BRACK. A wrestling-match. Ladies *and* gentlemen. Fortunately, at this point the police arrived.

HEDDA. The police?

BRACK. Things look hot for Master Løvborg. Master fool!

HEDDA. What d'you mean?

BRACK. He resisted. Fiercely. Boxed one constable's ears. Ripped his uniform. So he ended up at the station too.

HEDDA. Who told you all this?

BRACK. The police.

HEDDA (*gazing straight ahead*). So that's how it was. No vine leaves.

BRACK. Vine leaves?

HEDDA (*change of tone*). Your Honour, tell me. Why do you care so much what Ejlert Løvborg did?

BRACK. For one thing, my position. If it comes out at the trial that he began at my house.

HEDDA. There's going to be a trial?

BRACK. So they say. Maybe so, maybe not. In any case, as a friend of the family, I felt I really ought to tell you and Tesman exactly what went on last night.

HEDDA. But why?

BRACK. I've a feeling he may use you as a kind of . . . screen.

HEDDA. I don't understand.

BRACK. For heaven's sake! Mrs Tesman, we're none of us blind. I'm telling you, Mrs Elvsted won't be hurrying out of town.

HEDDA. Ridiculous! If there is anything between them, there are a dozen other places they can meet.

BRACK. Nowhere else respectable. Every respectable door will be closed to Løvborg now.

HEDDA. Including mine, you're suggesting?

BRACK. I have to tell you I'd be most displeased to find him admitted here. To find him making his way, uninvited, unwanted –

HEDDA. Into the triangle?

BRACK. It would be like losing one's home.

HEDDA (*smiling at him*). Just one cock of the walk, you mean.

BRACK (*nodding slowly and lowering his voice*). Exactly. That's exactly what I mean. And what I'll fight for, any way I can.

HEDDA (*no longer smiling*). You're a dangerous man, when the going gets rough.

BRACK. You think so?

HEDDA. I'm beginning to. And I'm heartily glad you've got no hold or power over me at all.

BRACK (*laughing ambiguously*). You may be right. But who knows, Mrs Tesman? One day I may find both.

HEDDA. Your Honour, are you threatening me?

BRACK (*getting up*). Not in the least. The triangle depends for its strength entirely on free will.

HEDDA. Exactly.

BRACK. Well, I've said what I came to say. I'll be getting home again. Good morning, Mrs Tesman.

He goes to the screen door.

HEDDA (*getting up*). You're going through the garden?

BRACK. It's quicker.

HEDDA. And a back way, too.

BRACK. I've nothing against back ways. Sometimes they're quite . . . exciting.

HEDDA. For example, when someone's shooting?

BRACK (*laughing, from the doorway*). Whoever shoots the cock of the walk?

HEDDA (*laughing*). Especially when it's the only one.

Still laughing, they nod goodbye.

BRACK *goes, and* HEDDA *closes the door behind him. She stands for a moment looking out. Then she goes to the main door, peeps through the curtains, and takes* LØVBORG's *envelope from the writing-desk. She is just about to open it when* BERTA's *raised voice is heard in the hall.* HEDDA *turns and listens, then quickly locks the envelope in a drawer and puts the key on the inkstand.* LØVBORG *throws open the door from the hall and comes in. He is wearing an overcoat and carrying his hat. He seems beside himself with worry.*

LØVBORG (*to* BERTA, *behind him in the hall*). Get out of the way. I'm going in.

He closes the door, turns, sees HEDDA *by the writing-desk, controls himself and bows.*

HEDDA. My dear Mr Løvborg, you're a little late to be fetching Thea.

LØVBORG. Or a little early to be making social calls. Do excuse me.

HEDDA. How did you know she'd still be here?

LØVBORG. They told me at her lodgings that she'd been out all night.

HEDDA *goes to the table.*

HEDDA. And when they told you, did you notice anything about them?

LØVBORG (*with an enquiring look*). Notice anything?

HEDDA. As if they had . . . views about it?

LØVBORG (*suddenly understanding*). Yes, that's true too. I'm dragging her down with me. Tch, I didn't notice anything. Is Jørgen up?

HEDDA. I don't think so.

LØVBORG. When did he come home?

HEDDA. Late.

LØVBORG. Did he tell you anything?

HEDDA. What a jolly evening you all had at His Honour's.

LØVBORG. Nothing else?

HEDDA. I don't think so. I wasn't really awake.

Enter MRS ELVSTED *through the curtained rear doors. She runs to him.*

MRS ELVSTED. Ejlert! At last!

LØVBORG. At last. Too late.

MRS ELVSTED (*with a wild look at him*). What d'you mean, too late?

LØVBORG. Too late for me. All of it. Finished.

MRS ELVSTED. Don't say that.

LØVBORG. You'll say it yourself when you hear –

MRS ELVSTED. I won't hear.

HEDDA. Would you like to talk to her in private? If you like, I'll –

LØVBORG. No. Stay. Please.

MRS ELVSTED. I won't hear. I won't.

LØVBORG. I don't mean last night.

MRS ELVSTED. What then?

LØVBORG. Our . . . ways must part.

MRS ELVSTED. Part!

HEDDA (*blurted*). I knew it!

LØVBORG. Thea, I don't need you any more.

MRS ELVSTED. How can you say that? Don't need me! You mean I can't go on helping you? We can't still work together?

LØVBORG. I shan't be working now.

MRS ELVSTED (*in despair*). And my life now? What use is that?

LØVBORG. You have to try to live as if you'd never met me.

MRS ELVSTED. How can I do that?

LØVBORG. Try, Thea. Go home –

MRS ELVSTED (*violently*). I won't. Never again! I'll be where you are. I won't be sent away. I'll stay here. When the book comes out, I'll be at your side.

HEDDA (*low, agog*). Aha. The book.

LØVBORG (*looking at her*). Our book. Mine, and Thea's. For that's what it is.

MRS ELVSTED. It is, it is. That's why I've the right to be with you then, when it comes out. To see them showering you with respect again, with honour. And the pleasure, the pleasure – to share that too.

LØVBORG. Thea, our book will never come out.

HEDDA. Ah!

MRS ELVSTED. What d'you mean?

LØVBORG. It can't.

MRS ELVSTED (*with terrified foreboding*). Ejlert! What have you done with the manuscript?

HEDDA (*looking narrowly at him*). That's right. The manuscript.

LØVBORG. Don't ask me.

MRS ELVSTED. Of course I'll ask. I've a right to know. Now.

LØVBORG. The manuscript. Well. I've torn it to a thousand pieces.

MRS ELVSTED (*shrieking*). No. No.

HEDDA (*involuntarily*). But that's –

LØVBORG (*looking at her*). Not true, you mean?

HEDDA (*recovering*). Oh. True. Of course. If you say so. It seemed . . . astounding.

LØVBORG. Still true.

MRS ELVSTED (*wringing her hands*). Oh no. Oh God. His own work, Hedda. His own work, to pieces.

LØVBORG. His life. I've torn my life to pieces. So why not my life's work too?

MRS ELVSTED. You did this last night.

LØVBORG. I keep telling you. A thousand pieces. And threw them in the fjord. Into deep, clean sea. Let them drift there. Drift in the winds, the waves. Then sink. Deeper, deeper. As I shall, Thea.

MRS ELVSTED. Ejlert, what you've done, to this book – all my life I – it's as if you'd killed a child.

LØVBORG. A child. Yes. I've killed a child.

MRS ELVSTED. It was my child too. How could you?

HEDDA (*almost inaudible*). Oh, the child . . .

MRS ELVSTED (*breathing heavily*). It's over. I'll go now, Hedda.

HEDDA. Back home?

MRS ELVSTED. I don't know what I'll do.

Exit through the hall. HEDDA *stands there. Pause.*

HEDDA. Mr Løvborg, I take it you're not seeing her home.

LØVBORG. In broad daylight? You want people to see her with me?

HEDDA. Naturally, I don't know what else went on last night. Something . . . irrevocable?

LØVBORG. Last night won't be the last. I know. And I don't want to live like that. Not again. I squared up to life . . . took it by the throat. She's smashed that.

HEDDA (*looking straight ahead*). Such a silly little goose, and she's changed another human being's destiny. (*To him.*) Even so, you can't be so heartless to her.

LØVBORG. Don't call it heartless.

HEDDA. Not heartless? You gave her . . . you filled her soul . . . and then you burst it apart.

LØVBORG. Hedda, listen.

HEDDA. I'm listening.

LØVBORG. First, promise, give me your word. What I tell you now, Thea must never know.

HEDDA. I promise.

LØVBORG. Thank you. Then – it wasn't true, the tale I told before.

HEDDA. The manuscript?

LØVBORG. I didn't tear it to pieces. Didn't throw it in the fjord.

HEDDA. Good gracious. Where is it, then?

LØVBORG. Destroyed. Just the same, destroyed. Entirely.

HEDDA. I don't understand.

LØVBORG. Thea said . . . what I'd done . . . to her it was like murdering a child.

HEDDA. That's what she said.

LØVBORG. For a father to kill his child . . . that's not the worst he can do.

HEDDA. It isn't?

LØVBORG. I didn't want Thea to hear the worst.

HEDDA. What is this worst?

LØVBORG. Imagine a father, Hedda, a husband . . . next morning . . . after a night of . . . wildness, recklessness . . . went home to his child's mother and said, 'I went there and there. I took the child. There and there. And I lost him. Lost him. Devil knows who's got him now. Who's got their hands on him.'

HEDDA. This was a book, that's all.

LØVBORG. Thea's soul was in that book.

HEDDA. Yes.

LØVBORG. You see why there's no future now? For her and me?

HEDDA. What are you going to do?

LØVBORG. Nothing. Finish it, somehow. Now.

HEDDA (*one step closer*). Listen, Ejlert Løvborg . . . Try to . . . Make it . . . beautiful.

LØVBORG. Beautiful?

He smiles.

With vine leaves in one's hair. D'you remember . . . ?

HEDDA. Not vine leaves now. But still, beautiful. For once! Goodbye. Go, now. Don't come again.

LØVBORG. Goodbye, Mrs Tesman. My regards to Doctor Tesman.

He makes to leave.

HEDDA. Wait. I want you to have . . . a keepsake.

She goes to the writing-desk, opens the gun-case, and gives him one of the pistols.

LØVBORG (*looking at her*). A . . . keepsake.

HEDDA (*nodding slowly*). Don't you recognise it? It was aimed at you, once.

LØVBORG. You should have used it then.

HEDDA. You use it now.

LØVBORG *puts the pistol in his breast pocket.*

LØVBORG. Thank you.

HEDDA. Ejlert Løvborg, beautiful. Promise me that.

LØVBORG. Goodbye, Hedda Gabler.

Exit through the hall. HEDDA *listens a moment at the door. Then she goes to the writing-desk, takes out the manuscript in its envelope, pulls out a page or two and looks at them. She goes to sit in the armchair by the stove. The envelope is in her lap. Pause. Then she opens the stove door and the envelope, and begins stuffing the pages into the stove.*

HEDDA (*whispering to herself*). Look, Thea. I'm burning your baby, Thea. Little curly-hair!

Stuffing more pages in.

Your baby . . . yours and his.

Stuffing the whole manuscript in.

The baby. Burning the baby.

Curtain.

ACT FOUR

The scene is the same. Evening. The main room is in darkness. The inner room is lit by a lamp hanging over the table. The curtains before the screen door are drawn. HEDDA, in black, is pacing the floor in the dark room. She goes into the inner room and out of sight, left. We hear a chord or two on the piano before she returns to the main room. BERTA brings a lighted lamp right from the inner room, and puts it on the table in front of the corner sofa. Her eyes are red and she has black ribbons in her cap. She slips quietly out right. HEDDA goes to the screen door, moves the curtain a little aside and looks out into the darkness. After a short pause, MISS TESMAN comes in from the hall. She is dressed in black, with hat and veil. HEDDA goes to her, hand outstretched.

MISS TESMAN. Dear Hedda, I come to you all in black. My poor sister's torments are over at last.

HEDDA. As you can see, I know already. Jørgen sent a note.

MISS TESMAN. He said he would. But all the same I thought: I ought to go myself, to Hedda, in the house of life, and break the sad news in person.

HEDDA. Very kind.

MISS TESMAN. Ah, Rina should have stayed. Not passed away now. This is no time for grief in Hedda's house.

HEDDA (*changing the subject*). A peaceful death?

MISS TESMAN. Peaceful . . . beautiful. She had the inexpressible pleasure of seeing Jørgen once more, just before the end. To say goodbye . . . He's not back yet?

HEDDA. He said in the note that he might be some time. Do sit down.

MISS TESMAN. Dear, sweet Hedda, no. Thank you. I wish I could. But there's so little time. She must be prepared, made ready, as best I can. When she goes to her grave, she must look her best.

HEDDA. Is there anything I can do?

MISS TESMAN. No, no. That's not for Hedda Tesman now. Not to do, not even to think about. At a time like this? No, no.

HEDDA. Thoughts. Who can control them?

MISS TESMAN (*running on*). Lord knows, that's how things are. At home, we'll be sewing Rina's shroud. And there'll be sewing here, too. Very soon, I'm sure. Of a very different kind, God send it so.

Enter TESMAN *from the hall.*

HEDDA. Thank God you're here at last.

TESMAN. Aunt Julia! Here, with Hedda! Here!

MISS TESMAN. I was just going. Darling boy. Have you done everything you promised?

TESMAN. Forgotten some of it, I'm afraid. I'll pop round tomorrow, see you then. My head's in such a whirl today, I can't keep my thoughts in order.

MISS TESMAN. Darling Jørgen, you mustn't take it this way.

TESMAN. How, then?

MISS TESMAN. You must be happy in your tears. Happy. As I am.

TESMAN. Oh, for Aunt Rina, you mean?

HEDDA. It'll be lonely for you now, Miss Tesman.

MISS TESMAN. For a day or two. But not for long, I hope. Poor Rina's little room won't stand empty long.

TESMAN. Are you moving someone in?

MISS TESMAN. There's always some poor, sick soul to nurse, to care for. Alas.

HEDDA. You'll take on that cross again?

MISS TESMAN. God bless you, child, why should you think it was a cross?

HEDDA. I mean, this time, a stranger –

MISS TESMAN. With sick people, one soon makes friends. I must have someone to live for. And here: God be praised, there may be one or two things here, too, for an old aunt to do.

HEDDA. Leave us out of –

TESMAN. We could be so happy together, the three of us. I mean if –

HEDDA. If?

TESMAN (*uneasily*). Nothing. It'll be all right. Let's hope so. Hope so.

MISS TESMAN. Well, I expect you've lots to talk about. (*Smiling.*) Hedda may even have news for you, Jørgen. Goodbye. I'll get back to Rina. (*At the door.*) It's so hard to take in. She's with me now, Rina, and with poor dear Jochum too.

TESMAN. Imagine that, Aunt Julia. Imagine.

Exit MISS TESMAN *through the hall.* HEDDA *is following* TESMAN *with cold, sharp eyes.*

HEDDA. You're more upset by this death than she is.

TESMAN. It's not just Aunt Rina's death. It's Ejlert.

HEDDA (*quickly*). What about him?

TESMAN. I popped round this afternoon to tell him the manuscript was safe and sound.

HEDDA. Wasn't he there?

TESMAN. He was out. But I met Mrs Elvsted, and she said he came here this morning, early.

HEDDA. You just missed him.

TESMAN. Apparently he said he'd torn that book to pieces.

HEDDA. He did say that.

TESMAN. He must have been beside himself. I suppose you didn't like to give it back to him.

HEDDA. He didn't take it.

TESMAN. You told him we had it?

HEDDA. No. (*Quickly.*) Did you tell Mrs Elvsted?

TESMAN. I didn't want to do that. But you could've told him. The state he's in – what if he . . . hurts himself? Give me the manuscript, Hedda. I'll take it round right now. Where is it?

HEDDA (*like stone, leaning against the chair*). It's gone. I haven't got it.

TESMAN. Haven't got it? What on Earth d'you mean?

HEDDA. I burned it. All of it.

TESMAN (*horror-struck*). You burned Ejlert's manuscript?

HEDDA. Stop shouting. Berta will hear you.

TESMAN. God in heaven. Burned. You can't –

HEDDA. I can; I did.

TESMAN. D'you realise what you've done? Destroying lost property – it's a criminal act. Ask Brack.

HEDDA. Don't tell anyone, then. Not Brack, not anyone.

TESMAN. But how could you do it? How could you, Hedda?

HEDDA (*hiding a smile*). I did it for you, Jørgen.

TESMAN. For me!

HEDDA. You came home this morning. You said he'd read to you.

TESMAN. Yes.

HEDDA. And you were jealous. You said.

TESMAN. I didn't mean it literally.

HEDDA. That's not the point. I still couldn't bear it: the idea of someone else putting you in the shade.

TESMAN (*in an outburst: half unsure, half glad*). Hedda? Is this true? What you're saying . . . ? I . . . you've never shown your love like this before. Never.

HEDDA. You might as well know. The thing is –

She breaks off.

Oh, ask Aunt Julia. She'll explain.

TESMAN. I . . . I think I know. (*Clasping his hands.*) Oh God, oh God, is it really true?

HEDDA. Stop shouting. Berta will hear you.

TESMAN (*laughing, overcome with happiness*). Berta! Oh, Hedda, you're priceless! Berta! It's Berta! I'll tell her myself.

HEDDA (*clenching her fists in despair*). I can't stand this. I can't stand any more.

TESMAN. Stand what, Hedda?

HEDDA (*cold, controlled*). All this . . . fuss.

TESMAN. But I'm delighted, I'm overjoyed! Well, perhaps, not a word to Berta.

HEDDA. Why not? Why ever not?

TESMAN. Not now, this minute. But Aunt Julia must be told. And you've started to call me Jørgen. Jørgen! She'll be so happy, Aunt Julia, so happy.

HEDDA. To hear that I burned Ejlert Løvborg's book – for you?

TESMAN. No, well. Not the book. But that you burn for me, Hedda – that's what Aunt Julia needs to know. Hedda, darling, is this what all young wives are like?

HEDDA. You could ask Aunt Julia that as well.

TESMAN. Good idea. I will. (*Worried and hesitant again*). Even so, that manuscript. Poor Ejlert. Even so.

MRS ELVSTED, *dressed as on her first visit, with hat and coat, comes in from the hall. She greets them quickly and with agitation.*

MRS ELVSTED. Hedda, I'm sorry to come again so soon –

HEDDA. Thea, what is it?

TESMAN. Ejlert Løvborg? Something new?

MRS ELVSTED. I'm afraid. I think something terrible's happened.

HEDDA (*takes her by the arm*). You think so.

TESMAN. Good heavens, Mrs Elvsted, what makes you think that?

MRS ELVSTED. When I got back to the boarding house just now, they were talking about him. There are rumours about him everywhere!

TESMAN. I thought he went straight home to bed.

HEDDA. In the boarding house – what were they saying?

MES ELVSTED. Nothing definite. Not to me, anyway. Either they didn't know, or . . . they stopped talking when they saw me. I didn't dare ask.

TESMAN (*pacing restlessly*). Let's hope . . . let's hope you heard wrong, Mrs Elvsted.

MES ELVSTED. It was him they were talking about. I'm sure it was. I'm sure someone mentioned the hospital –

TESMAN. Hospital!

HEDDA. They can't have.

MRS ELVSTED. I was so terrified for him. I went to his lodgings and asked for him there.

HEDDA. Thea! You dared do that?

MRS ELVSTED. What else could I do? Not knowing – I couldn't bear it.

TESMAN. He wasn't there?

MRS ELVSTED. They knew nothing about him. He hadn't been home since yesterday afternoon, they said.

TESMAN. Yesterday! What do they mean?

MRS ELVSTED. There's only one explanation: something dreadful's happened.

TESMAN. Hedda, shall I go . . . make inquiries?

HEDDA. No. No. Don't get involved.

BERTA *opens the hall door, and* BRACK *comes in. She closes the door behind him. He looks grave, and greets them solemnly.*

TESMAN. Brack. It's you. It's you.

BRACK. I had to see you this evening.

TESMAN. I see from your face, you've heard Aunt Julia's sad news.

BRACK. That too.

TESMAN. A tragedy.

BRACK. Depends how you look at it.

TESMAN (*with an enquiring look*). Something else?

HEDDA (*intent*). Judge Brack, another tragedy?

TESMAN. Depends how you look at it, Mrs Tesman.

MRS ELVSTED (*unable to contain herself*). It's about Ejlert Løvborg.

BRACK (*glancing at her*). Why d'you say that? Mrs Elvsted? You've heard something already?

MRS ELVSTED (*confused*). No . . . I . . . no . . .

TESMAN. Good Heavens, tell us!

BRACK (*shrugging*). I'm sorry to say . . . Ejlert Løvborg's been taken to hospital. He . . . won't last long.

MRS ELVSTED (*screaming*). Oh God, God.

TESMAN. Hospital? Not long?

HEDDA (*blurting it*). So soon?

MRS ELVSTED (*wailing*). Oh Hedda, we parted in anger.

HEDDA (*aside to her*). Thea!

MRS ELVSTED (*not noticing*). I must go to him. I must see him before he dies.

BRACK. Mrs Elvsted, impossible. They won't allow visitors.

MRS ELVSTED. At least tell me what happened.

TESMAN. He hasn't . . . hurt himself? Has he?

HEDDA. I'm sure he has.

TESMAN. Hedda, how can you know?

BRACK (*giving her a straight look*). Unfortunately, Mrs Tesman, you've guessed quite right.

MRS ELVSTED. No!

TESMAN. Hurt himself.

HEDDA. Shot himself.

BRACK. Right again, Mrs Tesman.

MRS ELVSTED (*fighting for self-control*). Your Honour, when did it happen?

BRACK. This afternoon. Between three and four.

TESMAN. Good Heavens! Where?

BRACK (*after a slight hesitation*). My dear man, at his lodgings.

MRS ELVSTED. That can't be right. I was there myself between six and seven.

BRACK. Somewhere else, then. I don't know exactly. All I know is that someone found him. Shot. In the chest.

MRS ELVSTED. How dreadful. That he should die like this.

HEDDA (*to* BRACK). In the chest? You're sure?

BRACK. Certain.

HEDDA. Not the temple?

BRACK. The chest, Mrs Tesman.

HEDDA. Well . . . the chest will do.

BRACK. Pardon?

HEDDA (*evasively*). Nothing.

TESMAN. And the wound was serious, you say?

BRACK. Beyond cure. He's probably . . . gone already.

MRS ELVSTED. He has! I know it. Gone! Oh Hedda . . .

TESMAN. But who told you all this?

BRACK (*curtly*). The police. I had . . . business there.

HEDDA (*loud*). At last, success.

TESMAN (*horrified*). Hedda! Whatever d'you mean?

HEDDA. I mean that this is beautiful.

BRACK. Mrs Tesman . . .

TESMAN. Beautiful?

HEDDA. Ejlert Løvborg has closed his account with himself. Had the courage to do . . . what had to be done.

MRS ELVSTED. It's not true. Not this. A moment of madness.

TESMAN. Despair.

HEDDA. I'm sure it wasn't.

MRS ELVSTED. It must have been. Despair. Like when he tore our book to pieces.

BRACK (*astonished*). Your book? The manuscript? He tore it up?

MRS ELVSTED. Last night.

TESMAN (*whispering*). Hedda, we'll never get out of this.

BRACK. What an odd thing to do.

TESMAN (*pacing*). Fancy Ejlert, leaving the world like this. Not even leaving behind the book that would make him immortal.

MRS ELVSTED. If it could only be reconstructed.

TESMAN. Reconstructed. Oh if only –

MRS ELVSTED. Dr Tesman, perhaps it can.

TESMAN. What d'you mean?

MRS ELVSTED (*going through her bag*). Look. I've still got his notes. The ones he dictated from.

HEDDA (*closer*). Oh.

TESMAN. Mrs Elvsted! You kept them!

MRS ELVSTED. They're here. I brought them when I came to town. They've been in my bag ever since.

TESMAN. Let me see them.

MRS ELVSTED *hands him a sheaf of notes.*

MRS ELVSTED. They're out of order. All mixed up.

TESMAN. Still we might be able to . . . If we helped each other . . .

MRS ELVSTED. Oh, do let's try. Let's try.

TESMAN. We'll succeed. We must! I'll devote my life to it.

HEDDA. Jørgen? Your life?

TESMAN. Well, as much as I can spare. My own work can wait. D'you see, Hedda? I must. I owe it to Ejlcrt's mcmory.

HEDDA. Perhaps you do.

TESMAN. Mrs Elvsted, we must take ourselves in hand. No use brooding on the past. We must clear our minds –

MRS ELVSTED. Doctor Tesman, I'll try. I'll try.

TESMAN. Come on then. We'll start right away. Where shall we work? In here? No: in there. Excuse me, Brack. This way, Mrs Elvsted. This way.

MRS ELVSTED. Please God it works!

She and TESMAN *go into the inner room. She takes off her coat and hat. They sit at the table under the lamp and begin a feverish examination of the papers.* HEDDA *sits in the armchair by the stove. After a moment,* BRACK *goes beside her.*

HEDDA (*murmured*). Freedom, Your Honour. That's what it means, this Løvborg business. Freedom.

BRACK. He's certainly set free.

HEDDA. Freedom for me, I mean. I'm free, because I know it's still possible to choose. Free will! Still possible, and beautiful.

BRACK (*with a smile*). Ah, Mrs Tesman –

HEDDA. I know what you're going to say. You're a kind of expert too. A kind of . . . Well.

BRACK (*looking intently at her*). Ejlert Løvborg was more important to you than you like to admit, even to yourself. Or am I mistaken?

HEDDA. I can't answer that. All I know is that Ejlert Løvborg had the courage to choose the kind of life he wanted to lead. And now this, this triumph, this beautiful deed. He had the strength, the will, to tear himself away from the banquet of life . . . so early.

BRACK. It's a charming fantasy, Mrs Tesman, and I'm sorry to shatter it –

HEDDA. Fantasy?

BRACK. It would've been shattered anyway, quite soon.

HEDDA. What d'you mean?

BRACK. He didn't . . . choose to shoot himself.

HEDDA. I don't understand.

BRACK. Things weren't exactly as I described.

HEDDA (*tense*). Something else?

BRACK. For poor Mrs Elvsted's sake, I kept a few details back.

HEDDA. What details?

BRACK. First: he's dead already.

HEDDA. In the hospital?

BRACK. Without regaining consciousness.

HEDDA. Anything else?

BRACK. His . . . accident . . . wasn't at his lodgings.

HEDDA. Not important.

BRACK. Maybe not. I'll tell you. They found him, shot, in Mamzelle Diana's boudoir.

HEDDA *starts up, then falls back.*

HEDDA. Not today, Your Honour! He can't have gone back there today.

BRACK. This afternoon. He was looking for something they'd taken from him. He was raving: a lost child -

HEDDA. And that's . . .

BRACK. I wondered if he meant his manuscript. But now I hear that he tore it up himself. It must have been his wallet.

HEDDA. So that's where they found him.

BRACK. With a pistol in his breast pocket. It had been fired. It had wounded him fatally.

HEDDA. Yes, in the chest.

BRACK. In the . . . lower parts.

HEDDA (*looking up at him in disgust*). Even that! Mean, sordid, like everything else I touch.

BRACK. Mrs Tesman, there's something else. Just as sordid.

HEDDA. What?

BRACK. The pistol –

HEDDA (*holding her breath*). What about it?

BRACK. He must have stolen it.

HEDDA (*jumping up*). Stolen it! No! He didn't!

BRACK. It's the only explanation. He must have stolen it. Sh!

TESMAN *and* MRS ELVSTED *come in from the inner room.* TESMAN *has both hands full of papers.*

TESMAN. It's no use, Hedda. I can't see a thing under that lamp. Not a thing.

HEDDA. You can't see a thing.

TESMAN. Could we sit in here for a while, perhaps, at your writing-table?

HEDDA. Of course. (*Quickly.*) Just a moment. I'll tidy it first.

TESMAN. No need. There's plenty of room.

HEDDA. No, no, I'll clear it. All this can go on the piano. There.

She has taken something from the bookshelf, covered with sheet music. She puts some more music on top of it and carries the whole armful through to the inner room. TESMAN *puts his papers on the table, and fetches the lamp from the corner table. He and* MRS ELVSTED *sit down and begin work again.* HEDDA *comes back, and stands behind* MRS ELVSTED's *chair, gently stroking the woman's hair.*

Any progress, Thea? With the Ejlert Løvborg memorial?

MRS ELVSTED (*looking up disconsolately*). It's going to be very hard.

TESMAN. We've got to try. It's essential. Sorting out someone else's papers — I know about that.

HEDDA *sits on one of the stools by the stove.* BRACK *stands over her, leaning on the armchair.*

HEDDA (*in a low voice*). What were you saying about the gun?

BRACK (*low*). He must have stolen it.

HEDDA. Why stolen?

BRACK. There's no other explanation, Mrs Tesman.

HEDDA. Oh.

BRACK (*looking at her*). He came here this morning. Didn't he?

HEDDA. Yes.

BRACK. You were alone with him?

HEDDA. For a while.

BRACK. While he was here, did you leave the room at all?

HEDDA. No.

BRACK. Think. Not even for a moment?

HEDDA. Perhaps a moment, into the hall.

BRACK. Where did you keep your pistol-case?

HEDDA. I . . . well, on the –

BRACK. Mrs Tesman, where?

HEDDA. There, on the writing-desk.

BRACK. Have you checked it since, to see if both pistols are there?

HEDDA. No.

BRACK. No need. I saw the pistol on Løvborg's body. I recognised it at once, from yesterday. And from before.

HEDDA. Did you bring it?

BRACK. It's with the police.

HEDDA. What will they do?

BRACK. Try to trace the owner.

HEDDA. D'you think they'll succeed?

BRACK (*bending over her, whispering*). No, Hedda Gabler. So long as I hold my tongue.

HEDDA (*looking sideways at him*). And if you don't?

BRACK (*shrugs*). You could still say it was stolen.

HEDDA (*firmly*). Rather death!

BACK (*with a smile*). People say that. No one does it.

HEDDA (*not answering*). Suppose the pistol wasn't stolen. And the owner was traced. What then?

BRACK. Mrs Tesman: scandal.

HEDDA. Scandal!

BRACK. The one thing you're afraid of. You'd have to appear in court, of course. You and Mamzelle Diana. She'd have to explain how it happened. Was it accident . . . murder? Did he reach for the pistol to threaten her, and shoot himself? Did she snatch it from him, shoot him and put it back in his pocket? She could have done that. She's a strong young woman, Mamzelle Diana.

HEDDA. These sordid details have nothing to do with me.

BRACK. But you'll have to explain why you gave him the gun in the first place. And what possible conclusion d'you think they'll draw from what you say?

HEDDA (*lowering her head*). I never thought of that.

BRACK. Luckily there's no danger, so long as I hold my tongue.

HEDDA (*looking up at him*). You mean I'm in your power, Judge Brack. You . . . own me.

BRACK (*low whisper*). Hedda, darling, trust me. I won't take advantage.

HEDDA. I'm still in your power. At your disposal. A slave.

She gets up impatiently.

I won't have it. I won't.

BRACK (*with a half-mocking glance*). You will. What can't be cured . . .

HEDDA (*returning his glance*). We'll see.

She goes to the writing-desk. Hiding a smile, and imitating TESMAN's *way of speaking, she says:*

Well now, Jørgen, how does it look? Eh? Look?

TESMAN. Heaven knows, Hedda. There's months of work, that's for sure.

HEDDA (*as before*). Months of work.

She strokes MRS ELVSTED's *hair.*

How marvellous for you, Thea. To sit here with Tesman – as once you sat with Ejlert Løvborg.

MRS ELVSTED. If I could only inspire your husband too.

HEDDA. You will, in time.

TESMAN. Already, Hedda. Already. I think so. You go and talk to His Honour.

HEDDA. You don't need me here, either of you?

TESMAN. There's nothing you can do. Nothing at all. (*Turning his head.*) Brack, you don't mind keeping Hedda company?

BRACK (*glancing at* HEDDA). My pleasure.

HEDDA. Thank you. But I'm feeling rather tired. I'll lie down a moment, in there on the sofa.

TESMAN. Do that, darling. Yes.

HEDDA *goes into the inner room and draws the curtains behind her. After a moment, we hear her playing wild dance-music on the piano.* MRS ELVSTED *jumps up.*

MRS ELVSTED. Oh! What's that?

TESMAN *runs to the entrance.*

TESMAN. Not tonight, darling! Think of Aunt Rina. Not to mention Ejlert.

HEDDA (*looking through the gap in the curtains*). Not to mention Aunt Julia. All of them. I won't make a sound.

She draws the curtains closed behind her.

TESMAN (*at the writing-desk*). She's upset to see us at such a tragic task. Mrs Elvsted, I tell you what: why don't you move in with Aunt Julia? I'll come round every evening. We'll sit and work there. Work there!

MRS ELVSTED. It might be best −

HEDDA (*from the inner room*). I hear what you're saying, Tesman. And what will I do, every evening, here?

TESMAN (*turning over the papers*). I'm sure His Honour will be kind enough to call.

BRACK (*calling cheerfully from the armchair*). Mrs Tesman, every evening! We'll have such a jolly time . . .

HEDDA (*clearly and audibly*). You really hope so, Judge Brack. Cock of the walk −

We hear a shot, inside. TESMAN, MRS ELVSTED *and* BRACK *jump to their feet.*

TESMAN. She's playing with those guns again.

He pulls the curtains and runs in, followed by MRS ELVSTED. HEDDA *is lying dead on the sofa. Noise and confusion. Enter* BERTA *right, beside herself.* TESMAN *shrieks at* BRACK.

Shot herself! In the temple! Shot herself!

BRACK (*slumping in the chair*). No one does that. No one.

Curtain.